THE GATEWAY TO THE MIDDLE AGES
MONASTICISM

The Gateway
to the Middle Ages

MONASTICISM

by Eleanor Shipley Duckett

ANN ARBOR PAPERBACKS

THE UNIVERSITY OF MICHIGAN PRESS

TO
MARY ELLEN CHASE
AND
OUR CAMBRIDGE FAMILY
CAMBRIDGE, ENGLAND
1934–1936

ABBREVIATIONS

PL	*Patrologia Latina*
PG	*Patrologia Graeca*
M.G.H.	*Monumenta Germaniae Historica*
M.H.B.	*Monumenta Historica Britannica*
R.I.S.	*Rerum Italicarum Scriptores* (Muratori)
Script. rer. Merov.	*Scriptores Rerum Merovingicarum*
Script. rer. Lang. . .	*Scriptores Rerum Langobardicarum*
C.S.H.B. . . .	*Corpus Scriptorum Historiae Byzantinae*
C.S.E.L.	*Corpus Scriptorum Ecclesiasticorum Latinorum*
P.L.M.	*Poetae Latini Minores*
P.W.	*Real-Encyclopädie*, ed. Pauly-Wissowa
C.M.H.	*Cambridge Medieval History*
H.S.C.P.	*Harvard Studies in Classical Philology*
C.P.	*Classical Philology*
Schanz	Schanz-Hosius-Krüger: *Geschichte der römischen Literatur*, IV, 2, 1920
Manitius . . .	M. Manitius: *Geschichte der lateinischen Literatur des Mittelalters*, I, 1911
Bardenhewer . .	O. Bardenhewer: *Geschichte der altkirchlichen Literatur*, V, 1932

PREFACE

THE GATEWAY TO THE MIDDLE AGES is made up of three parts. This one deals with monasticism in the sixth century.

Monasticism at that time followed one of two disciplines, according to the race, country, and temperament of its followers: Celtic or Roman.

Celtic monks belonged to the British, in Wales and the southwest of Britain; to the Irish in Ireland and in Scotland; and to those of the British who in fear of Saxon enemies or through love of wandering had crossed the Channel to find their peace abroad.

In Wales there was at this time the monastery of Abbot Illtyd at Llantwit Major; of David at Mynyw or Menevia, St. David's in Pembrokeshire; of Cadoc at Llancarfan. From Wales monks journeyed in their frail wicker boats to Cornwall and thence to Brittany, where we meet, with many others, Samson at Dol and Paul Aurelian at Saint-Pol-de-Leon.

For the Irish this sixth century was a Golden Age of monks and monasteries, established in their multitude up and down the land: by Finnian at Clonard in Meath; by another Finnian at Moville in County Down; by Comgall at Bangor on Belfast Lough; by Ciaran at Clonmacnois on the Shannon; by other founders without number.

The rule followed by these Celtic monks was common only in its fundamentals, and these were hard; fasting and vigil, prayer and penance, filled the hours of the day and many of the night. To holy observance was added zeal of scholarship; each of the greater Irish abbeys had its school, in which students of the Bible and the Latin fathers, of Christian doctrine and pagan Latin texts, listened to their teachers and pondered their few manuscripts whenever they could turn from fulfilling their round of prayer, from the carrying out of those manual tasks which gave them the bare necessities of life. Many men, also vowed to the same monastic ideal, were seeking it in the solitude so beloved by the Celtic spirit, on isles off Irish and British shores, on islets in lake and river, wherever their wandering had led them.

It was the monks of Roman discipline, however, who prepared the way for the coming of the great monastic orders of the Middle Ages. Among these we find in our sixth century those of the congregation established by that Cassiodorus who had been minister to Theodoric the Great, in his own country house, "Vivarium," "Fishpools," amid the meadows of southern Italy. Here his leisure from political labors has left us writings of high importance on his training of his monks in discipline both sacred and secular.

From Italy we come to Arles in southern France, to find its bishop, Caesarius, drawing up his *Rule* for nuns, for women living the monastic life under his guidance. Caesarius had a gift of common sense as well as sanctity, and in his provisions we come upon much of interest in regard to these good sisters, some of humble, others of most aristocratic birth. Even more interesting, however, were the sermons in which with scathing rebuke he stripped bare during mass the hidden consciences of his guilty flock.

And now we come to the climax: to the life of Saint Benedict of Nursia and to the *Rule* compiled by him for his monks of the sixth century in the abbey of Monte

PREFACE

Cassino, between Rome and Naples: the *Rule* followed since these, its earliest days, all down the ages by men and women of every kind and class and quality, small and great. Here we learn of the discipline which, unlike the harsh austerity, the vague prescriptions of Celtic codes, laid down its instructions for the needs of spirit, mind, and body, in clear and exact precision, that none who willed might fail to climb the steep hill of chastity and poverty, of stability and religious obedience.

Among these we see here Benedict's follower, Saint Gregory the Great, Pope of Rome: the father of rich and poor, simple and learned alike, who sustained his people firmly while the Lombard invaders came down toward Rome from their northern kingdom; who ruled his Papal Patrimony with a strong and masterly hand; who wrote for his bishops his famous *Pastoral Rule;* who taught his monks to follow the Benedictine life in a distracted world; and who, in his scant hours of freedom from toil, delighted in the legends of bird, beast, and serpent which fill the pages of his *Dialogues,* as well as in composing literature of a far sterner sort.

When he died, in 604, the gate to the fields and thickets of medieval religion, of medieval philosophy and debate, lay well and truly open.

E.S.D.

Northampton, Massachusetts, 1960

CONTENTS

THE GATEWAY TO THE MIDDLE AGES
MONASTICISM

CHAPTER I

ROMAN MONASTICISM

THE course of Christian monasticism before the sixth century has been told again and again and only needs a few words here.[1] From the fourth century it took its rise. It was then that St. Anthony pointed out the way of solitary living in contemplation of God which countless hermits in central and northern Egypt were to follow during the next two hundred years. During this same century southern Egypt saw the beginning of the life in community, induced by the example of St. Pachomius and his famous Rule. This discipline gained ground swiftly in Asia and was formulated for Greece and the Eastern Church in Europe by St. Basil the Great, Bishop of Caesarea, who died in 379. His teachings definitely ranked the practice shared in common as preferable to the practice in solitude, and laid down works of charity and a Rule suited to their performance as a true and holy part of the monastic aim. Here, then, we find already a form of religious discipline far different from the lonely pursuit of contemplation and mortifying of the flesh for this end which had been the burning desire of Egyptian monks of the desert after the example of St. Anthony.

Thus by the end of the fourth century this monasticism was firmly established in the East. The same period saw its

[1] See Montalembert, *The Monks of the West*, I, pp. 211–385; Hannay, *Christian Monasticism,* chs. iv–vii; Workman, *Evolution of the Monastic Ideal,*[2] ch. ii; Cuthbert Butler, on *Monasticism* in *Encycl. Brit.*

introduction to Rome by St. Athanasius, who practised and
taught the precepts of the religious life there from 340 on-
wards with the help of the monks he had brought with him.
As the East, so now the West caught the fire of its fascina-
tion, and, individually or in common, men and women
throughout Italy and Gaul and northern Africa gave themselves to its dedication in poverty, chastity and obedience.
St. Martin kindled the world by the spirit of his life at
Marmoutier and at Tours; St. Jerome preached indefatigably
the glory of the Three Counsels in Italy and drew around
him a devoted circle of men and women; St. Augustine
laid down in northern Africa his Rule, instituted for the convent over which his sister presided in Hippo, though it was
to bear its witness down the ages.

In the fifth century Cassian with wise discretion adapted
for Western use the rigorously ascetic practice of the East,
where he himself had been trained, in the books of instruction which he compiled from his own memories for his Abbey
of St. Victor at Marseilles. At the same time to and from
the monastic school of the island of Lérins near this coast
scholars and holy men went in and went out to teach and
to preach as bishops throughout southern Gaul. By the sixth
century the Christian monk was a familiar figure, settled in
solitude or in congregation; in the West, life in community
was the prevailing form. The fourth century had sown, the
fifth century had bedded out the seedlings, the sixth century
was to devise the methods and manners under which the
fields of the future should yield their fruits.

We read of many attempts in the West during this time
to draw up Rules and to formulate the practices which mul-
titudes in different places were following in their different
ways. Cassian had actually written: "We see almost as
many types and rules set up for use as we see monasteries

and cells." Each new founder in the West either desired to emphasize austerity in his own thirst for mortification, or thought it prudent to relax something of Eastern ascetic practice for the hope of perseverance in his Western disciples, unable in their cold damp winters to meet the standards of the Egyptian desert. Among these many Rules three stand out for their wider currency and special appeal: that of Caesarius of Arles, that of Columban of Luxeuil, and that of Benedict of Nursia, destined in his foundation to outlive both these his contemporaries.

But first we may linger a moment to look at two other individual pictures of monastic life. They are widely separated in locality and in character, but are of equal interest here.

The first belongs to the Roman province of Noricum on the south bank of the Danube, where Bavaria and Austria now lie. It brings us to those years in the latter part of the fifth century when Rome was giving up her unequal struggle with the barbarians. As she relaxed her grasp, her provincials were left unprotected, to defend themselves as best they might against these invaders who were steadily encroaching here and there, step by step, till the quickly coming day should arrive when they were to make the region their own.[2] Various names distinguished their peoples: Heruli, Rugi, Alamanni, Thuringi, Suevi and Goths; but all were fired by the one purpose of advance in search of a permanent home. They rushed in constant raids from the land lying across the Danube on the north, from the lands on the west and the north-west, from Pannonia on the east, against the miserable inhabitants of Roman territory, subjects of an Empire that had no ear for distant appeals in her own hour of crisis.

[2] Some excellent observations are found on this subject in Julius Jung, *Römer und Romanen in den Donauländern,* ed. of 1877, pp. 188ff.

Things had not been so bad while Attila and his Huns kept their rival barbarians in check. But after his death in 453, the motley hordes were delivered from this menace, free at last to wander and ravage where they would without fear.

Into this region of Noricum there came at this time a man of God, a worker dedicated to monastic discipline, who by his holiness and his zeal for his brethren gradually now made himself a Father for the distressed provincials in things both spiritual and temporal. His name was Severinus, and our knowledge of him comes from his *Life*, written in 511 by Eugippius, one of his disciples.[8] This *Life*, like the *Complaint* of Gildas, stands as a candle in the night of our ignorance and is, therefore, of rare value. It is our only source of information for the history of these last days of the Roman province on the banks of the Danube.

If Rome could not govern and help her citizens in these critical years, Severinus both would and could. Soon the terrified and distracted people looked on him as their only guide and support. His word became their law, and for their own good he ruled them with a firm hand. No one knew the land of his origin, and he would never tell it; though many, both priests and lay people, natives of the district as well as strangers from a distance, were possessed by a curiosity that longed to ask whence came this man of such extraordinary goodness. No one even dared to ask, till one day a priest of Italy called Primenius, who had been a friend of Orestes and had fled to Severinus when Orestes was murdered, presumed upon the friendly reception given him. He received no satisfaction. "What matters it," replied the Father, "to a servant of God, where or of what family he was born? If you think me worthy to be called a citizen of our native land

[8] ed. H. Sauppe, *M.G.H.* Auct. Ant. I, 2; P. Knöll, *C.S.E.L.* IX, 2; see also *PL* LXII. For trans. see G. W. Robinson, *The Life of Saint Severinus,* 1914.

on high, why should you know from what earthly land I come? Of a truth God, Who gave it you to be His priest, also Himself bade me dwell among these men here in their perils." But the Saint's conversation with his friends showed him to be one of pure Latin race, though sometimes he spoke of cities of the East and of perils and adventures of travel; he spoke always as though these places and perils had been experienced by another, but so intimately that men judged he must have visited them himself.

It was a hard calling, for, like all the Saints, he longed for solitude. But always the voice of duty drove him back from the dear peace of his cell, that his presence might comfort his appointed charges. These he trained by his acts rather than by much preaching. Prayer, repentance, alms-giving and fasting were the means by which he tried to lead both himself and his people to God, and these, too, were the means by which he taught them to meet their barbarian enemies. Even from a worldly point of view resistance was vain, and repeatedly he bade his sheep give way before invasion, as town after town was attacked.

Their hardships were his. He always went barefoot, even in mid-winter, when the ice on the Danube was so thick that waggons could cross it; he slept on a mat of haircloth and wore one and the same garment, night and day. He never took any food till sunset, except on certain Feast Days. His fame quickly spread, and disciples flocked to learn from him. Some he kept in community life near him at Favianis, where he made his home: possibly the modern Mauer, on the Danube between Tulln and Lorch.⁴ With these he used regularly to say Matins, Lauds and Compline; the remaining Hours he said alone in his own little cell hard by the

⁴ The old theory that Favianis was on the site of the modern Vienna has been abandoned. Eugippius shows his mediaeval Latin in this form, indeclinable, for Faviana.

monastery. For other disciples he founded other monasteries in the neighbourhood, that all might live a common life of prayer and good works, probably after the manner of Saint Basil which he had learned in the East.[5]

His biographer tells of terrible punishments that fell from God on those who dared to disobey the Father's command, issued in times of menace and attack. Severinus is pictured as forewarned of peril by a strange understanding of the future. Without in the least denying this power, common to many who have entered more deeply into the mind of the Lord, the suggestion may well be true that he did obtain information as to the movements of the enemy from secret sources.[6] It is certain that he was held in awe far and wide; even the kings of the barbarian races feared him. But the poor and suffering found a ready way to his heart. He was always striving to ransom those taken captive, to feed the hungry, to recall the erring; for "he wept for the sins of others as though his own."

Thus through these days he ruled his charges prudently and fed them with his own hand, content with the ministry of his stern Rule; refusing the call to become their Bishop with the answer that he had come thither to live in solitude and to aid the distressed without official honouring of the Church. And as he lay dying of pleurisy in 482, he reminded his monks gathered round him at midnight of what he had so often taught: "Let us, therefore, be humble of heart, tranquil of mind, on our watch against all sins, and ever mindful of the Divine commands. Let us remember that neither our humble dress nor the name of monk nor the appearance of piety will help us at all if we are found relaxed in our keeping of counsels and reprobate. Let our manners, most dear sons, be in keeping with our profession.

⁵ Rettberg, *Kirch. gesch. Deutschlands,* I, p. 231.   ⁶ *ibid.* p. 232.

It is a grave sin for even a man of the world to walk in the way of errors. How much more for monks, who have fled from the attractions of the world as from a fierce monster and have preferred Christ to all affections, whose outer habit and behaviour is believed to be a proof of their virtue within!" [7]

In his story preaching and precept found their fulfilment. At his word the inhabitants of Comagenis (near the modern Tulln), when the barbarians had actually posted a guard over its walls under pretence of a pact they had forced upon the citizens, betook themselves for three days to penitence and fasting and prayers for aid in their church. On the third day at time of Vespers there came suddenly a terrific earthquake and the barbarian soldiers rushed in panic from the town. At the same time the men of Favianis were earnestly begging the man of God to help them procure food in a winter famine, and he hastened to them with the same words: "By the fruits of penitence shall ye gain rescue from so great strait of hunger." But he did not only preach. He heard during the same winter that a rich widow of high-born family was keeping hidden a quantity of grain for her own use. A sharp rebuke in public was accompanied by a threat to throw her store into the Danube, "that she might be kind to the fish if she would not be to men." The lady promptly showed herself full of charity to her starving fellow-citizens. Soon afterward the ice melted, and abundant supplies of food came down the river on boats.

No wonder that towns and fortresses on the Danube all sought help from Severinus, since they believed that God was with him for their salvation. He delivered the land of Kuchel from a plague of locusts by ordering all its inhabitants to assemble in the Church and sing psalms, men, women and

[7] Eugippius, *Vita Sev.* c. 43.

children, down to the babies who could only pray without words! One man, indeed, who was very poor, could not endure this passive resistance and stole out of church to scare away the scourge from his own tiny patch of corn. Then he went back to join in Mass with his neighbours. Alas! next morning the locusts had devoured his corn alone and had spared all the rest. Severinus had mercy, and when the sinner had humbly confessed his fault and begged his happier brethren to pray for him, the Father commanded a collection made, and went on commanding till his penitent had enough to keep him for the rest of the year. And, in general, he made a practice of requiring the faithful who were better off in the various cities of Noricum to give tithes of their produce and clothing for the needy.

Soon town after town had to be abandoned. Astura, where now Klosterneuburg stands, was destroyed; the inhabitants of Quintanis, a town of Raetia, represented now perhaps by Osterhofen,[8] were forced to retreat before the Alamanni to the city of Batavis, built on the site of the modern Passau at the juncture of the River Inn with the Danube. There for a while the Alamanni were held at bay; but soon this stronghold, also, yielded to the Thuringians, after its citizens had been commanded by Severinus to flee in their turn to Lauriacum, the modern Lorch. All the people of Noricum who had not been killed or captured by the different barbarian forces now gathered in this city to make one last fight for their lives and freedom. For military garrisons slowly disappeared, till only a few soldiers still held their posts. At last these, too, became desperate, as pay constantly failed to arrive from headquarters, and some of them actually started off for Italy to ask for arrears for all. But

---

[8] For theories of identification of these towns on the Danube see Sauppe, ed. (index at end); Mierow, *C.P.* X, 1915, pp. 166ff.; Robinson, *op. cit.*

they were killed every one by roving barbarians as they went.

Among the many savage neighbours that slowly engulfed this province on the Danube, the Rugians played a considerable part. They lived across the river to the north, and their Kings and people held Severinus in special honour. He not only helped them in time of sickness but also in their distress through the depredation of their fellow-barbarians. Their King Flaccitheus sought aid of the holy man against the menace of the Goths; for he lived, he declared, in daily fear of death. The answer of Severinus is interesting, as Eugippius tells it. "If the one Catholic faith bound us together, it had rather been your duty to ask me how you might gain life everlasting. But since you are only concerned to ask me about safety for the present, which we do share, hear my assurance. Be troubled neither by the multitude nor by the assault of the Goths. They will depart quickly and leave you in peace to reign with the prosperity you crave, if only you will obey the commands of my humility. Do not, therefore, chafe at seeking peace even from the least of your brethren, and never rely on your own merits." [*]

The Goths were, as we know, Arian in their faith. It must be noted here that Severinus found, and did not make, a Catholic province in Noricum. It had its priests and its churches throughout its towns long before he arrived, as we can see from this *Life,* and to him belongs rather the honour of fostering the monastic life within its boundaries.

So Flaccitheus died peacefully in his bed, and his kingdom passed to his son Feletheus, sometimes called Feva. He, too, reverenced the Father and often visited his cell. But he had a wicked wife, Giso, who even dared try to rebaptize certain Catholics into her own Arian calling, and took prisoner some

[*] c. 5.

of the Romans in Noricum. When Severinus commanded her to let them go, she answered in all insolence and would not abate her pride till trouble came upon her. Certain men whom she was holding prisoner seized her little son, Frederic, in a desperate attempt to negotiate for their own freedom. The intercession of Severinus brought about the boy's liberty and his mother's repentance for the time being.

Then Feletheus advanced from his land across the Danube with a great force of soldiers against the last of the Roman population of Noricum, huddled together in Lauriacum. He had already compelled Favianis and other towns of Noricum to pay tribute to him, and he now proposed to carry off the Romans into these, that he might himself be lord of the riverside province. The only hope for these wretched survivors lay with Severinus, who travelled in haste all night and fell in with the hungry chieftain twenty miles outside Favianis. Feletheus declared that he wanted to protect the Romans, and Severinus retorted that his own fatherly care, rather than a military control, would better suit this people committed to him by the Lord. So the invader retreated, and some of the Romans even dared to creep out from Lauriacum to the towns they had deserted in their panic.

Before Severinus died, he called King Feletheus with the Queen to his presence and bade them, as they valued their own souls, not to harm the Roman people in Noricum. He laid similar injunction on Ferderuch, brother of Feletheus, to whom this King had made a present of the town of Favianis, though the Saint prophesied at the time that his words would be disobeyed. Eugippius tells us that Ferderuch was "poor and wicked, of barbarian greed and always inclined to violence." As soon as he heard that Severinus was dead, he seized property of the church, destroyed the monastery which Severinus had founded at Favianis, and carried all its belongings with him across the Danube. Punishment came on him, as Severinus had declared. Before a month was over he had lost his possessions, and his life as well, at the hand of his nephew Frederic, now man and soldier.

The last chapter in these annals of Roman Noricum finds war proclaimed upon the Rugians by King Odovacar, of whom a pleasant story is told earlier in this same *Life*: "Certain barbarians, drawn by the renown of Severinus, turned aside from their road toward Italy to seek his blessing. One of these was Odovacar, afterward King of Italy, but then a tall young man most shabbily dressed. He bowed his head to avoid striking the low roof of the cell and was told of his future fame by the man of God. 'Go on your way to Italy,' said Severinus. 'Now you are clothed in common skins, but soon you will give of your abundance to many.' " [10]

Long afterward Odovacar fell upon the barbarians of the land north of the Danube. It was the winter of 487, and Severinus had been dead now five years. The invasion was prompted by fear; Zeno, Emperor at Constantinople, had invited the Rugians to march into Italy in order to keep Odovacar from attacking lands of his in Illyricum; and Odovacar had decided to strike the Rugians in their own home first. His campaign was entirely successful. Feletheus and his Queen were captured and carried off to Italy, where the King was put to death. [11] A second expedition sent out under Odovacar's brother, Onulf, completed the work by the flight of Frederic.

Yet Odovacar realized that Noricum was doomed, that Rome could no longer hold this land by the river, and he commanded Onulf to bring its surviving inhabitants to Italy. In 488 the melancholy procession set out, bearing the relics

[10] c. 7. Valesianus Anonymus gives this story and acknowledges his indebtedness to Eugippius: *R.I.S.* XXIV, 4, p. 14.
[11] Paul Diac. *Hist. Lang.* I, 19.

of their Father, Severinus. So he had bidden at his death, foreseeing the destruction of this land, and hoping that about his grave another monastery of his disciples might be established in Italy. This actually came to pass. The relics were first of all placed in a fortress, thought with some probability to have stood on the site of the present Macerata di Monte Feltre, near San Marino. From there by permission of Gelasius, Pope from 492 till 496, they were transferred to the Castellum Lucullanum, the fortress where that unhappy boy Romulus "Augustulus" had been imprisoned by Odovacar after the attempt of his father Orestes to hold him on the throne of the West. An Italian lady of noble birth named Barbaria gave a splendid tomb for their reception, built at Naples, where now the Pizzofalcone lies. A third transference in 903 bore the relics through fear of the Saracens to the Benedictine monastery of San Severino inside Naples. Yet a fourth, after the dissolution of the monastery, saw their removal in 1807 to the town of Frattamaggiore, some miles north-west of Naples, where they rest now in the Parish Church. The tomb still stands there, with a painting of the saint in the presence of our Lady.[12]

Noricum Mediterraneum, the land south of this Noricum on the river, was still under Roman authority in the time of Theodoric the Great, who wrote through Cassiodorus to the people dwelling there as their Lord about 507.[13]

Before we leave this "Apostle of Austria" a word may, perhaps, be said about other miracles of his, though their stories must be read by the light of faith firmly planted in the candlestick of reason. Severinus himself refused to honour relics of the Saints, much as he longed for such, unless they came to him on credible authority. He even refused to pray

[12] Brunner, *Das Leben des Noriker-Apostels St. Severin*, pp. 167ff.; Lucy Menzies, *The Saints in Italy*, p. 403.
[13] *Variae*, III, 50.

for the healing of one of his monks who was troubled by
weak eyesight; but admonished him somewhat severely: "It
is no good for you, my son, to have keen eyes of the body and
to prefer clear outward vision. Pray, rather, that your inner
sight may be vigorous." Doubtless this particular servant of
Christ also suffered from distractions in prayer!

But the legends have their lessons for us. There is the
picture of the people of Juvao, now Salzburg, gathered in
their church for Vespers one summer evening, when all the
efforts upon flint and stone could produce no spark for the
lighting of the candles. At length Severinus knelt, absorbed
in prayer, and suddenly three men of God who were present
saw a flame blaze from the wax taper which he held in his
hand. Another story shows him watching with his brethren
through the night over the dead body of a much revered
priest in the church at Quintanis, identified, as we have seen,
with Osterhofen. At dawn Severinus sent the tired clergy
to rest after the long labour of the Office of the Dead,
smelled out by his spiritual nose and promptly ejected a holy
nun lurking in a corner in hope of seeing some miracle, and
with only four companions as witnesses, a priest, a deacon
and two door-keepers, prayed the Lord to vouchsafe
once again to show the virtue of His supreme majesty.
The narrative goes on: "Then, when the priest had ended
the appointed prayer,[14] Severinus of blessed memory addressed the dead: 'In the Name of our Lord Jesus Christ,
speak with thy brethren, holy priest Silvinus!' At this call
the dead man opened his eyes, and the Father could hardly
keep his companions from crying out in joy. Again he spoke
to him: 'Wilt thou that we ask of the Lord to grant thy

[14] Severinus, apparently, was not even a priest: cf. cc. 9, 16, and 23:
Zeiller, *Les origines chrét. dans les provinces danubiennes*, p. 375. An
engraving by Sadeler is found of this scene in Matthaeus Rader, *Bavaria
Sancta*, 1615–1627, p. 27.

presence still unto His servants here on earth?' But Silvinus
answered: 'By the Lord I beseech thee that I be no longer
held here, deprived of that perpetual peace in which I did
find myself.' At once prayer was made again, and the dead
man was at rest."

Not all the clergy of Noricum, however, had progressed
so far! We read of one who shocked the faithful badly. The
Saint's constant harping on fasts and vigils had got somewhat on his nerves, or, as Eugippius puts it, the devil had
seized him when Severinus was dealing firmly with the re-
fractory people of Batavis. He suddenly shouted: "Go away,
holy man, go away quickly, and let us have a little peace!"

The monastery in the Castellum Lucullanum near Naples
was first ruled by a certain Marcian, who had been a monk
under Severinus in Favianis, and after him by Eugippius himself.[15] There he wrote this *Life,* which the German historian
Wattenbach described as "the last ray of the sun before the
days of utter darkness." [16] In a letter to his friend Paschasius, a deacon of the Church of Rome, Eugippius tells that in
the consulship of Importunus, that is, in 509, he happened
to read a life of a monk of Italy named Bassus, written by a
layman of high rank, and was fired by desire for similar
honouring of his own first Abbot. He set to work, and finished two years later, in 511, a plain record of the life of
Severinus from the many narratives he had received from
the Father's disciples and from his own recollections. For
he had also been with Severinus in Noricum and had accompanied the relics on their journey to Italy.[17]

But who could embellish this simple story of his in a way

---

[15] *Vita,* c. 37; Isid. of Sev. *De vir. ill.* 34.
[16] *Deutschlands Geschichtsquellen,* I, p. 51.
[17] *Vita,* c. 44. The old theory (*e.g.* see *Dict. Christ. Biog.*) that Eugippius belonged by origin to Africa has been given up, and he is thought
to have come from a Roman family of the district near the Danube:
Jülicher, in *P.W. s.v. Eugippius,* 989.

worthy of its subject? Not, indeed, some learned layman,
trained in the obscurities of secular rhetoric which uneducated people would not understand. Paschasius at length
seemed the proper person, and to him Eugippius sent his
"Commemoratorium" or "Notes," that he might make them
into a lovely whole.

We know something of Paschasius from one of the *Dialogues* of Gregory the Great.[18] He wrote a work *On the
Holy Spirit,* now lost, though Gregory knew it and held it
"most correct and illustrious." Later authorities wrongly
looked upon a work of the same title by Faustus of Riez as
his. Gregory praises also this deacon of the Apostolic See
as a man of great holiness and much charity. But, he goes
on, Paschasius fell into trouble. He foolishly took the side
of Laurentius in the strife of Laurentius *versus* Symmachus
during the Papal election of 498, and persisted in his error
even after Symmachus had been seated on the throne of
Peter, right up to the very day of his death. Some time later
a Bishop of Capua, called Germanus, was ordered by his
doctors to take treatment in the hot baths at the site of the
modern Città Sant' Angelo, in the land of the Abruzzi. The
first day he entered he was horrified to find the ghost of this
late most highly revered Paschasius once again clad in mortal
flesh and suffering tortures, boiled up to the neck in the
steaming water. "My Father, what means this?" asked the
astonished Bishop. "To do penance for my fault have I
come," was the answer. "Wherefore do thou pray the Lord
for me, and if thou see me not here tomorrow, thou shalt
know thy prayer heard." The prayer was heard, and the
next day the distressing vision had vanished.

Paschasius, doubtless, was stubborn, but he seems to have
been gifted with good sense. He refused to touch the "Notes"

[18] IV, 40. Bardenhewer, IV, pp. 584f.

of Eugippius and told him to publish them as they stood.[19]
In the seventh century Isidore of Seville wrote of the "concise
style" of this same work, and mentioned a "Rule for monks"
written by Eugippius, of which we have now no trace. Probably it did not travel beyond the bounds of the monastery
over which Eugippius ruled.[20]

Eugippius was also held in honour by Fulgentius, Bishop
of Ruspe in Africa, who wrote to him a letter on the virtue
of love;[21] by Ferrandus, a deacon of Carthage, who addressed to him as to a master his treatise against the Arians
and other heretics, written in 533;[22] and by a monk of far-
reaching influence, Dionysius "the Humble," as he styled
himself. The works of this Dionysius, however, were neither
little nor poor. He came from Scythia, but was thoroughly
conversant with Roman culture through long stay in Italy,
and became renowned for his translation from Greek into
Latin of the canons of Greek Councils. He made them under
the Papal rule of Hormisdas and of Symmachus early in the
sixth century, and his collection was of infinite service to
the prelates of the Western Church in after days, when the
study of Greek was somewhat where it is now.[23] He took,
moreover, an important part in the calculations for the date
of Easter.[24] Altogether, a man of much intellectual merit,
and a scholar in whom Cassiodorus placed much confidence.[25] Eugippius was held by him worthy of receiving a
translation of a work of Gregory of Nyssa, *On the Creation
of Man;* and Dionysius prefaced it with words of deep
respect.[26]

[19] It does not seem necessary to read into this letter of Paschasius the
irony traced by Leclercq: *Eugyppius, Dict. d'arch. chrét.* ed. Cabrol, pp.
702ff.

[20] *De vir. ill., ibid.*   [21] *PL* LXV, 344.

[22] Angelo Mai, *Script. Vet. Nova Collectio,* III, 2, pp. 169ff.

[23] For his works see *PL* LXVII.

[24] Bede, *H. E.* V, 21; Paul Diac., *Hist. Lang.* I, 25.

[25] *De inst. div. litt.* 23.   [26] Mabillon, *Vetera Analecta,* 1723, p. 59.

The numerous manuscripts made of this *Life of Severinus* show how widely it was read in Italy and in the region of the Danube. Another work by Eugippius is also preserved in our libraries: a collection of passages from the works of Augustine of Hippo, made for those who had no access to these many tomes.[27] In itself this book of excerpts provides no mean feat of spiritual reading, with its roll of columns in the *Patrologia* and its exposition of the multitudinous problems known to students of this Saint. But the maiden lady Proba, to whom it was dedicated, was no ordinary daughter of the Church. She possessed on her shelves those works of Augustine from which Eugippius had made his three hundred and forty-eight extracts; he had borrowed some of them for his purpose and now repaid her zeal with the gift of this anthology. Cassiodorus had no reason to be ashamed of his kinswoman's love of sacred learning. This book, too, was eagerly read, and we find Cassiodorus and after him Notker, "the Stammerer" of St. Gall, recommending it for instruction.[28] Among the many copies made of it, one of the eighth century is of special interest for its different specimens of handwriting.[29]

It is rather a far journey from the banks of the Danube to the south of Italy, where our next monastic community awaits us. This one belongs to the sixth century both in its founding and in its literary work; it was the fruit of the calm and happy labours of the old age of Cassiodorus. No Order in later years carried on its name, and we know nothing of its monks after their Founder died. But it stands in history with an importance all its own.

[27] ed. Knöll, *C.S.E.L.* IX, 1.
[28] *De inst. div. litt.* 23. For Notker see Bernard Pez, *Thesaurus anecd. nov.* I, 1721, c. 1, col. 2.
[29] Leclercq, *ibid.*

We left Cassiodorus a weary man, looking back over those many years of civil service in Italy which he had rendered to her barbarian rulers. All had ended in disappointment, and, "sick to death" of "most bitter occupations and worldly cares seasoned with noxious flavour," [30] he resigned office and turned his thoughts to what had long been cherished in his heart as the real ambition of his life.

Even while he was immersed in the political swirl of Ravenna, he had had one place of retreat, the land in the region of the Bruttii where he himself had been born. This he not only visited from time to time, but fostered with all his care and eager plans for improvement, dwelling fondly on its beauty in one of the letters he wrote as Praetorian Prefect. [31] It lay near the Roman Scyllacium, originally a Greek foundation: a town which Cassiodorus calls "the first city of the Bruttii," famed in legend as built by Ulysses. The name still lives in the modern Squillace, an interesting place of some two or three thousand inhabitants, thought to be a few miles distant from the site of the old town; the estate of Cassiodorus we may imagine somewhere between this modern village and the shore of the Golfo di Squillace. A heavenly climate was its lot, sunny in winter, cool in summer, so equable that here no one ever feared unexpected changes of weather, and everyone's temper was as even as the temperature that soothed and yet braced his mind and body. Hence all a man's energy, freed from vexing problems of the barometer, was gloriously his own for higher thoughts. Guests in this place of peace looked out upon wide-spreading vineyards laden with fruit, on olive orchards, on fields of grain, and on the barns where threshing occupied its seasons of harvest. But the special joy of the host was his fish-ponds, hollowed out of the living rock at the base of the Moscian Hill

[30] *Exp. in Psalt.* Preface, 1.   [31] *Variae,* XII, 15.

under which his gardens rested. Deep pools lying in shadow, fed by the Pellene river, gave a delightful and natural home to a multitude of fish of various kinds, sporting as they would; now rising to take crumbs from the hands of Cassiodorus and his friends, now darting off to hide in caverns under the mountainside. From these pleasant waters the place received its name of "Vivarium."

Here Cassiodorus dreamed of working toward his great desire, secluded for the rest of his life from the world. It was a sorry world, this Italy about the year of grace 539 A.D.[32] Rome was in the hands of Belisarius, victorious after the year-long blockade by Witigis; Narses had already entered Italy. No wonder that Cassiodorus despaired of Courts and fled to dwell with spiritual eternities. But other thoughts, too, spurred him on. In the welter and turmoil of things political, when nothing could be thought of as safe from invaders and free-booters, what of the treasures laid up in books? Manuscripts, once destroyed, could not be replaced. Was the culture of the West, so hardly won, to be lost with the creatures of its soil and the bricks and stone of man's working? Why not devise a House of Prayer, in which men might both plead for the peace of the world during this distracted time and find occupation for leisure hours in the preserving of these precious works for ages to come? In such a home of religion the Queen of Sciences, Theology, should be honoured still with due reverence and care, attended and served by all the ministrations of those seven handmaidens, the liberal arts of secular learning.

For years Cassiodorus had been troubled by the lack of teachers skilled to interpret Biblical and patristic writings to

[32] It is thought that Cassiodorus must have left Ravenna before 540, when Belisarius entered the city, or he would surely have been mentioned as present there by Procopius, who accompanied Belisarius. He appears to have been for some time in Constantinople before he settled in Vivarium, and probably matured the plan for his monastery there: Bury, *Lat. Rom. Emp.* II, p. 222; van de Vyver, *Speculum,* 1931, p. 260.

the young men of his time, as contrasted with the attention still given to secular studies of rhetoric. Justinian in his zeal against heretics had closed the gates of the University of Athens ten years since. Although Greek scholars were still found to educate the sons of Italian noblemen, it was only in the house of some older member of the clergy, often a bishop, that instruction in their future calling was given to the more fortunate candidates for the priesthood. There was a grievous dearth in Italy of schools of religious training such as the monasteries of Ireland showed in such abundant splendour during this century. With this perplexing problem in mind Cassiodorus had already consulted Agapetus, Pope from 535 to 536, with regard to the building by public subscriptions of a theological college at Rome. Would it not be possible for Rome to follow the example of Alexandria, or, to bring the matter to their own day, to build a school such as that raised for Hebrew education at Nisibis in Syria? [33]

But the strife of war beating about the city of Rome made such hopes a vain dream, and he was forced to wait till in the leisure of retirement he could throw open his house at "Vivarium" to men who would follow his leadership in prayer and study. Life, he planned, should be lived there in common under a discipline laid down by himself, centred in the chapel and the libraries. For those who showed desire for yet deeper retreat he established a separate cloister at a little distance from the general monastery. There, on the Castle Mount, such who had duly prepared themselves might live the hermit's life, enclosed by ancient walls.

For all his family, "my monks," as he calls them,[34] Cas-

[33] *De instit. div. litt.* Preface, 1. For the later works of Cassiodorus see *PL* LXIX–LXX. The two books of the *Institutiones* are now available in the edition (1937) of R. A. B. Mynors.

[34] *De orthog.* Preface, 1. He writes of his "conversio" at the time of his retirement to Vivarium. The word, for one already a Catholic Christian, regularly means "entrance upon the monastic life," whether Cassiodorus literally assumed the tonsure or did not: see van de Vyver, *op. cit.*, pp. 261ff.

siodorus wrote precepts and instructions in two books. These contain no systematized Rule, and we read of none of this kind in connection with the monastery. A question of interest for students of Cassiodorus has seen considerable discussion: whether he was indebted to the Benedictine Rule in his discipline? The chief argument against this is his silence with regard to Benedict. Yet this is not by any means conclusive, and on the other side we have the facts that the two Houses were near each other in the south of Italy; that Cassiodorus, like Benedict, tells of eight Hours of monastic devotion in place of the seven generally observed in Italy before Benedict drew up his Rule; that both Founders made intellectual study an integral and important part of the daily task; that certain resemblances have been traced between the written words of Benedict and of Cassiodorus. It is true that Cassiodorus wrote for those who, like himself, might be engrossed in study of holy texts; Benedict had a far larger vision for his sons. But the facts seem to make it impossible that Cassiodorus should not have paid reverent attention to the Abbot of Monte Cassino, already some ten years or more a monastery when he himself retired from the world to establish his own. It is pleasant to imagine that Cassiodorus fostered the seed of learning planted by Benedict for some thirty years after the Father had gone to God, and that Vivarium holds its own place in the devotion to sacred scholarship which has always been the glory of the Benedictine Order.[35]

The Founder of Vivarium had read with great care his

[35] For reff. to the Hours in Cassiodorus see *PL* LXX, 10 and 547. See on Cassiodorus and Benedict, Dom John Chapman, *St. Benedict and the Sixth Century*, pp. 88ff., and Dom Cuthbert Butler's assent in *The Downside Review*, 48, 1930, pp. 185f. See also the collection of parallel passages made by Abbot Amelli: *Cassiodoro e la Volgata*, 1917, pp. 42f. On the intellectual influence of Cassiodorus see Dudden, *Gregory the Great*, II, pp. 172f. For the contrary view, the influence of Cassiodorus on Benedictine life, see Otto Zöckler, *Askese und Mönchtum*, II, p. 373.

Cassian on the *Training of Monks,* as adapted from the East for Western novices, and his disciples filled much of their day and night with the "work of God," the monastic Offices. But he laid down principles and methods of realizing these great aims, rather than articles of a programme for general and daily use.

The first of his two books, *On Training in Sacred Literature,*[36] prescribes the more important instruction and study. The basis and the end of all education is found in the Bible, explained by patristic commentaries: "Beloved brethren, let us ascend the divine Scripture through the teachings of the Fathers as by a ladder of vision, that, led and carried forward by them, we may merit to come to the contemplation of God." At the foot of this "ladder of Jacob" lie the Psalms, with which the recruit is to begin. The Psalms were the particular joy of Cassiodorus. Directly he had retired from politics he had turned with a sigh of relief to composing a *Commentary* upon them, and at the time of starting on his "Instructions for Monks" he had reached Psalm twenty.[37] His motive for writing was to give in somewhat shorter form the interpretations made by St. Augustine in the *Enarrationes.*

Yet his own *Commentary* embraces more than a thousand columns in Migne![38] Such was his delight in his subject. To him the Psalms were "a garden enclosed, a paradise full of all fruits," giving food and solace to the soul in all its needs, telling of penitence and prayer and prophecy, enlightening every Hour of day and night with a peculiar and proper message. In them, he declares, men and angels unite to pour forth their praise of God, whether as from a vessel filled with varied fragrance or as in an orchestra of living sounds. In them the coming day is welcomed with the joy of

---

[36] *De institutione divinarum litterarum: PL LXX,* 1105ff.
[37] *ibid.,* c. iv.
[38] *PL LXX,* 1–1056.

morning; they dedicate the first hour and consecrate the third; in them the breaking of bread is blessed at the sixth hour and fasting is ended at the ninth; in them the day finds its close; in them men hold a light to lighten the darkness until dawn.[39]

Each Psalm is treated in due order of explanation of its title, of its divisions, of its content, of its moral. The version used is the "Roman Psalter," in union with the translation of St. Jerome and even the Hebrew text. Much stress is laid on the mystical interpretation of numbers, to which Cassiodorus, too, was especially partial. Thus the body of one hundred and fifty Psalms is divided into a first part of seventy, representing by symbol of the Sabbath the Old Testament, and a second part of eighty, representing by symbol of the eighth day the Resurrection and the New Testament: "For, though we must avoid impious astrology with all our power, yet we ought to remember that the Psalms contain matter of arithmetic and other arts."[40] This is in keeping with the declaration made by Cassiodorus again and again, that from the source of Holy Scripture arises for men their knowledge of the human and the divine.[41]

The work is not original. Besides its basis in Augustine, it contains much teaching taken from the writings of others of the Fathers. It stoutly maintains that all the Psalms are the work of David, and that other names placed at their head must be understood as referring to singers or interpreted mystically. Its length did not prevent it from becoming famous in the Middle Ages, and it was frequently copied.

We return to our manual of training. After the Psalms, Cassiodorus continues, the rest of Holy Scripture must be read

---

[39] *De instit.* c. iv; *Exp. in Psalt.* 10. A third simile is of the varied colours and "eyes" of a peacock's plumage.
[40] *PL* LXX, 505.
[41] *ibid.*, 175; 20; Franz, *M. Aurelius Cass. Senator,* pp. 100f.

and digested. Here the matter of text assumes immense importance, "lest faults of copyists become ingrained in your untutored minds." Next he prescribes the study of commentaries in Latin, with an exhortation that constantly recurs. Let the monks themselves search on their own account for fresh light. If Latin commentaries leave a problem still dark, turn, if possible, to Greek, turn to Hebrew! Above all, never grow weary of hunting for truth, and use every fair means of attaining it. Of course, as Cassiodorus remarks, prayer *can* work miracles, and "meditation, frequent and intent, is the mother of understanding." Did not Cassian tell of the aged monk who solved a bitter problem, not of his own little learning, but of seven days and nights of prayer? And St. Augustine praised an uneducated servant who through grace of this same prayer could translate from an unknown language as well as if he had studied it for years. All the same, in common life let us not try to tempt the Lord our God. The monks of Cassiodorus will stick to grammar and dictionary, and pray for diligence as well as light.

Those who have had the necessary education will devote themselves to preparing emended texts of the Bible for the use of all. Here Cassiodorus himself set an example, by collating texts of the Psalter, the Prophets, and the Epistles. For the benefit of this more advanced section he gives a detailed account of commentaries and aids to sacred study: works by Ambrose and by Origen, by Augustine and by Jerome, by Hilary of Poitiers, and by Rufinus of Aquileia. He includes also Greek works, such as those by Basil, by Chrysostom, by Eusebius, which the monks are to read; some, by the aid of a translation, others, better equipped, in the original. Most of the books mentioned were to be found in the Monastery Library, which Cassiodorus had taken extraordinary pains to make as complete as was possible in that time of continual war. He had sought in Italy, in Greece, and even in Africa, for the manuscripts he needed for himself and for the copyists among his brethren.[42] For some commentaries he prescribes cautious handling, as suspected of heretical passages. The work of Ticonius the Donatist is one of these, also that of Origen; even that of Cassian, whom, however, in general, the monks are to read with diligence. Treat such writers, the Founder advises, as Vergil treated Ennius, and pick out the gold from the dung-heap. His own practice was to mark dangerous passages with the word *"Unsound"* in the margin. At the beginning of each work he placed a table of contents for the assistance of the less practised reader; blank pages, also, were left for future finds.

But the brethren who shall dare to enter upon the work of copying and of emending sacred texts must extend their studies still further. Church history must be read in Josephus, in Eusebius and Rufinus, in Orosius, and so on. To aid these workers Cassiodorus not only had the *Jewish Antiquities* of Josephus translated "with great labour" into Latin, but also gave to a certain scholar, Epiphanius by name, the task of translating from the original Greek many selected passages from the Church historians Socrates, Sozomen, and Theodoret. He himself chose the passages. The result was the *Tripartite History*, a confused medley, marred by many omissions and redundant statements; even more seriously at fault because of errors due to the translator's little knowledge of Greek. But, doubtless, the whole was very useful at Vivarium, as it was in the Middle Ages, for which it reproduced for Greekless readers much of the Church's record after the Council of Nicaea.[43]

[42] *PL* LXX, 1120 and 1109ff.
[43] Manitius, I, p. 51. For detailed criticism see Franz, pp. 104ff.

There is, moreover, in this same handbook of training some brief mention of those four Councils of the Church that the fourth and fifth centuries had known; the *Encyclical*, published after the Council of Chalcedon to deal with Monophysite heresy in the East, Cassiodorus had also had translated into Latin for his Library,[44] and other *Acta* of the Councils he had laid up there in their original Greek. A short account is given here as well of the Latin Fathers whose commentaries he prescribes; also of Eugippius, as excerptor of St. Augustine's volumes, and of Dionysius "the Humble." Dionysius was a friend and fellow-student of Cassiodorus, who gives him praise for his knowledge of the Bible. From the words: "Dionysius, who read dialectic with me and passed many years of his life as a splendid professor of learning," it has been thought that he may have lived for a time at Vivarium.[45]

The student of sacred texts must know of secular matters, too. His reading must include geography, that he may identify places named in holy works, and orthography, that he may himself understand the rules of writing if he is to criticize texts composed by others. Long after Cassiodorus had written his two books for the training of his monks, he tells us that they complained: "What good is it for you to write about ancient authors for us when we don't know how to write ourselves?" So in his ninety-third year the Founder set to work for the last time and extracted from twelve well-known grammarians passages dealing with this subject.[46] Those curious to know more he refers here, as ever, to the complete works of these authorities, collected on the

---

[44] *PL LXX*, 1123.

[45] Franz criticizes this suggestion: p. 39, note 4; cf. Mabillon, *Ann. Bened.* I, p. 126.

[46] He only gives the names of ten. For this collection in the *De Orthographia* of Cassiodorus see Keil, *Gr. Lat.* VII, pp. 143ff.

monastery bookshelves. "It is a glorious art," he bursts out, "to be able both to write decently what you would say and to read aloud properly what has been written!" [47]

Instruction in the art of copying also begins here. These are some of the rules prescribed: "Never meddle with the metaphors of Holy Scripture by trying to reduce them to common speech. Do not decline Hebrew proper names. Do not interfere with the properly supported text of manuscripts, even though you find expressions contrary to ordinary usage, as:—*For the people who shall be born whom the Lord hath made.* When in doubt examine several manuscripts, and refer to a Greek or a Hebrew text, if your knowledge admits of this. Retain in your copy even expressions contrary to the accepted usage of good prose, if they are found in good texts, as:—*"inflabitur ventrem"* for *"inflabitur ventre,"* and *"obliti non sumus te."*

On the other hand, the student must be careful to detect errors made by careless copyists. Look out especially, Cassiodorus urges, for mistakes in ablatives and accusatives, but be sure you are right yourself before you venture to correct. The MS. will not look nice if you stick in or cross out the letter *m* at random! Be sure to correct a *b* written wrongly for *v*, or a *v* for a *b*, or an *o* for a *u*, or an *n* for an *m*, and keep a sharp lookout for the letter *h*, wrongly omitted or added. Leave *ae* for the genitive, but not for adverbs. Remember that we write *illuminatio, irrisio, immutabilis, impius, improbus.* Omit the *g* in such words as *gnarus.* Write *quod* for* the pronoun, but *quot* for the numeral adverb; *quicquam* rather than *quidquam.* Divide your text for the help of your readers' minds by points between words, after the manner of Donatus; [48] and for their souls' sake follow me in placing the warning *"Unsound"* against passages which may worry their orthodox sense of creed!

[47] *PL* LXX, 1241.　　　　　　[48] Keil, *Gr. Lat.* IV, p. 372.

These instructions are naturally still of interest to students of the Latin of this time.

Even these hints, however, did not satisfy the Founder's zeal, and he added a second book, *On the Arts and Disciplines of Liberal Letters,* containing in seven brief chapters the principles of the seven liberal arts.[49] These, too, the student must know if he would accomplish his task aright. It is not surprising that Cassiodorus met with criticism for trying to encompass precepts on the science of sacred and secular letters within the space of two short books of instruction; he himself lamented the difficulty of his task. But he held it a necessary one in the lack of monastic schools in Italy, and strengthened his courage with an appeal to the Lord in two lines of Sedulius, poet of sacred song in the fifth century:

> Grandia posco quidem: sed tu dare grandia nosti,
> Quem magis offendit, quisquis sperando tepescit.[50]

These seven arts are treated here in order of Grammar; Rhetoric; Logic; Mathematics, comprising Arithmetic, Geometry, Music, Astronomy, and are described by the aid of recognized Greek and Latin authorities. To the translations of Boethius Cassiodorus owes much;[51] Martianus Capella is nowhere named. In both Cassiodorus and Boethius, of course, the aim has veered from pagan culture to Christian search for truth. Did not David praise the Lord seven times a day? Even so has Wisdom hewn out her seven pillars, and Revelation has raised on high her seven lamps for the lighting of the science of God.

The double text-book lived on for some centuries. Isidore of Seville drew on its author for the teaching of rhetoric;

---

[49] The two books are known in one work as *Institutiones divinarum et saecularium lectionum* (or *litterarum*). For the history of the text and its various recensions see Mynors, ed.

[50] *PL* LXX, 1141.   [51] See *e.g. PL* LXX, 1171B.

Bede called him a "teacher of the Church" and praised warmly his *Commentary* on the Psalter; his writings found their place in Alcuin's Library at York. Raban acknowledged his debt to him, among other learned authorities, in the preface to the manual *On the Training of the Clergy.* Erasmus admired his character, but criticized the comprehensive reach of his subject.[52] It must be confessed that the secular second part was better known in the Middle Ages than the first, to which it was added afterward as a preparation; the greater space devoted in it to rhetoric and dialectic shows the greater importance attached to those studies. The section on music is of interest in connection with the remarks of Cassiodorus on this subject in his letter written as Secretary of Theodoric to Boethius.[53] A reference in this section to a former Latin authority on music, Albinus, has been thought to provide some kind of date for this book on secular arts: "Among the Latins Albinus, a man of much distinction, composed a book on music, brief but comprehensive. I have it in my library at Rome and remember reading it carefully. But, in case it has been destroyed in the inroad of the barbarians, you can use Gaudentius translated into Latin by Mutianus. If you read and re-read this with diligence, it will open for you the halls of this science." If Cassiodorus is referring here to the capture of Rome by Totila, this second book must have been written after 546.[54]

We have remarked that Cassiodorus spent all his energy on the collecting of books for his Library. Texts of the Bible,

[52] For Isidore see Halm, *Rhet. Lat. min.,* pp. 508ff.; for Bede, *PL* XCI, 849; for Alcuin, *PL* CI, 843; for Raban, *PL* CVII, 296; for Erasmus, *Epist.* ed. Allen, tom. VIII, p. 128. See on all, Franz, pp. 122ff.

[53] *Var.* II, 40.

[54] See L. Traube, *Vorles. und Abh.* I, 1909, p. 105. The mention in *De instit. div. litt.* I of the condemnation of Origen by Vigilius and the fact that Cassiodorus does not mention the Fifth Council of the Church at which Origen was again condemned seem to point to a date between 543 and 553 for that book: Franz, p. 47.

including the Septuagint version of the Old, and the Greek text of the New Testament, and, in Latin, the Old Latin version, the *Itala,* in different forms, and the Vulgate of St. Jerome, took the most honoured places, supported by an extraordinary variety of works. A catalogue of this "first monastic library" has been drawn up for us by the skilled imagination of Adolph Franz.[55] Several manuscripts of kindred contents were often filed together for greater ease in studying, and for the same end books were massed in different sections. We read, for instance, of the Greek manuscripts as housed in the eighth section. Various covers were provided for the codices, "that a fair exterior might clothe, as with a wedding garment, the beauty of sacred literature." Moreover, a choice of covers was given, in a collection of specimen varieties from which the copyists of new manuscripts might select according to their own taste. Other material aids to comfort in study included oil lamps, ingeniously constructed to replenish their own fuel from a little reservoir, sundials for daytime, and water-clocks for cloudy days and the hours of night. Thus no one would miss by concentrated study the more direct "work of God."

He did not, however, forget his weaker disciples. For the sick he provided baths, and admonished those who cared for them to be sympathetic, thinking more of their brother's trouble than of their own. Skill was requisite also here, as in all parts of a monk's life. The infirmarian must understand the properties of herbs and study authorities on medicine, such as Hippocrates and Galen in a Latin translation. But let him remember, withal, to trust in the Lord above all simples and potions of human device. Similar thought for humbler folk is enjoined upon the two "Abbots" of this community, Chalcedonius and Geruntius. Cassiodorus did not,

[55] pp. 8off.

it seems, assume the office of Abbot himself, and we may well understand that his thought of literary things left him little time for practical administration, even were he a monk himself in very fact. The "Abbots," then, are instructed to administer alms, to clothe and to feed the poor. They are to train in good habits the peasants of the countryside around their walls: "Let these know nothing of thefts, and of the worship of heathen places. Let them live in innocence and happy simplicity. Let them come frequently to the monastery and be ashamed to be called yours if they be not known as of your training. And tell them that it is God who gives fruitfulness to the fields of men if they call upon Him faithfully."

In similar manner those of the Community whose hearts shivered within them when they entered the Library, and, in spite of diligent perseverance, really could not master texts and codices, were sent to till the fields and to tend the gardens and orchards. Such manual labour, Cassiodorus admits, is not unfitting for monks nor without its blessing: "To give fresh fruit to the weary and to nourish the hungry with sound meat is, indeed, a work of heaven, though it may seem to savour of earth." Even these sons of toil, however, are to seek for enlightenment in the written page; from Columella, or from other authors, if he be found too difficult.

More glorious, nevertheless, the task of perpetuating works of holy scholars.[56] "Happy is the aim, praiseworthy the eagerness, to reveal tongues with the fingers, silently to give salvation to men, to fight with pen and ink against the attacks of the devil. Satan receives a wound in every word written by him who makes fresh texts of the ancient law of the Lord. Though, indeed, the scribe must sit in one place,

[56] Of course, the encouragement of study in the cloister was no new movement of Cassiodorus or of St. Benedict; cf. the school of St. Jerome and of the congregation of Lérins.

yet by the scattering of his labour he walks through divers provinces."

So for the former Praetorian Prefect his latter days were full of peace. From about his sixtieth year till he was well over ninety he laboured on, first to learn and then to teach; for, as he warned his two Abbots, "it is a burden of great shame to have books to read and not to know whereof you may teach." In addition to the works described above he wrote also some minor treatises on grammar, and commentaries on the Epistles and on the Acts of the Apostles as well as on the Apocalypse, works which attained little or no fame in later years.[57]

The thought which he leaves with us, whether we see him in Ravenna, in Rome, or in the retirement of the Bruttian land, is of one who, above all, saw everywhere an ideal of harmony and concord. If his long toil to unite Roman and Goth under the leadership of Rome was in the end doomed to failure, he will always be remembered in that he taught his disciples to link the things of God with the things of men, mindful that all things are of God, and, therefore, as the Stoics said before him, must work in sympathy for the common good. Only let Reason ever be obedient to Faith. Here we come back to Boethius, who, like his contemporary, looked back upon the old and forward to the new. The last words written by Cassiodorus for "his monks" shortly before his death show the undeviating purpose of these thirty years of retreat: "Farewell, my brethren, and do you grant me remembrance in your prayers, to whom among other things I have given this brief counsel on the excellence of orthography and on its distinctions of right proven value; for

[57] Cassiodorus himself gives a list of his writings at the beginning of his *On Orthography,* but does not include the *Historia Tripartita,* perhaps because Epiphanius, the translator, had done so much of the work: Franz, p. 106.

whom I have written in great abundance of the understanding of the Holy Scriptures. This was my will, that you might be separate from the number of ignorant men; even so may God in His grace suffer you not to be joined with the wicked in the company of punishment."

He died, we may think, about 575. What matter if his monastery did not survive? The activity of his youth has left us a collection of rather tedious letters, of value to his period's history alone. The peace of his old age enriched the power of the cloister unto all time: concretely by the legacy of his collected manuscripts; in the abstract, by his enthusiasm for learning, so fruitful for the unbroken tradition of monastic scholarship.[58]

From the south of Italy we make our way lastly to the south of France and reach Arles, converted to the Catholic faith by the great Trophimus, according to Gregory of Tours,[59] and famous for the labours of Hilary, its Bishop in the fifth century. At this time it was also renowned throughout Gaul for its vigour in commerce and politics, which had raised it in Christian times to a city of the first rank, and held itself a rival of Marseilles in matters of the world, of Vienne and Narbonne in ecclesiastical importance. The story of the struggle in the fifth century for pre-eminence between these sees of southern Gaul is a truly complicated one, and it must content us to remark that in 417 Pope Zosimus had raised the Bishop of Arles to the dignity of Metropolitan [60] and thereby intensified the keenness of Vienne and Narbonne to assert their enjoyment of the same standing.

---

[58] See G. H. Putnam, *Books and their Makers during the Middle Ages*,[2] pp. 16ff.
[59] *Hist. Franc.* I, 30.
[60] Mansi, IV, 359. See Scott Holmes, *The Christian Church in Gaul*, pp. 363ff.; Malnory, *Saint Césaire*, pp. 38ff.

The sixth century saw further glory for the Cathedral of Arles, when in 514 Pope Symmachus conferred on its Bishop Caesarius the honour of Vicar Apostolic throughout Gaul and Spain.[61] Henceforth it was for him to act as intermediary between the clergy and bishops of these countries and the Holy See. It is this Caesarius with whom we are concerned here. He ruled over the diocese of Arles for forty years; he saw the standards of three nations raised, one after another, over its towers; he corresponded with seven Popes, presided over six Councils of the Gallican Church, and watched the developing of a national Church in Gaul under the determined hand of the Frankish monarchs. His wise and energetic administration introduced many reforms into ecclesiastical government. His passion for orthodoxy in doctrine laid an impress on the Church at large which has lasted permanently. He ranks with Augustine as one of the most diligent and able preachers in the Western Church of the first six centuries. And it is to him that we owe the first definite Rule for nuns in this Church, a document that held wide authority in this time and would doubtless have been of influence in far later days, had it not been lost in the increase of Benedictine progress.

His work was made none the easier in that he was Burgundian by birth, son of a noble and devoutly Catholic family residing near Chalon-sur-Saône. Historians as well as Churchmen have reason to be grateful to him, since his official *Life,* related at the prayer of the second Abbess in his religious foundation for women and of her nuns, is a document in itself of importance, as written by men of his own time.[62] Its first part, dealing especially with his work as ruler of the Church, was composed by three bishops, whose Father in God

[61] Mansi, VIII, 227; *PL* LXII, 66.
[62] Its editor, Krusch, *M.G.H. Script. rer. Merov.* III, p. 451, dates Book I of this *Life* between 542 and 549.

he himself had been. The most important part in this triple authorship was taken by Cyprian, Bishop of Toulon; he was aided by Firminus, Bishop of Uzès, and by Viventius, whose see is not known. The second part, telling of more personal details, was entrusted by these to a priest, Messianus, and a deacon, Stephen, who had both held responsible positions in the house of Caesarius, and had known him intimately for many years.

The narrative is simple and unadorned; it is also a record of great piety. At the age of seven the future Saint gave away his clothes to beggars, and when sternly questioned by authority on his return home, declared that "they had been taken away by passers-by." At eighteen, without consulting his family, he begged Silvester, Bishop of Chalon, to receive him into his clergy-house; with shaven head and his lay garments discarded for the cassock, he would begin there to learn the way of religion. The Bishop consented, and for two years Caesarius served the Church in his own city. But this was not hard enough for his ambition, and when he was twenty, he entered the monastery founded by Honoratus in the fifth century on the larger of the Isles of Lérins off the south coast of Gaul, near Marseilles. Porcarius was its Abbot at this time, and under him Caesarius kept its Rule with admirable fervour. For his merit he was promoted to the office of cellarer. But, unhappily, certain of the brethren were not equally virtuous and did not brook patiently the discipline in matters of food and drink imposed on them by this youthful ascetic. They even went so far as to complain to the Lord Abbot, and Porcarius, who was getting old and infirm, thought it prudent to send Caesarius back to his private life of devotion as simple monk. He returned, and his passion for abstinence and his hours for prayer now flowed on unchecked. We read that on Sundays he used to cook for himself a few vegetables and a little porridge to do duty for meals all the rest of the week. The result was a sharp attack of quartan fever, and the Abbot, finding that the doctors were talking to no purpose, decided to send off this zealous disciple to the care of specialist physicians at Arles.

Here he was hospitably received and persuaded to follow a course of secular learning under Pomerius, a celebrated African professor of rhetoric. But Cicero and Vergil were not the sustenance his mind craved. One night he fell asleep with his lesson-book under his arm and dreamed that a fearful serpent was gnawing him at the place where the heathen volume lay. Like Jerome before him he jumped up in terror and forswore pagan studies. We may think, however, that the decision did not give him the trouble it caused Jerome. Long afterward he wrote humbly to a learned Lady Abbess that he, alas! had been a lazy student.[63]

But dreams were of great importance in the sixth century, and our student marched off at once to consult Aeonius, Bishop of Arles, who received him with open arms as a kinsman and a fellow-citizen of Chalon. With permission from Porcarius, Aeonius ordained the young man deacon and priest, and finding that he still kept strictly the Rule of Lérins, judged him worthy to reform the ways of a small monastery on an island not far away. Its Abbot had lately died, and discipline had relaxed. For three years Caesarius held office, and successfully, till by desire of Aeonius and his clergy he was elected Bishop of Arles on the death of Aeonius in 502. The election took place in his absence, and when he heard of it, he ran away to hide in the old Roman cemetery at Aliscamps.

Arles at this time was under the dominion of King Alaric the second. Although he had consented to the election of

[63] *PL* LXVII, 1136.

Caesarius, yet he was ruler of the Visigoths and Arian by creed; Caesarius was not only of the Catholic Church, but also a native of the hated Burgundy. What easier than that he should be suspected of harbouring treacherous designs in the interests of Gundobad, then King of Burgundy? Suspicion was brought to a head by the false accusation of one of the secretaries of Caesarius, Licinianus by name, and the Bishop was sent into exile at Bordeaux in 505. But the charge was soon refuted, and the guilty secretary only rescued from death and the devil's maw by the prayer of Caesarius that he might not depart this life impenitent.

Alaric now turned to a better mind. He received Caesarius with respect and willingly gave the grace which the Bishop was obliged to ask of his secular and heretic Lord, that he be allowed to convoke a Council of Gothic Bishops at Agde in 506.[64] In preparation for this, the first of the series of Gallican Councils over which he presided, he gathered together with long labour a collection of the ancient Statutes of the Church for his guidance.[65] We will not tarry over the collection here, since its details belong to Church history and not to the special writings of Caesarius. Not all the Bishops arrived for the Council. We have a letter from Ruricius, Bishop of Limoges, saying that the climate of Agde was altogether too hot for his health, and would the Bishop of Arles kindly let him know earlier, next time he wanted a Council? The whole tone of the epistle breathes envy and bitterness. We may note, however, that those who gathered at Agde asked earnestly of the Lord God long life for the "most glorious, most magnificent, most pious King, through

[64] For its acts see *Concilia Galliae*, ed. Sirmond, I, pp. 16off.
[65] *Statuta Ecclesiae antiqua*, PL LVI, 879ff. See on these Duchesne, *Christian Worship*[5], p. 350, and, for the work of Caesarius, Malnory, pp. 50ff.; Lejay, *Dict. de théol. cath.* II, 2171.

whose permission they had assembled";[66] and we know that
the next year, 507, Alaric was dead at the hand of Clovis.[67]
The Franks then proceeded with the aid of Burgundy to
besiege Arles, and Theodoric, equally determined, sent an
army to oppose them.[68]

It is here that the *Life of Caesarius* becomes of special
interest to history.[69] The Bishop had among his minor clerics
a relative of his, who also belonged to the Burgundian nation,
now more than ever held hostile. Unfortunately this young
man, terrified by all that was happening, climbed one night
over the walls of Arles and went to parley with the enemy.
Suspicion again fell on Caesarius, this time that he had sent
his kinsman to arrange the surrender of Arles to Burgundy.
The Bishop was haled from his residence and kept under
close guard, while his captors debated whether they would
drown him promptly in the Rhône or carry him by boat to
the fortress at Beaucaire. The streets were filled with citizens
screaming, "Death to Caesarius!" as he was led to his temporary place of waiting, and none shouted louder than the
heretics, the Arians and the Jews, whose creeds, of course,
he had consistently opposed.

Once more the tide turned. One day a Jewish sentry,
standing at his post on the city walls, threw down a large
stone into the enemy's land; it was recovered by the defend-
ers from within, and to good purpose. For it bore, securely
fastened, a letter proposing to the Franks that they scale the
walls under cover of night at a place designated by the writer,
whose name and race were given; as reward immunity was
to be given to all Jews. The shouts of "Death and destruction!" now changed their attack from Caesarius to the

[66] Sirmond, p. 161. For the letter from Ruricius see Sirmond, *Supple-
ment*, p. 46.
[67] See my pages 87 and 216.
[68] Cf. Cass. *Var.* I, 24, a.508.   [69] *Vita*, I, 29ff.

Jewish soldiers and citizens of Arles, and the Bishop once more returned safely to his Palace. Soon afterward the besiegers were put to flight by the Ostrogothic army, and Arles passed under the rule of Theodoric the Great.

Caesarius now threw himself into his life-long works of charity and giving of alms, distributed to all alike. He sold the treasures of the Church themselves, thuribles, chalices, patens, for the ransom of heretic captives, for food and for clothing for the hordes of prisoners in need. Distress was naturally terrible in the city after the siege. In one of his sermons he pictured its horrors: of women carried off and of babies tossed carelessly aside, of the dead lying unburied and of streams of prisoners departing from their homes.[70] Theodoric in pity remitted tribute due from Arles to his exchequer.[71]

In 513 Caesarius met this great ruler in the Palace at Ravenna. For some unexplained cause Theodoric, also, had seen reason for offence in his behaviour and summoned him now to Italy. When he entered the audience chamber, the King rose to greet him with reverence, doffed his crown, and talked with him of his journey, of his work in Arles, and of the King's own Ostrogothic subjects. After he had left, Theodoric turned to the officials who waited near, and said: "Now God punish those who gave this innocent and holy man the trouble of this long journey! Why, I trembled from head to foot when he came in and I saw that face of an angel, that man looking like one of the Apostles themselves!"[72] And immediately the King sent off to the Bishop's lodging a present of silver plate and money, begging him to accept them as a father from his son. Caesarius, of course, sold the plate to get money for his poor at home and thereby increased

[70] *PL* XXXIX, 2316.
[71] Cass. *Var.* III, 32, a.510.   [72] *Vita*, I, 36.

the reputation he had gained by the royal greeting. The Pope himself, Symmachus, received him in audience, confirmed his standing as Metropolitan, allowed him to wear the *pallium,* and gave his deacons the right to wear at Arles the dalmatic, already in use at Rome.[73]

Other Councils of the Church in Gaul over which Caesarius subsequently presided were those of Arles (the fourth), in 524; of Carpentras, in 527; of Orange (the second) and of Vaison (the second), in 529; of Marseilles, in 533.[74] Those of Arles and of Vaison dealt with the details of Church administration so dear to this orderly mind; at Carpentras and at Marseilles the Gothic Bishops met to try charges against their episcopal brethren. The Council of Marseilles is of interest because, after convicting Contumeliosus, Bishop of Riez, on a charge of grave offence against moral law, and sentencing him to make restitution of stolen property to the Church and to retire to repent of his sins in a monastery, its action was confirmed by Pope John the second and sharply rebuked by Pope Agapetus, who succeeded John in 535.[75] Most important of all in our eyes is the Second Council of Orange, at which in 529 the assembled Bishops pronounced the death-blow of the "semi-Pelagian" doctrine which had raged so vehemently in southern Gaul. This was a milder form of the heresy which Pelagius and his school in the fifth century had dared to maintain against Augustine and his follower, Prosper of Aquitaine, stout upholders of the orthodox Catholic creed that man can avail nothing of himself, but is wholly dependent for good on the grace of God.

There was a personal aspect for our Bishop in this Coun-

[73] *M.G.H. Epist.* Tom. III, pp. 37ff.; *Vita,* I, 42.
[74] Maassen, *Concilia aevi Merov.* pp. 35, 40, 44, 55, 60. For the Council of Orange see also *PL* LXVII, 1141ff.
[75] *PL* LXVI, 25; 46ff.

cil. The monastic School of Lérins was accused of sending out clergy who leaned toward the Pelagian views, especially Faustus, once its Abbot, now Bishop of Riez; and Caesarius himself, as trained at Lérins, had fallen under suspicion in the minds of Bishops of the See of Vienne, that rival of Arles, when they gathered for debate in 528 at Valence.[76] In vindication both of the Catholic creed and of his own firm adherence to it, he assembled the following year the meeting at Orange.

There is evidence that for a long time before this Council met he had once again been at work on the writings of the Fathers, gathering pronouncements on this all-important subject of Divine grace. It seems that he had sent to Rome a collection of nineteen extracts, assembled especially from the works of Saint Augustine; that the Papal See had then subtracted part, retained part, added seventeen sentences from the work of Prosper, and sent the amended document back for the assent of the Bishops, who signed it at Orange.[77] Its declarations were confirmed by Pope Boniface the second in 531, and thereby passed into the body of the doctrine of the Church.

As a learned authority on Caesarius has remarked, there is interest in comparing these canons, signed by Caesarius as President of the Council of Orange, with more outspoken teaching given by him in a little work on the same subject, discovered by Dom Germain Morin in the Bibliothèque Nationale at Paris. Here Caesarius is shown as upholder of the strictest Augustinian belief. To the question: "Why does God give grace to some and not to others?" he answers with Augustine that we should rather give earnest thanks to God for those to whom in His mercy He does vouchsafe this

[76] *Vita*, I, 60.
[77] See Krusch, ed. p. 442; Dom Germain Morin, *Revue Bénéd.* XXI, 1904, pp. 225ff.; Mansi. VIII, 722ff.; Maassen, *ibid.*, pp. 45f.

necessary gift through His own inscrutable will. Without it all are lost; none can attain it save God desire this; and the entrance to its salvation comes by way of Holy Baptism. Babies who die unbaptized, through the lack of belief or the carelessness of their parents, through misfortune, or hindrance due to war, pestilence or famine, are none the less damned for all eternity. There is a story in these few pages of parents hastening to the font with a sick child in a race against Death. But Death wins, and the babe, shut out forever from spiritual bliss, pays for the sin of its natural guardians.[78]

Other dogmatic writing of Caesarius lately brought to light deals with the Mystery of the Holy Trinity, containing much matter extracted from patristic writings.[79]

This practice of culling material from the Fathers Caesarius followed zealously in the preparation of his sermons. Preaching was to him one of the chief duties of a pastor of souls, and not only did he diligently visit the multitudinous parishes of his diocese at the cost of, at least, one sermon a day, and often more, but he drove home the extreme importance of this duty, in season and out, and sometimes, probably, to the discomfort of his brother bishops and priests. We have a paper called "A Humble Admonition or Suggestion," which he sent round to his suffragans and colleagues in the episcopate, as well as to the minor clergy.[80] Bishops, he reminds them, are the watchers in the lofty towers of the Church, posted as sentries in the citadel to

---

[78] See the Latin text of Dom Germain Morin and comment by Dom Urbain Baltus: *Rev. Bénéd.* XIII, 1896, pp. 433ff. The detailed studies which Dom Germain Morin has carried on for many years in preparation for an edition of Caesarius are found in the *Rev. Bénéd. passim,* and in the *Anecdota Maredsolana,* in which see especially Series 2, I, 1913, pp. 41ff., 489ff.

[79] ed. A. Mai in 1852, and G. Morin in 1934; *Rev. Bénéd.* XLVI, pp. 192ff.

[80] ed. Malnory, pp. 294ff.

guard the gates on which knock boldly great and deadly sins; and the little doors, too, through which tiny venial faults are forever trying to creep. The Bishops' means of defence is the preaching of the Word in their churches. "My Lords," the exhortation continues, "you are not consecrated merely or primarily to care for the harvesting of broad acres of land, even though you do this in the name of the Church their owner. Yours it is to cultivate souls, not soils. And so you must preach, evermore and constantly, on Sundays and high Feast-Days, the mighty Bible truths to those for whom you will be required to give account at the last great Day. And that you may be fitly prepared thereunto, study the Holy Scriptures diligently and the canon laws of the Church. See to it that sacred reading be carried on always during your meals, instead of vain talk, and lead your own clergy in these same paths. . . . Do I hear some one say: '*I* am not eloquent. *I* cannot attract a congregation by my skill in speaking?' Does the Lord *require* this of you? Surely not! But the simplest priest can rebuke the faults he finds among us"—and here Caesarius gives an enlightening catalogue of the chief sins prevalent among his various flocks—"lies, drunkenness, revelry by night, pagan rites and superstitions of all kinds, the cult of trees and of watersprings, consulting of augurers and fortune-tellers, magical ceremonies, carrying of mascots, bribery, abortion, refusal of women to bear children." The last offence is condemned as a gainsaying of Nature that is pure homicide, and that, save she repent, shall land the recalcitrant wife straight into Hell. Only covenant on religious grounds with her husband may make such refusal lawful. . . . "Who is so simple that he cannot preach these things? Tell your people," the Bishop storms on, "to come to Church earlier in the mornings, to keep from getting drunk on Saints' Days, to stop bawling lewd songs and dancing indecent dances! Tell your married folk to observe continence from the first day of Lent till after Eastertide, and for shorter times before the other great Feasts of the Church, that they may come with a pure conscience to the altar of the Lord! Tell your boys and girls to live cleanly and honestly! Tell all to learn the Creed and the Lord's Prayer and to say them regularly, and to give from their means the tenth which is their bounden duty as alms for the poor!"

We may pause a moment here to remember that the sixth century in Gaul was a time of gravest sin and immorality. This is also clear from the pages of Gregory the Great; and the labours of the Bishop of Arles before his time were no less strenuous in the continual fight against evil. Standards were grievously low, and consciences had constantly to be awakened to an understanding of what decency and devotion demanded of ordinary people.

If the Lord Bishops find it hard to write their own sermons, Caesarius goes on, why not read one composed by some one else? Or, if this be not consistent with their dignity, allow one of their deacons to do so? Why not use the treasures of the Church for this purpose? "I fear," he observes, "lest the Library of the Fathers confront us priests for our confusion at the Day of Judgment. The priests are the eyes of the Church, and what shall the body do if the eyes refuse to see for it? The Bishop is the helmsman to guide the ship of the Church over the waves of this life, rebuking, admonishing, instructing, that those sailing thereon may reach safely the haven where they would be."

This use of metaphors, so frequent in Caesarius, springs entirely from a desire to drive home his words. He refers constantly to the medical art of spiritual physicians in his talks to his simple parish audiences, or tries to interest farmers by begging them to break up and weed and sow the fields of their souls. Humble folk were his special love, and he ends this discourse to the clergy by reminding them that the Lord did not entrust his Church to scholastics or rhetoricians, but to unlettered fishermen, poor and unknown.

His own sermons are written in the simplest Latin, short, definite, and full of vivid instruction. They would make an admirable model for modern homilies on the truth and precepts of the Gospel, though the matter would be somewhat strong meat for our refined palates. Caesarius used to give them away, singly or in collections, to priests who visited him in Arles, and from time to time would send them to his friends in the Gauls and Italy and Spain. Occasionally they appeared under the name of the Father who had proved most useful in preparation, frequently they bore no name at all. In consequence the labours of recovering the sermons of Caesarius and of sorting them out from those of other writers, especially Augustine and Faustus of Riez, have been truly herculean, and scholars owe an immense debt to the Benedictines for the valiant courage and skill which has separated out some *corpus* of these works. Several lists have been made of sermons accounted the genuine writing of Caesarius among the three hundred and seventeen of the Appendix to the fifth volume of Augustine's works in the *Patrologia,* and students may consult the works of Malnory or Arnold or Lejay and compare their findings.[81]

The Benedictines have divided them into homilies on the Old and on the New Testament, on the various seasons of the Church's year, on Feasts of individual Saints, and on a number of abstract subjects. The clear and definite exposition of the Church's teaching given by Caesarius to his

[81] *PL* LXVII, 1041ff.; XXXIX, 1735ff.; Malnory, pp. xiff.; C. F. Arnold, *Caesarius von Arelate,* pp. 491ff.; Lejay, p. 2168; Morin, *Rev. Bénéd.* X, 1893, pp. 62ff.

people has led to his inclusion among possible authors of the
so-called "Athanasian" Creed.[82]

When his people have digested these truths of doctrine,
they must learn afresh that the basis of all progress in Christianity is penitence. As the Bishop is a really excellent
teacher, he knows that, first, all must understand of what
to repent! So we find most detailed and definite instruction
on what, in the sixth century, as at other times, the Church
deemed mortal, and what she considered venial sins, their
nature, effects, and remedies. Mortal sin, which causes the
death of the soul and leads, if not repented of, directly to
eternal fire, was found in murder, fornication, robbery and
theft, false witness, pride, envy, greed, consulting of soothsayers, attending indecent or sanguinary entertainments, and
anger or drunkenness, if persistently indulged. In southern
Gaul of this sixth century the remedy for gravest sin was
public penitence. So Caesarius exhorts that such an offender
should make confession of his sin to the priest, and afterward,
clad in goatskin as belonging rightly to those on the Lord's
left hand at the Last Day, should appear in church in witness of his penitence, and of his desire for the prayers of the
congregation that he may finally be readmitted to the communion from which his sin has excluded him. Public penance
before the congregation is fitting, the Bishop declares, for one
who by his wicked life has outraged his fellows.

Such public offering of penitence was followed in due
time by public reconciliation, received from the hands of the
Bishop himself. It was not a common practice, in spite of
exhortations in church. Caesarius does, indeed, allow that
sin, even deep sin, may be expiated by determined amendment, and by constant practice of prayer, fasting, and giving

[82] See Lejay, 2177, and cf. Morin, *Rev. Bénéd.* XVIII, 1901, pp.
337ff., and A. Cooper-Marsdin, *Caesarius, Bishop of Arles,* p. 82.

of alms, without public humiliation. Such a manner of penitence might even be recommended in cases where the public penance seemed unadvisable; as, for instance, in the case of a young married man, whose wife might be unduly scandalized if he went about with shaven head in mourning dress, or of a soldier in service of the State.

Many people, however, though their consciences were troubled by some grave matter, deliberately postponed penitence till they lay dying in their beds, when the Church naturally counselled private confession before the priest rather than a bad death. Such sinners, when hale and vigorous, had preferred to run the risk of dying unshriven rather than ask guidance of the Church, lest, as was probable, the public ordeal be recommended. On such deathbed penitence Caesarius preaches a specially sane sermon. If genuine, it is better than nothing: "But, O man of intelligence, do you really think it decent that you should be a slave to vices and failings all your earthly life, and then at last try to pull yourself together to gain eternal life when you are only half-alive to do it? You wouldn't stand such conduct from *your* servants!"

Practice of the three great Christian precepts is prescribed as penance and prophylactic for venial sins, from which no one, not even of the Saints, is ever free in this life, but must struggle on daily, trying to ward off and heal their tiny mosquito bites. Such are eating and drinking too much on occasion, idle and unkind gossip or off-colour stories at dinner-parties on the one hand, protracted and selfish silence on the other, unkindness to the poor, refusing to observe Fast Days when quite well, arriving too late for early services, lack of charitable works, selfishness at home, flattery, breaking promises, brief indulgence of unworthy thought, and so on.

In general the Bishop counsels: "Never despair; rise quickly from your sins. But never presume upon God's mercy, and never imagine for a moment that penitence without good works is worth anything. The last day of our lives must find us far further on the road to Heaven than the day of our Baptism did, innocent though we were then. *Christiani nominis non facit sola dignitas Christianum.*"[83]

Prayer, in its simplest form, includes the saying of the Lord's Prayer and the Creed; in its highest, attendance at Mass. The faithful must not be absent from Mass on Sundays and greater Feast Days, and when possible should come to Matins and Vespers. They are forcibly admonished not to leave the Church during Mass after the reading of the Epistle and Gospel, which seems to have been a regrettably frequent occurrence. They *can* read the Bible at home; they cannot assist at Mass there! To whom is the priest to bid *Sursum corda* if the congregation has already left? Moreover, it is the people's duty to hear the sermon after the Gospel.

The congregation stood for a good part of Solemn Mass, lasting perhaps two hours. We can imagine what it was like from an account left us of the Gallican Liturgy of Germanus, that Bishop of Paris in the sixth century whom we have already met.[84] An antiphon was sung during the entrance of the officiating Bishop, who began the service, after the deacon had bidden silence, by the *Dominus sit semper vobiscum,* and was duly answered *Et cum spiritu tuo.* Then came three canticles: the *Trisagion,* the *Kyrie eleison,* and the "*Prophecy,*" the *Benedictus Dominus Deus Israel.* These were followed by a Collect; two Lessons, one from the Old Testament and one from the Epistles; the Hymn of the Three

[83] *PL* XXXIX, 1896. See on all this matter O. D. Watkins, *History of Penance,* II, pp. 506ff.; 55off.
[84] See Duchesne, *Christian Worship*[5], pp. 190ff.

Children, the Response, and the Gospel. During the Procession of the Gospel, both going and returning, the *Sanctus, Sanctus, Sanctus* was again sung, and the congregation answered the announcing of the Gospel with the *Gloria tibi, Domine*. After the Gospel the Sermon was preached, followed by a Litany of intercessions, a Collect, and the Procession of the Oblation, the bringing in of the bread and the wine mingled with water. Two chants accompanied this part of the ritual. The *Preface* was then addressed to the congregation. Next came another Collect; the solemn reading of names among the Faithful Departed, with prayer; then the Kiss of Peace, exchanged by the people. Now followed the *Sursum corda*, another Preface, the *Sanctus*, and another Collect. The Bishop then offered the Prayer of Consecration with the *Epiclesis*, or Invocation of the Holy Spirit. Another anthem was chanted during the Fraction of the Host, followed by the Lord's Prayer, the *Commixtio*, and the solemn Pontifical Blessing. Now came the Communion of the Faithful. They advanced into the sanctuary as far as the altar, where the men received the Host in the bare hand, the women in the hand covered with a *dominical*, a linen cloth which they brought with them to church for this purpose. During the Communion a hymn was sung, such as that given in the *Bangor Antiphonary*:

Sancti venite, Christi corpus sumite:

familiar to us in the version:

"Draw nigh and take the Body of the Lord."

After the faithful had communicated, the Prayer of Thanksgiving was said and all were dismissed.

The service was long; the people were fasting; and the Bishop administers constant rebukes for whispering. Those who *will* talk in church had better not come! Also, please arrive there in time. If workmen of the world can get up early, surely the servants of the Lord can do equally well. And will all be good enough not to pray their private prayers aloud, remembering blessed Hannah, whose lips alone moved and her voice was not heard? Remember, too, that bodily presence in church does no good if thoughts are far away. Men do not behave thus in the presence of earthly dignities. Please follow the service, and when the deacon cries *Flectamus genua,* don't remain stuck upright like pillars of stone. If your knees hurt you, you can at least make a little bow. Remember the Pharisee and the Publican. Or perhaps you are afraid of spoiling your clothes? Well, it is worse to stain the soul than the body.

Precepts of fasting are taught by Caesarius with broad understanding and tolerance of human frailty. Abstinence from wine and meat is prescribed, naturally; but none is obliged to do more than his health will allow, and consideration is given to the circumstances and conditions of individuals. More importance is given to the duty of almsgiving, which is continually inculcated with great vehemence. Not only the tenth is expected, as a matter of course, but from the remaining nine-tenths each is bidden give what he can for the aid of the poor. An Advent sermon counsels for the same reason due moderation in meals. Luncheons and dinner-parties may occasionally be indulged in, especially at Christmas time, but only within limits, that there may be food for the needy and the stranger. This forms, too, an excellent subject for a sermon at time of harvest, in preparation for St. John's Day.

A sermon to farmers in a rural parish bids all to read the Bible. If you can't read yourself, get some one to read to you. If you think you haven't time, stop gossiping so much,

and don't sit over your meals so long! These winter nights,
the Bishop continues, are so lengthy that it wouldn't hurt some
of you to have some good Bible reading early in the morning! You say your farming takes all your time and thoughts?
Well, how then do you manage to learn all those vulgar love
songs you are always singing? Much better to learn and say
frequently the Lord's Prayer, the Creed, and some Psalms,
such as the *Miserere mei, Deus* and the *Qui habitat in adiu-
torio Altissimi*. Another discourse preaches the value of
retreat: "If a man does not try to free the wings of his soul
from the hindrances of this world and the sticky mire of sins
he will never come to true rest. Let us try to cut down something from our worldly occupations that we may gain a few
hours for prayer and sacred reading."

When seasons of worldly festivity approach, such as New
Year's Day, the faithful are warned earnestly against the
pagan practices still current at this time. Such are the cult of
trees and of springs, with ritual bathing at night or early
morning, the exchange of gifts as mascots, the consulting of
omens for the future. Spiritual seasons have their own
lessons. Lent, for instance, is described as a time of spiritual
gathering in of harvest for the rest of the year.

General sermons give a store of practical thoughts. On the
keeping of content: Don't grumble at the weather, because
it rains, or because there is a drought, or because it is too
windy, or your vines do not ripen as they should. On
humility: Don't grumble at rebukes in sermons; a priest is
a physician, and must administer medicine nasty as well as
pleasant. On thoughts: Of course you can't *always* be actually
thinking about God; I know you have all those daily duties
to think about. But you can leave some little time free. And
don't deliberately embrace a low thought. You wouldn't want
to embrace a public prostitute in the streets if all your friends

were looking on; so remember that God is witness to all that you do secretly in your minds.[85]

We turn now to consider the Bishop with his clergy. His ordinances for them were as definite as his teachings of the universal precepts of the Church. Some of his ruling was incorporated in the *acta* passed by Bishops of the Gallican Church in council; as, for instance, his requirements that none be ordained deacon before he reach his twenty-fifth year, none raised to the office of priest or bishop before he be thirty years old; that, moreover, no layman be honoured by Ordering of the Church before he shall have proved his worthiness in Christian living for at least a year.[86] This was aimed against the scandal of forced and sacrilegious consecrations and ordinations so frequent in the fifth and sixth centuries. Another salutary condition laid down by Caesarius for his diocese was that every ordinand should have read the Bible, both New and Old Testament, at least four times before the laying on of hands. He instituted the singing of Tierce, Sext and None daily by his clergy in his Church of Saint Stephen, and perpetually reminded them of their duty to preach the Faith; whether in their own words, or in his, gathered in the collections he so willingly bestowed on them for their assistance, or in the *verba ipsissima* of the Doctors of the Church. Another marked feature of the services held under Caesarius in the diocese of Arles was his insistence on congregational singing. He made the laity learn psalms and hymns by heart and chant them in church, that none might have leisure for wanderings of thought!

In his own Bishop's House reading from sacred texts was always carried on during lunch and dinner, and the Bishop

[85] There are two interesting pictures of the Good and the Bad Christian in *PL* XXXIX, 2240f.

[86] Cf. Krusch, ed. *Vita*, p. 480; *Suggestio*, ed. Malnory, *Saint Césaire*, p. 301; Maassen, *Concilia aevi Mer.*, pp. 36f.

had a disconcerting way of examining his staff and his guests afterwards on the subject-matter of these feasts of the soul. Those who were aware of the practice could hardly notice what was put on their plates, in their anxiety to hear what the reader was gabbling. But he loved to be asked to explain the difficulties felt by his younger brethren in regard to the Bible or knotty points of theology: "I am sure you don't understand it all. Why don't you *ask* me for help? Don't you know that it is good for me, also, to have to answer questions and to search for spiritual honey on your behalf?"

All male visitors, of whatever race or station, were always welcome in the House; and such streams of hospitality issued thence to the poor of Arles that sometimes the steward was distracted with worry as to where he should find enough to serve the Bishop's dinner. But miracles, of course, happened. One night the episcopal cupboard was entirely bare, and the episcopal poor dreaded to see the dawn break on their hunger; when, lo! three ships came sailing in on the morrow, laden with wheat from the stores of Burgundy. It must have made life interesting to the clerical staff of the Palace; since no one ever knew whether they, or the Lord's poor in their stead, would lunch or dine. Young men were received in the House for training as ordinands, a practice included in the enactments of the Council of Vaison in 529. But no woman might show her face within its doors. Caesarius was true to the example of Martin and Augustine and the hosts of fearful Fathers of the Church to whom the confidence of Jerome stood out in exception. Once, however, the devil got the better of him. A beggar, trying by false means to wheedle charity out of the Bishop, sent him his little daughter dressed up as a boy. The tender heart of Caesarius was touched by the sight of the child, so ragged and forlorn, and he bent down and kissed the little face. His pity turned to horror and

Miserere when the child returned on a similar errand, this time as a girl! He bade her, who had been kissed by a priest, never to kiss another man, but to enter a convent and dedicate herself to God. But God, the biographer of Caesarius assures us, was wiser than the Bishop. He knew that her piety was not equal to this admonition, and so in His wisdom He removed her early from this difficult world.

However, Caesarius had no feeling against women in their proper place, as wives and mothers or as dedicated virgins of the Lord. He repeatedly tells his congregations that there is but one and the same standard of purity for both men and women, and that the world is entirely wrong in punishing the guilty woman and letting off the man with a tolerant laugh for his sins against society. And some of the best work of his life was done in the gradual working out of his *Rule for Nuns*.

He composed also a *Rule for Monks,* arranged on the basis of the community life at Lérins, for the brethren with whom he lived at Arles.[87] Rules for men, however, of these earlier days are more interesting in the pages of Cassian and of Benedict. The only rival of Caesarius in his *Rule for Nuns* was the letter of Augustine written for the Convent of nuns over which his sister once presided, and this can scarcely be called a definite Rule, though it formed the starting point of the Rule of the Augustinian Canonesses.[88] The Rule of Caesarius for women cost him long labour, as he subtracted, added, and emended in the light of growing experience. Before the Middle Ages had gone it was lost, and was only recovered and published again in the seventeenth century. But while it was famous important communities of women sought its help, and among them the Lady Radegund.[89]

[87] *PL* LXVII, 1098ff.
[88] S. Aug. *Epist.* 211: *PL* XXXIII, 958ff.
[89] For the petition of Radegund see Gregory, *H.F.* IX, 42; for the answer of Caesaria *M.G.H. Epist.* Tom. III, pp. 450ff.

For convenience we may briefly sum up its provisions from various writings of the Bishop: the Rule itself, a "Recapitulatio" added by him, a letter to the Abbess, and two letters addressed to both the Abbess and her nuns.[90]

Permanence strikes a first note of gravity. No nun, once professed, might leave the Convent before her death, when her body was carried into the church of St. Mary the Virgin adjoining, to lie beneath the flag-stones of the aisle. The door into the church was in the keeping of the Lady Abbess; other doors Caesarius himself had shut and sealed.

Those who aspire to enter the Convent, the Rule enjoined, are to hear its text frequently from the lips of the Abbess, that they may know so far as possible what will be expected of them. Those admitted as postulants are to remain for a year before their clothing, under the special instruction of one of the professed Sisters. All must give or will away their possessions, or claims to possessions, before being received.

The Abbess ruled her Community under the Bishop of the diocese, Caesarius and his successors, and was regularly elected from within it. Her first care was the souls of her nuns. As one who should give answer to God she must rebuke the restless, comfort the scrupulous, sustain the weak, and hold up an example to all in her own life. "Be first to enter the Chapel, and last to leave," Caesarius wrote to her, "be first to begin work and last to relinquish it. Be discreet in prescribing prayer and fasting, and eat yourself what your sisters eat. In the midst of your secular occupations let your soul in its longing fly as a winged creature to the things of God. For your responsibility is very great, and I cannot tell you, nor would you believe, how full my heart is of anxiety and fear for you." The secular duties of the Mother were to superintend in general the discipline and routine of the house, to

[90] All are edited by G. Morin, *Florilegium Patristicum,* XXXIV, 1933.

care for the conventual property, to receive visitors, accompanied by a guard of honour of two or three Sisters, to answer letters, and to deal with gifts on behalf of the Community.

Obedience was, of course, due to the Mother; deference was owed under her to the *Praeposita,* the "Prioress," her assistant and deputy. Other bearers of office were the *Formaria,* the Mistress of Novices, who was to set an example in the observing of the Rule and to keep watch over the younger women, especially those in any trouble of mind or body; the *Registoria,* or Treasurer; and the Cellarer, the Infirmarian, the Keeper of wools, and the Portress. A number of the professed nuns were also called *Seniors,* and were each given charge of one or more postulants. Spiritual offices were fulfilled by a Chaplain, assisted by other priests in the singing of Mass; charge of the property and its maintenance was in the hands of a male Steward (*Provisor*).

The nuns lived and slept in large common dormitories. The Rule ordered that no one was to have even a cupboard to herself, though a special room could be set aside to receive the old and the infirm. All the furnishings were very simple; no embroidery, no down cushions, no pictures. Silver was permitted only in the Chapel, where, also, no pictures were allowed, merely hangings of linen, not silk, marked by crosses in black or white. Any ornaments given for the Chapel were sold for the good of the Convent or given to the Church of St. Mary, built by Caesarius himself. The Sisters were habited in white, "fitting for the humility of virgins"; old clothing was passed on to junior Sisters or given to the poor. All garments worn in the Convent were made there, and spinning and weaving formed the chief manual labours of the nuns, in addition to necessary household duties. Everyone, except the Mother, took her turn in the work of the house, including the cooking.

All were obliged to eat in the appointed place; no one could eat or drink secretly. Wine—and decent wine—was allowed the sick, and Sisters "delicately reared" in the world; Caesarius, like Augustine, remembered that monastic austerities affected his novices differently. It shows common sense, but must have needed tact on the part of the Reverend Mother. All things, of course, were common property. Baths were prescribed for the sick, if the Infirmarian ordered them, whether the patient willed it or not; but the greediness of healthy nuns was not to be indulged in this matter. Fasting was ordered for every day (except Sundays and Greater Feasts) during Lent and the period from November the first till Christmas Day; for three days a week from September the first till November, and from Epiphany till the week before Lent; at the discretion of the Mother from Pentecost till the beginning of September. Animal flesh was never eaten "except in cases of desperate sickness," when one supposes that beef-tea or its like was administered. Chicken, however, could be given to invalids, an interesting instance from early times of a distinction between birds and beasts as food.

Silence was especially bidden. No one was to raise her voice at any time, and alms were only rarely to be dispensed from the Convent gate, lest undue noise arise within. During part of the time of meals one of the Sisters read aloud; when she ceased, all were expected to observe secret meditation on holy things. During the day only such talking was to be done as was necessary. We hear nothing of Community recreation.

Every nun had to know how to read, or begin to learn directly she entered the Convent. Two hours of the early morning were set aside for reading, and some of the Sisters were occupied in copying sacred manuscripts under the direction of the Abbess.[1] The first Abbess, Caesaria, sister of the

[1] *Vita,* I, 58.

Founder, had been specially trained for her work in the convent founded by Cassian for women at Marseilles during the fifth century. She was succeeded on her death by another of the same name, sometimes called Caesaria the younger. To her Caesarius addressed a letter which shows his high opinion of her learning in sacred studies. "Who could think that you, the Abbess whom I respect so highly, and at the same time my daughter in Christ, should be the same nun who used to love me so dearly from afar, in the cloister where you were deep in the study of Holy Scripture? I was a lazy youth, but you have followed learning from your cradle. And now the Lord has given it me to guide you and your nuns!"

Her thought and her words concerning him, however, were confined to conferences on Convent business and the colloquies of her secret heart with God. "So far as you may," he writes her, "remember not the face of any man, save in pure prayer, lest in your desire you set up an idol in your soul. Guard yourself when you must meet priest or servers within your walls, and be not led astray by the music of the voice that reads the Gospel. If you must discuss necessary business with the steward, do it in the presence of two or three of your sisters, or if your talk be private, at least in an open place. Let all your conversation be ever of God, your thoughts upon God; and, save when faults must be rectified, be compassionate to all, be gracious to all, be loyal to all, be affectionate to all, inspired by all good things."

Caesarius practised what he preached and hardly ever entered the Convent door, but gave his counsels to Caesaria and her family in writing. Male visitors were forbidden, except those requisite for the life and work. Neither were visits from laywomen allowed, unless they were received by the Lady Abbess or specially permitted to greet a near relative in the presence of a professed Sister. No man, not even the Bishop of Arles himself, might be asked to dinner, and no woman, except a Religious coming on some meet errand from another city; no one from Arles, except it be very rarely some Religious of very high distinction, whose presence might be accounted honour to the Convent.

Directions are given in the Rule for the daily Offices, with the titles of the hymns sung at Tierce, Sext, None and Vespers. Nuns who arrived in Chapel late for Office were sharply rebuked, and, if repeatedly guilty, banished for a time either from the Chapel or the Refectory or both, according to the gravity of the offence.

Other faults of which the Rule took cognizance were: receiving secret messages or letters or gifts from without the Convent, a most serious matter; scolding, upbraiding, or even hitting one another, which last misdemeanour, God forbid it to happen, laid the offender under possible penalty of corporal chastisement herself; carrying food or drink from the Refectory; disobedience or indocility of any kind. Grave sins were punished by placing the erring Sister in solitude under the eye of one of the Seniors.

Caesarius, with seven other Bishops, signed the Rule, and a Bull of Hormisdas, Pope from 514 till 523, gave enthusiastic approval to this new venture.[92] More than twenty years in all went to its making; from 512, when the first Convent of Saint John, as its dedication named it, received the tiny company who formed the beginning, till 534, when all was complete and more than two hundred Sisters were living under the Rule in the Convent now established near the Church of Saint Stephen in Arles.

By this time Caesarius had become greatly weakened through increasing age and sickness. Theodoric was dead.

[92] See for this Morin's edition of the Rule, pp. 28ff.

Athalaric, his successor, had had no power to hinder the flowing tide of barbarians, and under Witigis, anxious for support in his campaigns against Belisarius, Arles passed in exchange for goodly promises to the dominion of the Franks. The Emperor Justinian was compelled to assent to this, and Procopius states sadly that the Franks who rule Germany "now preside over the Games in the Circus at Arles, and stamp coins of Gallic gold, not as before was done with the head of the ruler of the Romans, but with their own impress." [93] Under them Caesarius attended no more of the frequent Councils of the Gallican Church, and death soon foretold its coming to this "Archbishop" of Arles. In 542 he was carried from his own Bishop's House to the Convent of Saint John, called in later days by his own name, to give his last words of counsel and comfort to the nuns he had cherished so long. He died directly afterward, at the age of seventy-three, leaving in his Will the care of his Religious to his successor in the See of Arles. [94]

The memory of Caesarius is still bright in the pages of his *Life,* studied by many, both high and humble. Among the latter the unlettered nun Baudonivia borrowed passages from it for her narrative of Radegund, whom Venantius Fortunatus pictures as "drinking in eagerly from Caesarius every word of his Rule." [95] Miracles, naturally, appear in it, as in all the lives of the Saints of these early days. Ennodius wrote of Caesarius as "a sun among the stars, in whom radiance of words meets radiance of works." [96] More delightful, surely, are the words of his biographer concerning him: [97]

[93] Procopius, *De Bell. Goth.* III, 33.
[94] The authenticity of this Will is now generally admitted: see G. Morin, *Rev. Bénéd.* XVI, 1899, pp. 97ff., where its text is printed, and Krusch, *Script. rer. Merov.* IV, pp. 770f.
[95] Baudonivia, ed. Krusch. *Script. rer. Merov.* II, pp. 383f., p. 391; Fortunatus, *Carm.* VIII, 3, lines 47f.
[96] *Epp.* IX, 33.   [97] *Vita,* I, 53; II, 35.

"He loved all men not only with a father's but with a mother's love," and: "To his clergy who saw him day by day in the Bishop's House at Arles he always seemed every morning some one entirely fresh and new."

CHAPTER II

CELTIC MONASTICISM

CELTIC monasticism has already met us in Wales. Gildas
as "historian" was always subordinate to Gildas the monk,
and we have seen something of the School of Illtyd, and of
the disciples whom he trained there for the founding of monasteries and schools and episcopal sees.

Side by side in British history with these monastic schools
of Wales there stands the earlier foundation of Ninian, who
about 397 had built his *Candida Casa*—"White House"—
where now the Isle of Whithorn lies off Wigtown in Galloway.
From this as centre he laboured to convert the wild Pictish
settlers of that region, the "southern Picts." He was himself
of British birth, and probably came from the district south
of the Firth of Clyde. The story goes that his father was a
Christian king, that he was sent to Rome in boyhood as
hostage, educated there, and at length consecrated Bishop.
We read also that he visited shortly afterward Saint Martin
in Tours, and there is a tradition, a rather frail one, that he
carried with him to Britain on his return masons from Gaul
to build him a church after the Gallic fashion.[1] The church,
certainly, was built of stone, and called "The White House"
in distinction from the rude huts of the neighbourhood; with

[1] Ailred of Rievaulx, *Vita Niniani* (12th century), in *Historians of Scotland,* V. See Bede, *H.E.* III, 4.

the aid of the monastery that clustered around its walls it gathered converts from far and near and became of high renown throughout Celtic lands.

The two streams of monastic life, from Wales and from Galloway, meet in Ireland during this sixth century. How, when and where Ireland first received the Christian creed cannot be described in exactness, but can in some measure be broadly guessed. Intercourse of trade by sea, active in the early days of our era between Ireland, Britain and Gaul, must have brought its teachings from one point to another, and captives from Britain, fruit of the raids of Irish pirates upon British coasts, no doubt furthered the work of conversion. It was in such a way that the missionary vision opened before the mind of St. Patrick.

The growth of Christianity in Ireland was aided by the traditional division of her people into clans; a converted chieftain meant, naturally, the Christianizing of those over whom he ruled. Moreover, the innumerable bards of Ireland, whose proud function it was to chant heroic lays of legend and history intertwined, turned on their conversion to sing the deeds of saints and apostles of the Lord Christ. The greatest enemy of the Church in the first centuries of Ireland was found in the Druids, who determinedly held over its peasants the terror of magic and superstition, centred, as in Gaul, in spirits of waters and of trees, in the sun and the stars, in awful *numina*, whose wrath was certain to fall on any who dared desert their rites for a foreign cult.[2]

Early in the fifth century Irish Christians were held worthy by Pope Celestine to receive a Bishop of their own, probably at their own petition. Prosper of Aquitaine tells of the zeal

[2] Bury, *St. Patrick,* pp. 76ff.; Warren, *C.M.H.* II, p. 504. This kinship by clan materially furthered the monastic religion of early Ireland: see Workman, *Evolution of the Monastic Ideal,*[2] pp. 192f. See, on Irish monasticism in general, the work of that title by Fr. John Ryan, 1931.

of Celestine "to keep the Roman island" (Britain) "Catholic and to make the barbarous island" (Ireland) "Christian." [8] It must be remembered that the secular power of Rome did not dominate Ireland. Prosper tells, also, that one named Palladius was consecrated and sent in 431 to the Irish who believed in Christ, as their first Bishop. [4]

The mission of Palladius ended within a year. Tradition has it that he could gain no hearing among the Irish and forsook his work to die among the Picts of Britain on his return journey. [5] Modern scholarship, however, has come to his rescue in thinking it likely that he died thus suddenly when trying to convert the Picts, not of Britain, but of northern Ireland, where his missionary enterprise had kept him from the first. [6]

At any rate, a new Bishop was required for the Irish believers and was found in Patrick, who was already preparing to spend his life in converting Ireland. We know that he, also, was of the British people, though the place of his birth has been vigorously disputed. [7] His father was a Christian and a deacon of the Church, Calpurnius by name. When he was sixteen years old, Patrick was carried off by pirates to Ireland and remained there six years in captivity. At last he escaped with some companions and, after an adventurous crossing of the sea and much wandering on land, entered the monastery of Lérins. At least, so the story goes. Some

---

[8] *Contra Collatorem,* XXI; *PL* LI, 271.

[4] *Chron.* in an. 431: *PL* LI, 595; cf. Bede, *H.E.* I, 13.

[5] *Vita S. Patricii,* H. and S. II, ii, pp. 290f. Meissner (*History of Church of Ireland,* ed. Phillips, I, pp. 84f.) holds that Palladius was sent as Bishop to the Irish "Scots" who had settled in the region north of the Antonine Wall.

[6] Bury, *St. Patrick,* p. 55.

[7] From the evidence available the district of the Severn seems most likely, rather than the district of the Clyde: see Bury, p. 17, pp. 322ff.; but cf. Meissner, *ibid.,* p. 77, note, and Gougaud, *Christianity in Celtic Lands,* p. 32. On the theory that Palladius and Patrick were identical see *ibid.,* pp. 29f.

years were spent there in religious practice, and then a visit to his relatives in Britain was marked one night by a vivid dream, which decided his future career. He returned to Gaul, and placed himself under Amator, Bishop of Auxerre, for the training and other preparations necessary for a missionary to the Irish people. Amator ordained him deacon, and the next ruler of the See of Auxerre, Germanus, consecrated him as Bishop of the Irish in succession to Palladius and sent him on his way. In 432 he landed at Strangford Lough and began his work.

So much of tradition it is needful to repeat, without dwelling on the various problems connected with Patrick's life and work. It is doubtless true that he found Christians already scattered here and there when he arrived in Ireland; yet so little had been done, so much was done by him, that his is ever the glory of Apostle of Ireland. He and his disciples carried the Gospel, founded churches, and established on firmer footing the place of the Irish Church among the others that looked to Rome as their centre and their head. In the eighth century a document was compiled known as "The Catalogue of Irish Saints," extending from the time of his arrival till "the time of the Great Plague" in 665.[8] In this list three Orders of Saints are distinguished: "most holy," "very holy," and "holy." The First or "most holy" Order, we read, lived in the time of Patrick and consisted entirely of Bishops, three hundred and fifty in number, founders of Churches. They had One Head, Christ, and one leader, Patrick; one Mass, one Rule of Office, one tonsure from ear to ear. They celebrated one Easter, from the fourteenth day of the moon after the vernal equinox, and what was excommunicated by one of their churches was excommunicated by all. They did not reject the administration and fellowship of women, because they were

[8] H. and S. II, ii, pp. 292f.

founded on the Rock of Christ and were not unduly afraid of temptation.

We learn from this statement that under Patrick bishops regularly ruled, tended and taught the Irish Christians; that they established centres or dioceses throughout the country; and that they were united in the form of Mass and of the Breviary.

It is, moreover, of importance to our subject to note that under Patrick Latin became also the language of the Church in Ireland, as it was throughout the Church of the Western Empire. Under him Ireland clung as closely as he could effect it to the Church centred in Rome, in spite of the remoteness of her island in these days.

We have two writings composed by himself in Latin. In his *Confession* he tells something of the story of his life, and much of his belief in God. Here we can read of his conversion during the days of his captivity in Ireland, and of the dream in his British home which called him to return.[9] Another writing in the form of a letter warns the Christians dwelling about the basin of the Clyde, in the district known later as Strathclyde, against the wickedness of their secular ruler, the chieftain Coroticus. He had sent a band of freebooters to raid the North Irish coast; and they had killed or taken captive some of Patrick's disciples just as they emerged from the waters of Baptism, still arrayed in their white garments, "with the Faith radiant upon their brows" in the mark of holy chrism. Patrick commands the Christians neither to eat nor to drink with such men nor to receive alms from them till they shall have repented before God with tears and set at liberty the servants and handmaids of Christ. He then seizes the opportunity to complain with bitterness of ill-feeling against him and his work in Ireland on the part of his British

[9] H. and S. *ibid.*, pp. 296ff.

compatriots, declaring that envy and contempt are his lot, and that "a prophet hath not honour in his own country." [10]

Both writings are given in a rude Latin style, with no evidence of training in composition or rhetoric; [11] Patrick describes himself as "a sinner untaught and most countrified." Nevertheless, it was he to whom Ireland owed great progress in the Latin scholarship that has ever marked her Churchmen.

During the time of Patrick and the episcopal organization of the Irish Church, monasticism flourished in Britain rather than in Ireland. His Bishopric, that of Armagh, destined to be foremost among the sees of Ireland in later days, was probably not a monastic church till long after his death in 461. The monastery founded by St. Brigit at Kildare, training both men and women, grew to renown in the sixth and was famous in the seventh century. The same is true of the House of St. Mochta at Louth. The life of monastic fervour was, indeed, already seething in Ireland in the fifth century, fed by the preaching of St. Patrick and by the example of monks trained in Britain by Ninian's "White House." But its flood-tide was not yet. [12]

For this we must come to the sixth century and to the Second Order of Irish Saints who belonged to its period. [13] Of them we read in the same Catalogue that they consisted of Catholic priests, with only few bishops. They had one

[10] *ibid.*, pp. 314ff. See also Whitley Stokes, *The Tripartite Life of Patrick*, II, pp. 357ff., 375ff.; N. J. D. White, *The Latin Writings of Saint Patrick*, *Proc. Royal Irish Acad.* XXV, Section C, 1905, pp. 201ff.

[11] The famous hymn, the *Lorica, Breastplate,* or *Cry of the Deer,* was written in Irish at a very early date and may well be the work of St. Patrick, though this is not certain; see Bury, *St. Patrick*, p. 246; Whitley Stokes, *Tripartite Life*, I, pp. 47ff. *The Canons of the Church,* attributed to him and two other Bishops, are now very generally assigned to a later date. See H. and S. *ibid.*, pp. 328ff. Bury, pp. 233ff., defends them as genuinely belonging to a Synod held by Patrick.

[12] The monastic character of Ireland in the fifth century and of St. Patrick's work is variously estimated: cf. for example, Gougaud, p. 226, with Kenney, *Sources*, p. 291, and Meissner, ed. Phillips, p. 200.

[13] The date, 544, given for its inception is too late: see Bury, p. 287.

Head, our Lord; they celebrated different Masses and kept different Rules, but observed the same date of Easter and wore the same tonsure as the First Order. They refused the administration of women, and separated them from themselves in monastic houses.

Here we find an Irish Church that differed widely from that of the fifth century. Three marks characterized it very strongly: its monasticism, its individuality, its learning.

In this Church it was the Abbot, not the Bishop, who in general guided administration; monastic, and not diocesan rule and care that prevailed for the cure of souls. Bishops were naturally held in reverence, especially as those to whom it had been given to ordain the priests and deacons of the Church. But very many of them possessed no sees and were no longer in actual command as Fathers of their people; they were individual bishops, exercising their episcopal functions in monasteries, under the jurisdiction of the Lord Abbot in each case. Sometimes the Lord Abbot was himself a bishop. Monasteries were now constantly increasing in number: each a centre of religious and intellectual attraction for the students and aspirants who came from all directions to be trained within its walls, and, in lesser degree, for the lay folk without who looked to its monks and priests for the fostering of their spiritual life. The standard was no easy one; for this Irish monasticism was characterized by a severity of standard worthy of the Fathers of the Egyptian desert themselves. Asceticism appealed to the Irish of early days, and those both inside and outside the cloister willingly submitted to its demand of penitential discipline for body as well as for soul.

Secondly, the Irish Church, as part of the Celtic, appears in this sixth century as marked by greater individuality, by a less strong union with Rome than had marked it in the days of Patrick. Two points of difference between the Roman

and the Celtic Churches stand out especially: the difference
in the date of keeping Easter and the difference in the manner
of wearing the tonsure. These differences had, indeed, existed
in the fifth century under Saint Patrick and his "First Order
of Saints," but in less degree, kept in subordination, we may
think, by Patrick's keen sense of loyalty to the Church of
Rome. At any rate, it was not till after his time that the
division between the Roman and Celtic usages became acute.

The Church of Rome from the second century onward had
ordered the rule of keeping Easter on a Sunday, as distinct
from the usage of those Jewish Christians who had been
accustomed to keep it on the fourteenth day of the month
Nisan, whether that day fell on a Sunday or a week-day. The
rule did not become universal without bitter strife; but it
did prevail, and those who refused to heed it were termed
"Quartodecimans" and held guilty as heretics. The Celtic
Church under Patrick and his successors also kept Easter on
the first day of the week.

Moreover, it was decreed in the fourth century at the
Council of Arles in 314, and at the Council of Nicaea in 325,
that this Sunday of Easter should be one and the same through
all the world. Now the Roman Church till the year 457 held
a method of dating Easter based on a cycle of 84 years,
although twice, in 343 and in 447, minor changes had been
introduced into this method. About that year, 457, it adopted
the calculation of Victorius of Aquitaine, based on a cycle
of 532 years. Thirdly, at a time placed variously by scholars
in the sixth and in the seventh century, it changed its method
to adopt that drawn up by Dionysius "the Humble" in 525,
founded on the Alexandrine cycle of 19 years.

The Celtic Church, however, was keeping its Easter in this
sixth century very determinedly according to the original
Roman 84-year cycle and, it seems, according to the older

reckoning of that cycle used by Rome before 343.[14] It had quietly gone on its own way in its islands, far removed from those bitter years in Italy, and it carried its usage wherever its leaders went forth to mission work without. The details of the different theories of calculation within the two Churches require skill in mathematics and immense patience for their right comprehension in all their solar and lunar maze.[15] But the simpler pages of the Venerable Bede show well how acute this Paschal argument still remained in practice during the seventh century. We read there of an Irish Bishop of that period refusing for this very reason even to eat in the same house with his Romanizing brethren of the episcopacy, and of King Oswy of Northumbria celebrating his Easter joyfully in the Celtic Church, while his Queen Eanfled in obedience to her Roman confessor was still keeping the fast of Holy Week with her maids.[16] At the same time, it is well to remember that small disagreements are often put forward as causes of strife that is born in reality of far larger differences: differences in this case, we may think, of race and blood.[17]

The second dispute centred around the wearing of the tonsure. In the Celtic Church the head was shaven from ear to ear; in the Roman the hair was allowed to grow in a crown around the shorn circle of the top of the head.

It is pleasant to turn from controversy on ritual to the monastic learning of Ireland, sown in the fifth, fostered and established in the sixth, destined to give light to Europe in the dark age of the seventh century. Enthusiasm for religion and its practice bore fruit in the numerous cloisters of Chris-

[14] It has been suggested that St. Patrick endeavoured to introduce into Ireland both the Roman dating of Easter in force during this time and the Roman tonsure: see Bury, *ibid.*, pp. 371ff.; pp. 239ff., and (for the dubious canons of St. Patrick) pp. 233ff.
[15] See Plummer, ed. Bede, II, pp. 348ff.; H. and S. I, pp. 152ff.; Gougaud, pp. 185ff.; Kenney, pp. 215ff.
[16] *H.E.* II, 4; III, 25.   [17] Plummer, *ibid.*, p. 353.

tian study to which men flocked in their hundreds and their thousands. Especially renowned among earlier monastic foundations was the School of Aran on the island of Aran Mor, at the entrance to Galway Bay. It was the work of St. Enda, and it drew to itself at one time or another most of those who were to be Saints of the Second Order.

Far more famous, however, in the sixth century was the school of Saint Finnian the Wise at Clonard on the River Boyne in Meath. We are told that Finnian received much of his training in Wales, and learned to know there the Welsh Fathers of this period, David, Gildas, and Cadoc. Here is some trace of the influence of the Welsh Church upon contemporary Irish monasticism. Further witness, as we have seen, is given in the *Catalogue of Irish Saints,* which declares that the Saints of the Second Order (those of the sixth century), received one of their differing forms of Mass from David and Gildas and Docus (perhaps to be identified with Cadoc). There is the story, too, that the three visited Ireland.[18]

We are to imagine, then, young Finnian in Wales at Llantwit Major, at Menevia and at Llancarfan. Under the guidance of an angel, tradition tells, he came afterward to Cluain Eraird in Ireland: that is, to Erard's Meadow or Clonard. There he built a little hut for his use, as Illtyd had done in his fruitful Welsh valley, and there he was joined by men of all ranks and callings. There he and his disciples built cells for their necessity, just large enough for a rude bed of stone or wood on which the monk could rest, covered by a rough blanket, during the hours of his brief night. His habit for all time, night or day, was made of coarse wool, girdled by a rope, and the rule of discipline denied all but absolute need in regard to food. The members of each common settlement

[18] See above, ch. VII, p. 342.

grew and ground their corn, added to their porridge milk from the cows they themselves kept on the pasture-fields by the river, supped on fish from the streams that abounded near at hand. The only conspicuous building was the church, built of the strongest material the region could provide, often, no doubt, of great stones piled together by the labour of the brethren. For the saying of the Offices we may, perhaps, imagine the monks assembled in small groups, and prayer held all, each in his solitary exercise, both night and day. Instruction was given by word of mouth in those days of few and precious manuscripts. A vast company sat on the grass outside the monastic village of scattered huts to hear Finnian expound from some little knoll the truths of the Church: bishops and abbots, priests, deacons, readers, laymen of every kind and fortune. Most renowned of all in later years were those destined to be "The Twelve Apostles of Erin"; among them were Ciaran of Clonmacnoise and Brendan of Clonfert and the great Columba of Hy.[19]

At Moville on Strangford Lough in County Down another Finnian founded his school some twenty years later in this sixth century. We find here the influence of monastic Galloway in northern Britain. For when this second Finnian was studying sacred writings under Saint Mocha on Island Mahee in Strangford Lough, monks from the "White House" came to visit his school, and he begged Mocha to allow him to accompany them on their return to Whithorn. At the "White House" he was prepared for his life's work at Moville, famous as the earlier training school of Columba. About the same time Ciaran founded his abbey and school of learning at Clonmacnoise on the River Shannon near Athlone. He died when he was but thirty-three, but his monastery became the

---

[19] See Healy, *Insula Sanctorum*, pp. 188ff.; Plummer, *Vitae Sanctorum Hiberniae.*

most celebrated in all Ireland; Alcuin was one of the multitude which filled its gates. The Irish still remember Ciaran,
and make pilgrimage to his shrine on his day, the ninth of
September.

Most romantic of all is the name of Brendan, the Voyager
Saint, who is honoured on the sixteenth of May. The tradition of his wanderings in search of an earthly Paradise comes
to us from the later Middle Ages, centuries after he lived and
died; it told among other legends one of his discovery of
America. Another story relates that he once landed on the
coast of Rhuys in Brittany one winter's night and made his
way with his companions to the monastery of Gildas. Snow
was falling, and the thought of a warm reception heartened
the weary men as they hurried on. But no admission was
given, as they arrived after dark had set in, and they were
obliged to stay in the snow outside all night long. The porter,
it seems, was conscientious rather than hospitable. Another
legend tells of a visit to Gildas in Wales. Brendan was invited
to say Mass, but was given for use at the altar a Missal in
Greek script, and he knew not a letter of Greek. But this was
a small problem for a man of God. He fell to prayer, and
shortly afterward sang his Greek Mass as to the manner
born.[20] About 556 he founded his monastery at Clonfert on
the Shannon in Connaught and lived to see it frequented from
far and wide.

At the same time Comgall, Father of many monasteries,
was presiding over his School at Bangor, revered at a later
time throughout the continent of Europe. It was founded
on the south of Belfast Lough, about seven miles from Belfast
and in full view of the sea. Here once again we are to imagine
the multitude of little huts built of wood piles plastered with

[20] Healy, p. 217; Baring-Gould and Fisher, *Lives of the British Saints*,
I, pp. 243f.

mud after the common monastic fashion. It was protected, as were all these settlements, by an earthen rampart or by a deep trench surrounding the whole, and sometimes by both. Each of these great Schools of Ireland, with its daughter monasteries, kept a Rule laid down by its Father Founder in every individual case. There were many monastic Rules, therefore, differing in lesser points, but similar in prescription of Mass and Office, of secret prayer and discipline of austerity and learning. The green banks and meadows of this early Ireland were crowded by men listening to the words of one or another of these Founders or to some one of their pupils trained to carry on their work.

The Bible formed the foundation of all study, interpreted by the works of the Fathers: the Latin ones in their original, and the Greek usually in Latin translation. Latin, to say nothing of Greek, was a privilege peculiar in Ireland to the scholar; for it was not the tongue spoken by the people, as was the case in Italy. There is, indeed, evidence that the Irish did know Greek in the sixth and seventh centuries before they flocked with the rest of the world to learn from Theodore of Tarsus at Canterbury; the matter is full of question, however, and in any event the Greek, we may think, was small in range and its serious study confined to the best students.[21] For the majority of learners a knowledge of Latin texts would be sufficient, and their subject-matter was secular as well as sacred, including works of history and of poetry. Moreover, the Christian monk of Ireland in the sixth century could himself write Latin prose and poetry, sometimes correctly according to classical standards, sometimes in a manner that foretells the mediaeval, sometimes, it would seem, in a strange and barbarous fashion peculiar to his age. Of this we shall

[21] See Bede, *H.E.* IV, 2; M. R. James, *C.M.H.* III, pp. 502ff.; Hauréau, *Singularités hist. et litt.* 1894, c. 1: *Écoles d'Irlande.*

read later. It was good for the world that the young novice in the Irish monasteries of these times could read his Horace, his Vergil, his Roman satirists, even although Jerome and Augustine had striven to overcome their natural love of beauty in secular words, and Gregory of Tours and Caesarius of Arles cared nothing for pagan literature. Thus in the following age Ireland was to uphold the scholarship of Europe.

But the monasteries of Ireland were not only places of prayer and of instruction for their own members and guests and for the peasant folk who lived and worked around them. The jurisdiction of the Father Abbot in each case was, of course, especially concerned with these matters, and he ruled concerning them with independence, as Lord of his own little world. A third and most important part of his office was that of Father Director of the number of penitents who flocked to his gates. These were of two kinds: First, the people of the countryside came to him and to the priests of the monastery over which he presided for the confession and the counsel they needed in repentance of sin. These penitents included both men and women, who returned promptly to their homes to work out there the penance assigned. Secondly, there were numbers, of those in Holy Order and of the laity, who came as grievous sinners to work out their penitence for months or for years under the direction of the monastery and in its enclosure.

For guidance in this work the Father Abbot, who had composed the Rule for his community, also composed for his sons and spiritual family a Penitential, which set forth clearly the various penalties to be assigned in reparation for the sins prevalent at the time, both greater and smaller. We have already seen one of these Penitentials as the work of Gildas. Another, and more interesting one, has come down to us under the name of Vinniaus, doubtless referring to some Finnian, and, very probably, to Finnian of Clonard. Critics are divided between this Saint and the Finnian of Moville as author. But the commanding position of Clonard among monasteries in the sixth century, and the fact that another Penitential, which we shall see later as the work of a monk connected with Clonard, shows intimate resemblance to this one, points to Clonard as its birthplace.[22]

This Penitential of Finnian establishes the penalties to be laid upon members of the clergy and of the laity, respectively, for their offences against Holy Church. Far heavier penance is assigned to the clergy: for "the blame to be attached to a layman in this world is lighter, even as his reward in the next will be less." If, then, a cleric has willed in his heart to strike or to kill his neighbour, he is to repent for six months on bread and water, strictly measured out, and to abstain another whole year from meat and wine before he may again be admitted to the fellowship of the altar. If he strike another and shed his blood, without killing him, he is to live on bread and water for a year without exercising his ministry. If he actually kill another, he must live ten years in exile, three of these on bread and water, four with abstinence from meat and wine, and three with bread and water in Lent. Satisfaction must also be made to the father or the mother of the slain man.

Penalties for the laity are seven days of fasting for murder in thought, forty days and a sum of money for bloodshed without murder. For the sins of fornication and bloodshed united in a layman the penalty prescribed is that he go unarmed, save for a staff, during three years and be deprived

[22] For its text see F. W. Wasserschleben: *Die Bussordnungen der abendländischen Kirche*, pp. 108ff.; for comment, O. D. Watkins, *A History of Penance*, pp. 606ff.; J. T. McNeill, *The Celtic Penitentials, Revue Celtique*, XXXIX, 1922, pp. 266ff.; T. P. Oakley, *Cultural affiliations of Early Ireland in the Penitentials, Speculum*, VIII, 1933, pp. 489ff.

of the society of his wife, with strict fasting on bread and water during the first year. After these three years he shall complete his penance by giving a sum of money to the priest and by giving a dinner to "the servants of God." Sins against chastity on the part of a cleric require penance varying from seven days of fasting for unworthy desire, to the heavy burden laid on one guilty of the murder of the child born of his sin. For this crime he must live three years on scant measure of bread and water, with tears and prayers day and night to God for mercy; three years he must abstain from meat and wine and take only a little bread and water in Lent. For seven years he is to live in exile and be denied the exercise of his ministry. Marked difference was made in the penalty according to the secrecy or publicity of such offences; for publicity caused scandal among the lay people. A cleric deposed under penance might be restored to the exercise of his office on its completion "at the judgment of the bishop or priest." The Abbot did not as such presume to take this power.[23] Much space is given to sins of layfolk against purity, both of men and of women, and a special warning is given for the protection of nuns. Penance for theft on the part of the clergy, in such cases as stealing of sheep or pigs and so on, requires fourfold restitution, as well as fasting.

At the end there is an interesting clause: "The death of a child unbaptized through negligence is a great crime, for it means the loss of a soul. But it may be redeemed by penitence; for there is no crime which may not be redeemed as long as we are in this body. Let the guilty parents repent a full year with fasting on bread and water, and let them abstain from marital intercourse for the same period." The last words of the pamphlet tell that Finnian (Vinniaus) has drawn up these rules for his beloved brethren, the sons of his

[23] See on this Watkins, p. 610.

heart, in accordance with the teaching of the Scriptures and of learned authorities.

Here, then, we notice a system of penance very different from that of the Church in Gaul. The Celtic practice described here expects that penitents, whether clerics, religious or lay-people, guilty of greater or of lesser sins, will make their confessions privately before the Father Abbot or some one of his monks in priest's orders, and that penance will be privately assigned and privately performed in accordance with the Penitential adopted by the monastery. Moreover, as sins provided for in this Penitential, doubtless typical of others, include sins of thought, we are to think that confession and penance were neither confined to flagrant offenders nor to the sick on their death-beds, nor was the penitence of an amended life alone held desirable. Lastly, the minister of reconciliation in this private office is, as a rule, not the bishop, but the priest who hears the confession.

The Penitential of Finnian shows us the character of penance as exercised in Ireland; that of Gildas may be held characteristic of Britain.[24]

Such, also, was the penitential discipline of Ireland taught and administered in northern Britain by Columba of Iona, himself trained at Clonard, as Comgall had been, and ranking with this Founder of Bangor as one of the Saints of the Second Order in Ireland. He was born where the mountain crags darken with their shadow the tarns of Donegal, a boy in whom the human wrestled fiercely with the divine. From his childhood he had loved to read the psalms alone in the church; so that, as the story goes, the name Colum received by him at his baptism was changed by his friends to Colum

---

[24] *ibid.*, pp. 603ff.; McNeill, *Revue Celtique*, XL, 1923, pp. 78ff.; G. Le Bras, *s.v. Pénitentiels, Dict. de théol. cath.*, 1163ff. See also, for other penitential records in connection with St. David, H. and S. I, pp. 116ff.

Cille, "Colum of the cell," or "church." And so Colum Cille is his name in old manuscripts. He received the diaconate at Moville and carried on his studies there under the Finnian of that place. In addition to his training in Latin works Columba must have drunk in all he could learn of his own native Irish literature and history; for tradition includes him among the bards of Ireland. This Irish learning he gained under a bard of great age, Gemman by name.

His preparation for the priesthood was made under the other Finnian at Clonard, and thus his discipline descended to him from both the Abbey of Saint Ninian in North Britain where Finnian of Moville had studied and from the Welsh monastic schools where Finnian of Clonard had dwelt as student. The last stages of his training were passed at Glasnevin, not far from Dublin, where he prayed and talked on matters spiritual with Ciaran and Comgall. When he left there as a priest, he turned his thoughts to the foundation of monastic schools of his own. We are told to imagine him tall and strong of limb, with fair hair cut in front in the Celtic tonsure, and gray eyes alight with the fire of his mind. The spirit of his proud fathers still burned in him, and he had a hard struggle before he could conquer himself, living a life of austere discipline and humbly bending to carry out his share in the laborious handiwork of the monastic day.[25]

His first foundation was the School of Derry, on the island encompassed by the River Foyle. Afterward, as Bede tells us, he established the Abbey of Durrow, the "Field of the Oaks," in Leinster.[26] Of his love for the monks of Durrow we read in the *Life of Columba* by Adamnan, Abbot of Iona in the

[25] See *Notes from the Lebar Brecc* in the *Calendar of Oengus*, ed. Whitley Stokes, *Trans. Royal Irish Academy*, 1880, I, p. ci, and the *Life of Columba* in the *Lives of Saints from the Book of Lismore*, ed. Whitley Stokes, 1890. On p. 301 the editor prints the passage from the *Speckled Book* telling of the origin of the name Colum Cille, "Dove of the Church."
[26] *H.E.* III, 4.

seventh century, who relates that he continued to watch over them from his island home in Scotland.[27] Later on this Abbey was famous for the illuminated copy of the Gospels known as the *Book of Durrow*. More celebrated is the *Book* of Kells, another Abbey renowned among the followers of Columba, said to have been founded by the Saint himself among his many religious houses. Tradition has connected the name of Columba with both these manuscripts. But they may be more safely dated in the eighth century when script and missal painting had reached a far higher excellence.

Record states that Kells was given to Columba by Diarmait, King of all Ireland, whose royal seat was at Tara, in the present Meath. Presently, however, the anger of Columba was raised against the King, either, so the Irish narratives tell, because Diarmait had put to death a young noble who had fled to Columba in penitence for manslaughter, or because the King had decided against him in a dispute with Finnian of Moville. The story goes that Finnian, who had spent some time in study at Rome, brought from there on his return to the monastery of Moville a most precious copy of the Scriptures, containing emendations from the Vulgate of Saint Jerome. Columba was then at Moville and begged to be allowed to copy this manuscript; but Finnian was afraid to trust his treasure to other hands. So Columba secretly gained possession of it and made his copy by night in the church, lighted by miraculous light from Heaven. An inquisitive peeper through the keyhole saw the sight, but was summarily punished when one of the birds that roosted there, a great crane, plucked out his eye. After Finnian discovered what had been done, he demanded the copy as his own, but Columba as valiantly clung to his work. The matter was referred to the judgment of the Great King of Tara, who

[27] *Vita Adamnani*, I, 23.

gave his decision in favour of Finnian, declaring: "To every cow belongs her calf, and to every book belongs its copy."[28]

A battle was fought in 561 at Cuil Dremne, now Cooladrummon, near Sligo, and we read that Columba incited the men of his clan to fight against Diarmait and his men, who were utterly defeated. The old narratives go on to say that the holy man was greatly vexed in soul afterward for his part in this work of blood and went off to confess his sin to his "soul-friend," Saint Molaise, who dwelt on Innismurray Island, but happened just then to be near at hand. Molaise prescribed a heavy penance: Columba was to leave Ireland for missionary work in another country and to win for God souls as many in number as the spirits of those who had died by his fault on the field of battle.

The biographer, Adamnan, tells nothing of this. But he does tell of a Synod held at Teltown in Meath where Columba was excommunicated "for some venial and very excusable reasons and, as it turned out, unjustly." He came to the meeting in person and was warmly defended by a friend named Brendan, founder, not of Clonfert, but of another monastery at Birr in King's County. Brendan declared it impious to excommunicate one whom God actually sent on his way escorted by angels and a pillar of fire! Had he not just seen this with his own eyes? So the Synod repented of its rash act and fell to great reverencing of the blessed man.[29]

There may be truth in some of this old tradition. But we shall be wise if we think that Columba went forth gladly and of his own free will to preach to the Irish Scots in Northern

[28] Reeves, ed. Adamnan's *Life of Columba*, 1874, pp. XLIff. For the stories given here see the *Life of Columcille* by Manus O'Donnell, dated 1532, ed. and trans. A. O'Kelleher and G. Schoepperle, 1918. Cf. R. Henebry, *Zeitschrift f. Celtische Philologie*, III–V, 1901–1905; A. Kelleher, *ibid.* IX–X, 1913–1915.
[29] *Vita Adamnani*, III, 4.

Britain.[30] He set sail with twelve companions, chosen from
the monks of Derry, and landed on the coast of the island of
Hy, now renowned as Iona, in the year 563.

This is not the place to repeat the story of Iona, so often
related and so well.[31] In many works one may read of the
arrival of the monks; of the gift of the island to Columba by
Conall, Lord of Dalriada in Scotland, and by the Pictish King
Brude; of the first beginnings in this wild and beautiful place;
of the rule of Columba; of his monks and their dress and
food and work; of their prayer; of the marvellous spreading
of truth from the little island to the numberless churches and
monasteries in Scotland which in later years held Columba
their Father and their Head.

It is rather our business here to look at the writings he left
in Latin. He wrote, it is said, poems in Irish, and songs attributed to him may still be read in Irish or in delightful English
rendering.[32] We have remarked that he was most probably
one of the Irish Bards, and it is told that he secured their
Order from abolition by his eloquent apology at the Assembly
of Drumceat in 575. The Bards, very numerous at this time,
had been accused of arrogance, tyranny and sloth. Columba
did not deny their faults, but pleaded for reform rather than
destruction. His victory won for him the famous song of his

[30] See, on exile as part of Irish asceticism, Plummer, ed. Bede, H.E.
II, p. 170. The "old Irish Life," dating probably from the 10th century,
given in the Speckled Book and in the Book of Lismore, merely states that
Colum Cille left Ireland on pilgrimage to preach the word of God to the
men of Scotland: see translations of this Life by Whitley Stokes, ed. Book
of Lismore, p. 178, and by W. M. Hennessy: Skene, Celtic Scotland, II,
p. 491.
[31] e.g., E. C. Trenholme, The Story of Iona; Lucy Menzies, Saint
Columba; Padraic Colum, The Legend of Saint Columba. For the Life
by Adamnan see also J. T. Fowler's edition[2], and, for the work of
Columba, John A. Duke, The Columban Church, 1932; Hist. of the
Church in Scotland, 1937.
[32] For Irish poems attributed to Columba and their translations, see
the Life, ed. Reeves, 1857, pp. 264–277, 285–289; and Kenneth Macleod,
The Road to the Isles, p. 144.

praises, called the *Amra of Colum Cille,* from the gratitude of the Chief Bard, Dallan mac Forgaill.[33]

Three Latin poems are connected with his name. Very interesting details are found in the old prefaces prefixed to them, which tell probably what scholars of the tenth century believed concerning their origin and authorship. These curious prefaces are written in a mixture of Irish and Latin; the *Irish Liber Hymnorum* gives a translation of the Irish with the original Irish-Latin of the prefaces and the Latin of the poems themselves.[34]

The best known of these three poems is one beginning *Altus Prosator,* generally considered a genuine work of Columba. Its preface gives two reasons for its composition: first, that the Saint composed it in penitence for the part he played in the battle of Cuil Dremne won from King Diarmait, and in other battles, also. For on two other occasions Columba is said to have incited men to war, and these, too, long after he had become Abbot of Iona: near Coleraine, about 579, where strife was said to have arisen between him and his brother Abbot, Comgall of Bangor, concerning possession of a church, and again in 587 at Cuilfedha, near Clonard. We are not to forget that we are concerned here with the sixth century, which fled readily to war as remedy for troubles, and with the martial spirit of the early Irish clans.[35] Nevertheless, it is a comfort at times to recall the frailties of the Saints, if frailty is the word, indeed, and not righteous wrath! This version of the poem's origin tells that it took seven years in the doing, and was written at Iona in a dark unlighted cell.[36]

The preface then gives a variant narrative. "Others say"

---

[33] *Irish Liber Hymnorum,* II, pp. 53ff.
[34] *ibid.* I, pp. 62ff., II, pp. 23ff.   [35] Reeves, ed. 1874, p. XXXIX.
[36] The Preface in *B* MS. understands from "Cellula Nigra" the Black Church of Columba at Derry, but the *TF* Preface distinctly gives Hi as the place of writing: *Ir. Lib. Hymn.* II, pp. 23ff., 140ff.

that it was composed extemporaneously when Columba was alone in Iona with only one brother monk, named Baithin. No food remained in the monastery except one sieve of oats, and guests were expected shortly, very important ones, messengers bringing presents from Pope Gregory the Great. Columba bade the brother stay in the Abbey to receive the visitors while he himself went off to the mill, carrying the oats to be ground. A song, he thought, would help on the work. So he chanted a verse of this hymn, just as the words came into his head, each time he put a measure of the oats into the mill for grinding. It is a pleasant story, though the other version seems more probable.[37] It goes on to relate that the poem was sent to Gregory in return for certain gifts from him, a book of "Hymns of the Week" and a cross known as the "Great Jewel"; and that Gregory liked it very much, except that he did not think it sang enough of the praise of the Holy Trinity. When Columba heard this, he set to work and wrote another hymn to make up for this fault.

The *Altus Prosator* consists of *capitula,* or verses, of six lines, each verse beginning with a letter of the alphabet.[38] The first, alone of all, has seven lines, explained by the author of the *Preface* as due to the pre-eminence of God, Whom it praises here at greater length than the works of His hand on which it dwells later. The lines are of sixteen syllables, and the halves of each line rhyme with one another. After the praise of the Holy Trinity, it goes on to sing of the creation and the fall of the angels, especially of the Dragon, Satan; of the forming of man, heralded by the glad angelic song; of the birth of

[37] II, pp. 23f.
[38] For the Latin text of the *Altus Prosator* see *ibid.* I, pp. 66ff.: for translations II, pp. 150ff.; *The Altus of St. Columba,* by John, Marquess of Bute; Jack Lindsay, *Med. Lat. Poets,* pp. 22f.; Trenholme, *op. cit.* pp. 157ff.

Nature; of the will of God dominant over the passing glory of this world; of Hell and of Paradise; of the Last Judgment, with the joy of the blessed and the doom of those who resist the Lord Christ.

Here is the song of the Angels at man's creation:

> Factis simul sideribus etheris luminaribus
> collaudaverunt angeli factura pro mirabili
> immensae molis dominum opificem celestium
> preconcio laudabile debito et immobile
> concentuque egregio grates egerunt domino
> amore et arbitrio non naturae donario.

And here the picture of the Last Judgment:

> Stantes erimus pavidi ante tribunal domini
> reddemusque de omnibus rationem effectibus
> videntes quoque posita ante obtutus crimina
> librosque conscientiae patefactos in facie
> in fletus amarissimos ac singultus erumpemus
> subtracta necessaria operandi materia.

The many references to the Bible show that Columba used an Old Latin, not the Vulgate, version. This is also true of the frequent quotations in the *Confession* of Saint Patrick. It is interesting to think that possibly the manuscript of tradition, source of so great strife between Saint Columba and Saint Finnian, may have been the first copy of Holy Scripture in the Vulgate version to reach Ireland.[39]

The Preface to the *Altus Prosator* promises great blessings to him who shall recite it piously. Angels shall attend him as he devoutly says its words day by day; evil spirits shall flee from him, and his house shall be at peace. His house shall know neither hunger nor nakedness; he shall be safe from assault and shall meet death quietly in his bed.

We do not know what hymn Columba wrote to make

[39] *Irish Liber Hymn.* II, p. 145.

reparation for his lack of lines on the Holy Trinity. The *Preface* to a hymn beginning *In te, Christe* tells that he composed it in Iona for this reason, but remarks also that some people believed that much of this hymn was not his work. It does not resemble the *Altus Prosator* in its matter or its style, though that is no certain reason why the same man should not have written it. Its form is a kind of litany of phrases descriptive of the glory of Christ as God and Man.[40]

A third hymn attributed to Columba begins:

> Noli pater indulgere tonitrua cum fulgore
> ne frangamur formidine huius atque uridine

It is a prayer against vengeance of God sent by thunder and lightning, and sings, moreover, the praise of John the Baptist. This strange mixture of themes has been explained in reference to an ancient legend that dread disaster would visit Ireland on the Feast of the Beheading of Saint John, August 29th. We are told that its recitation would protect men from harm by fire and by stroke of lightning, and not only him who recited it but also nine members of his household, whomsoever he should choose.[41]

There is a natural temptation to tarry in Iona, among memories of the days when its first Saint was kindling a flame that should blaze far and near. A line of abbots and scholars carried on his work till the ninth century, with rule over all the monasteries in Scotland and in Ireland which owed reverence to their Mother House. His spell still rests on the white sands where he beached his rough boats, over the meadows springing with wild flowers where he loved man and beast and bird, body as well as soul, over the church which still honours his name. It is pleasant to think of his

[40] I, pp. 84f.
[41] *ibid.* I, pp. xxiiif., 87f.; II, pp. 28, 171f.; *Zeitschrift f. Celt. Phil.* IV, p. 293.

meeting with his fellow-missioner, Saint Kentigern, who did much work on the Molendinar, where Glasgow now stands. Tradition tells that each gave to the other his own pastoral staff as a mark of the love they shared in Christ, that they talked long together of holy things before they broke their fast. "But," the biographer of Saint Kentigern goes on, "the depths of divine contemplation in those hallowed hearts it is not mine to fathom. Neither to me nor to those of my ilk has it been given to understand the manna hidden and, I think, all unknown, save to those who taste thereof." Others of their company, however, were more like ordinary sinners. It is sad to relate that two of Columba's disciples, being born thieves (so the *Life* frankly declares), stole the fattest ram from the flocks of Kentigern! [42]

Let us keep from temptation and deal with Latin writings. For a moment, however, we must glance at that extraordinary monument of preciosity known as the *Hisperica Famina,* the "Western Sayings." This is a collection of texts on various subjects, composed in a bizarre and artificial style that seems to have been in vogue among cultured writers of Britain and Ireland in the fifth, sixth and seventh centuries. Cardinal Mai, who first published its almost unintelligible jargon, threatened it with the rightful curses of all lovers of classical Latin, though he saw equally well that philologists would greet it with a cheer. [43] In England scholars of Cambridge have lavished on it special devotion, especially Henry Bradshaw, who found it "of immense help" in his linguistic studies, [44] and Francis Jenkinson, who edited all its four texts and added a summary of their contents for which we are truly grateful; [45] for its vocabulary makes its meaning as clear, shall we say?

[42] Jocelin, *Vita Kentigerni,* ed. Forbes, cc. XXXIXf.
[43] *Auctores classici ex cod. vat.* V, pp. 479ff.
[44] *Memoir* of Henry Bradshaw by G. W. Prothero, p. 341.
[45] *The Hisperica Famina,* 1908. For description see M. Rogers, *L'enseignement des lettres classiques,* pp. 238ff.; Kenney, *Sources,* I, pp. 255ff.

as the writings of Gertrude Stein to the uninitiated reader.
Moreover, in browsing on these ancient words the pasture so
rich for the philologist yields little grain for the student of
literature, either in fruit of meaning or in beauty of sound.
Here a background of the ordinary words used by writers of
prose and poetry in the sixth century is thickly sown with
Greek words, Hebrew words, words of unknown derivation,
words borrowed from the vulgar or colloquial Latin of the
day, technical terms of ecclesiastical use, words used in a
sense entirely different from their current meaning, and words
adorned with new endings.[46] The origin of some of these
strange growths is still obscure; but it seems as though
devotees of some literary cult had used all their ingenuity to
pick out from glossaries and all recondite and mysterious
sources a language of their own, foreign to the writing of their
time.[47] Scholars have differed on the question whether these
"Western Sayings" are prose or poetry. Cardinal Mai printed
them as prose; Henry Bradshaw judged them "assonant
rhythm," understood by their author as poetry;[48] Jenkinson
also saw in them a kind of crude verse, but with considerably
less assonance. Of the German writers, Stowasser, with whom
Jenkinson agreed, held this verse to be related to the Latin
hexameter;[49] each line, normally, completes a sentence,
making a style simple in structure. A consensus of authority
ranks the collection as Celtic Latin, and internal evidence
points to Ireland as the land of its origin.[50] Its patient and

[46] Roger, *ibid.* pp. 242ff.
[47] Roger traces the use of glossaries as source, which Jenkinson disputes.
For a dictionary of Hisperic Latin see the *Mediaeval Latin Word-List*,
Baxter and Johnson, 1934.
[48] Henry Bradshaw, *Collected Papers,* p. 463.
[49] Stowasser, *Archiv für lat. Lex. u. Gramm.* III, 1886, pp. 168ff.; Jenkinson, ed. pp. XVIIf.
[50] See Jenkinson, p. XI; Bradshaw in Prothero's *Memoir,* p. 341. H.
Zimmer once thought it came from S. W. Britain (*Nennius Vindicatus,*
p. 336), under the influence of Martianus Capella, but afterward preferred
to think that its contents were composed in Ireland by exiles from S. W.
Gaul (*Sitz. d. Preuss. Akad. d. Wiss.,* Berlin, 1910, p. 1119).

skilful editor tells us,[51] and few readers of Latin literature classical or mediaeval will care to dispute with him, that in the various parts of the A-text, the only one complete, we may read of praise of rhetoricians; of advice to a farmer, who would be a scholar, that he go home from school to aid his disconsolate family; of the errors made in Latin by those who try to write it, and of the writer's superiority in this respect over other men. A more entertaining section tells of the doings of a day, from morning till evening: its sun rising over trees and fields, over sheep and cattle and horses; its labourers, men of the farm and the forest, students of the school; its midday dinner; its twilight and evening meal.

Much of the interest of these texts lies in traces of their connection with more readable works, only slightly or partially "Hisperic." Such are the *Altus Prosator* attributed to Columba; the *Lorica* which bears the name of Gildas; some of the writing of Columban, whom we shall find next in our procession of writers of the sixth century; some of the writing of Aldhelm, and certain compositions preserved in manuscripts of a later date in the University Library at Cambridge: the *Rubisca,* the *Hymn of St. Omer,* and the *Cambridge Juvencus.* These all contain words seasoned with the "Hisperic" flavour.[52]

It is a relief to turn from artificial words to think of a man who came from Ireland to give new light to the continent of Europe: Columban, that Saint afire with Irish enthusiasm, whose zeal for his faith and the traditions of his country was stayed by no obstacle, not by fear of the Church and her bishops in Gaul, not even by his reverence for the Chair of Saint Peter itself. His love of the Gospel carried him on through every kind of peril and discomfort, wrestling against man and beast, against flood and fire and famine, if only he might stir anew monastic fervour in Europe and guide into

[51] Jenkinson, ed. pp. XIf.   [52] For these see Kenney, I, p. 257.

the fold the souls wandering unfed. He, too, struggled against immorality stalking unabashed by day and night in Gaul under the Merovingian Kings. And he was rewarded with extraordinary success. Through him Ireland invigorated countless centres of the Christian Faith for both men and women in the sixth and the seventh centuries, till finally his houses were merged in the great garner of the Benedictine Rule. Through him monastic learning on the continent of Europe, fruitful throughout the Middle Ages, was strengthened to carry on the work for which Cassiodorus had laboured so long in southern Italy.

We owe the *Life of Columban* to Jonas, a monk of Bobbio in the seventh century.[58] He tells us that he wrote at the command of his Abbot, Bertulf, and of his fellow-monks, who desired a record of their Father's acts. His information came from many who had known the Saint, especially from Eustatius, who succeeded him as Abbot of Luxeuil, and from Attala, second Abbot of Bobbio.

Ireland, then, gave birth to Columban: "a land," as Jonas described it, "apart from other countries in her laws and aloof from their wars; flourishing in vigour of Christian doctrine and pre-eminent over other nations in the power of her faith"—words which may well gladden those who look back on Irish lineage. His home was in Leinster, and as he grew up under the care of his mother he worked diligently at his grammar and literature; for he was a gifted boy. He was good-looking, too, we read, and when he was older, the devil began to tempt him by inciting wanton maids to desire his love. They worked in vain, for he only fell more resolutely than ever upon rhetoric and geometry and, above all, upon the Scriptures.

Yet something troubled him, some dissatisfaction with his

[58] ed. Krusch, *M.G.H. Script. rer. Merov.* IV; trans. D. C. Munro, *Trans. and Reprints,* Univ. Penn. II, 7.

present life, and one day he went to consult a holy anchoress of the neighbourhood in her cell. Her response was quick and fiery: "For fifteen years I have been homeless in the place of my pilgrimage and never by the aid of Christ have I looked back. Yes, and if my weak sex had not prevented, I would have gone on truer pilgrimage across the sea. And you, alive with the fire of youth, you will stay here at home in your native land with weaklings and women? Remember Eve and Delilah and Bathsheba and the tempters of Solomon! Go forth, young man, go forth, and avoid the road to ruin and to Hell!"

It was all that was needed. The lad only stayed a moment for a word of thanks, ran home to give a quick good-bye to his friends, and started out. His mother burst into tears and threw herself in this sudden misery across the doorstep of their cottage. But he jumped stoutly over her, crying farewell; she would never see him again in this life, for he was bound on the road to salvation! Christianity in the sixth century seems to have been so much simpler than to-day.

Thus he left Leinster and made his way to a hermit named Sinilis, renowned for his erudition. Columban stayed with him till he knew his Bible thoroughly; till he had even, so Jonas declared, progressed enough to make a marvellous commentary on the Psalter. It has been suggested that this was a revision in Latin of the commentary by Theodore, Bishop of Mopsuestia in Asia Minor, that Theodore of the "Three Chapters," who, as we noted in connection with the Emperor Justinian, caused a whirlwind of controversy in the fifth and the sixth centuries concerning the orthodoxy of his teachings. Perhaps Columban was perpetuating solid doctrine here while trying at the same time to correct errors; the suggestion is certainly of interest in connection with his later history. He was never afraid of his own opinion, and, though intensely

loyal to the Catholic Church, would scarcely have been afraid
to put his hand to re-editing a famous book because it was
held in bad repute. A Commentary of St. Columban on the
Psalms is mentioned in a catalogue of the Bobbio library of
the tenth century, and also in one of the library of St. Gall of
the ninth.[54]

A direct reading of Theodore would require in Columban
a knowledge of Greek, a matter not proved, in spite of his use
of Greek words. He may have used for this revision, if he did
make it, the commentary on Theodore's work made by Julian
of Eclanum, the Bishop renowned in the Pelagian warfare.
At any rate, Ireland now made of Columban an accomplished
classical scholar, as we shall see from his writings. Under
Sinilis, in addition to sacred learning, he is said to have studied
poetry and "many things useful for a teacher."

From Sinilis he went to learn monastic discipline in the
School of Bangor under Comgall, and made steady advance
till he felt himself ready for the petition, which his Abbot
heard with sorrow, that he be allowed to go forth on missionary labours. Consent was given, and he sailed with twelve
companions to the Breton coast.[55] Once safe on shore, the
little band journeyed on to Gaul, and, in the midst of lax
manners and morals, began to live anew their life of strictest
mortification in a foreign land. There they made their way
into Burgundy and under the protection of Guntram, its King,
whom we have seen as a keen son of the Church, chose to
settle in the forest land of Haute-Saône among the Vosges
mountains. In this wild and rocky region they took possession
of a ruined fortress and founded Columban's first monastery
of Annegray. It was about the year 591, and the leader,

[54] See Krusch, p. 18; Gougaud, p. 268; R. L. Ramsay, *Zeitschrift f.
Celt. Phil.* VIII, 1912, pp. 448ff.

[55] Krusch, p. 71, note 1, against the theory of some scholars that Britain
is meant here.

according to the most reasonable tradition, was now a man of mature years, possibly well on in middle life.[56]

We can see from the stories of Jonas that it was a desperately hard undertaking. The bleak tracts of the wilderness in which Columban and his disciples were encamped afforded but bare necessity of food and water. At one time, we are told, the brethren lived for nine days on wild herbs and the bark of trees, until a certain abbot called Carantoc, perhaps of Saulx in Haute-Saône,[57] was directed by the Lord to relieve their need. His convent cellarer, Marculf, was at once despatched with provisions, but lost his way and only reached the starving monks through the inspired sagacity of the horses which led his team. Another story shows the Saint pacing by himself in the depths of the forest with a book on his arm, making his meditation. Suddenly a question leaped into his mind, in the way so familiar to such exercises, born of the happenings of daily life. Would he, he wondered, rather meet with evil treatment at the hands of robbers or at the claws of wild beasts? An inspiring theme for a meditation, especially as both were well within reach! Columban crossed himself and decided to prefer the savageness of lower animals, because no sin of a guilty soul was to be presumed in them. The Lord took him at his word and promptly allowed twelve wolves to rush out and seize his clothing. But they retreated when they found the man of God entirely calm and self-possessed. Neither did the Lord allow a band of Suevian robbers, roving near at hand in search of prey, to molest him, though he could hear their shouts very clearly. He was puzzled, indeed, afterward as to whether these were real occurrences or illusions sent by the devil to interrupt his devotion. They seem quite real in the narrative. Once, too, during another quest into the heart of the forest he came upon a huge

[56] Kenney, p. 187.   [57] Krusch, p. 73, note 1.

precipitous crag. In its face there was a yawning cave; and
since Columban never lacked courage or zeal for knowledge,
he climbed up the almost impassable cliff and crawled into the
dark mouth of the tunnel till he came upon its tenant, a great
shaggy bear. Columban mildly remarked: "Please do not
frequent these trails in the future," and, of course, the bear
obediently ambled off. This was some seven miles from
Annegray.

But all sorts of people, sick in body and in mind, discovered
the Saint and flocked to him for healing. Many came who
longed to try the monastic vocation under his guidance. So
he decided to move to more suitable quarters and found them
in another disused fort at Luxeuil, about eight miles distant.
Jonas describes its scenery: "There were hot springs there,
held in devout reverence; stone images crowded its forest
glades, honoured in ancient days by the pitiful cult and
impious ceremonial of the heathen people of this countryside,
who offered before them their accursed rites; the place was
desolate, only frequented by savage wild life, a multitude of
bears and owls and wolves." Yet here again so many pilgrims
hastened after Columban that he was compelled to found a
third monastery, in the place where Fontaine now lies on the
banks of the stream La Roge.[58]

We will read first what Jonas tells us of the outer life of
the brethren in these houses. At last they had sufficiency of
corn, when they had broken up the hard ground, weeded,
sown and tended, threshed and gathered into barns. Columban took his own share in this toil, and all things were evidently done with order and decency. One day the Father laid
aside his working gloves at the door of the refectory, so the
story goes, before entering for dinner, and a raven was wicked
enough to fly down and carry them off. Columban knew it

[58] *ibid.* p. 76, note 2.

must have been a raven, the bird that never came back to the Ark! But this time the sinner was brought to penitence. Such stories earn gratitude, even from the historian, for what they reveal of the manners of the time. Thus we learn that the monks drank herb-beer at dinner from the legend of the monk who flew to answer his Abbot's call just as he was drawing it from a barrel into a flagon. His prompt obedience caused no harm; for the liquid was piled high on his return in a column above the neck of the flagon, and not a drop was spilled.

There were beasts of the forest here also, as Columban discovered when he resumed his solitary walks with God. Once he came upon another bear devouring the carcase of a deer slain by wolves, and rebuked this one, too, for harming the hide which must furnish the monastery with shoe leather. Fish were plentiful in the streams and made excellent food for the refectory. Columban could always tell, Jonas observes, where they lay hidden in the pools. Four-footed creatures and birds would come to him at his call, and the squirrels would jump from the trees to rest on his shoulder. The people of the district of Luxeuil still point out to travellers the cave and the holy well of the Saint, with the Chapel beside them on the mountain that rises from the village of Sainte-Marie-en-Chanois, Saint Mary of the Oak-Wood.[59]

Columban ruled supreme as Father Abbot after the manner of his Irish tradition within both Luxeuil and Fontaine; Luxeuil, which soon included a numerous company, was a Clonard or a Bangor in miniature so far as its monastic life went. It was afterward to recall the Irish monasteries in its fame of learning. Here under Columban in the sixth century we are to imagine the young men of Gaul, gathered from all ranks, hastening to learn of the life of the cloister; the

[59] Margaret Stokes, *Three Months in the Forests of France,* pp. 23f.

peasants, men and women, seeking comfort and direction in that tumultuous and disorderly age; the penitents striving in some way to atone for the past under the constant rule of a disciplined community.

The Abbot's relation to his monks is seen through his *Sermons* and his *Rule*, both composed for these houses he established in Burgundy. Of the seventeen sermons or "instructions" contained in Migne, four are held genuine on good authority, found together in one manuscript of Fleury-sur-Loire and dealing with one subject, the way of life for monks.[60] They are full, however, of goodly precepts for all travellers in this world of time. "Think not what you are, wretched man, but what you will be. . . . Do not be sure about things that perish and unsure about the better things that shall last. . . . Awake, my sons, from darkness, seek the light, that you may both see and be seen. . . . Sleep not, lest you believe the false to be the true. . . . Life is a wheel, it runneth today and waiteth not for thee, who should run with it. . . . Sell not your inheritance in heaven; sell your faults, above all, your pride, and buy virtues, buy humility. . . . Through things seen let us contemplate things unseen. . . . He tramples on the world who tramples on himself. . . . He who loves has accomplished all and never grows old and feeble. . . . Perchance by aid of love we shall escape the penalty of our folly in this world, of our ignorance of the things that really matter. So give of your charity to those who need. . . . Do not prize your wealth before yourself, your possessions above your soul. For what is really yours except your soul? Truly patience for one hour is better than peni-

---

[60] See for criticism O. Seebass, *Zeitschrift f. Kirchengeschichte*, XIII, 1892, pp. 513ff. Here he attributes most of these sermons to a pupil of Faustus of Riez. For the text of the four which he holds genuine writings of Columban (Migne, Nos. 16, 3, 17, 11, *PL* LXXX) see Seebass, *ibid.* XIV, 1894, pp. 76ff. Cf. also Kenney, pp. 196f.

tence throughout eternity." So in essence run two of these informal talks to the brethren. The third treats of the seven deadly sins, and the fourth, once again, of Christian love: "It is so easy to break the vessel of love by a little word of wrath. Let us therefore try not to talk much, not to feed our human appetite for gossip and slander. Whosoever tells lies, and evil lies, concerning his neighbour slays his own self with a dagger to the delight of his spiritual enemies. For if he who merely does not love is dead to Christ, what of him who breaks out into actual words of evil?"

The Rule, also, consists in its greater part of general principles underlying the monastic life.[61] It was no easy view of this that Columban laid before his disciples. Obedience must be immediate and entire. Directly the "Senior" bids, the junior brother must rise to fulfil the command, however hard it be, whether he judge it good or no. The responsibility lies with the one who commands, and the guilt with a junior who refuses to obey, even though his refusal be justified by lay standards. The younger's constant words must be: "Not what I, but what you wish." Mortification, indeed, Columban describes as a most important part of a monastic rule. Its prescription is threefold: Never rebel in your heart; never talk as you would; never go anywhere on your own account.

Silence was perpetual in Columban's monasteries except when necessity interrupted, that the monks might be free from chattering and, in consequence, from evil words. Fasting continued till the evening, and the dinner then served consisted of mean and frugal fare; vegetables and meal mixed with water and a small quantity of hard biscuit sustained the brethren during their long toil on the farm and during their watches in the chapel. Fasting, in the Founder's prescription,

[61] For the text see Seebass, *ibid.* XV, 1895, pp. 366ff., and for description and bibliography Kenney, pp. 197f.

is as much a part of the daily work as labour and reading and prayer. Other chapters tell of the driving out of greed by contempt of possessions and of the battle against vanity and pride. Chastity also receives its due share of instruction, with the hard saying that to be virgin in body avails nothing if one be not virgin in mind. Discretion, that queen of virtues in Cassian's instructions to monks, is described in the eighth chapter as the balance weighing appetite against necessity, body against soul, evil against good, the moderate against the perfect, the superfluous against the frugal. The ninth chapter, *On the perfection of a monk,* comes directly word for word from St. Jerome's letter to the monk Rusticus.[62]

One section, the seventh, is of special interest as giving us some account of the monastic Hours of day and night under Columban. Again we remember that this Irish Founder was doubtless reproducing the Rule he had learned under Comgall in Bangor; and, happily, we can compare the order for prayer given here with the order, remarkably similar, put forward in the Celtic service-book of the seventh century known as the "Antiphonary" of Bangor.[63] Still greater interest belongs to the whole Rule of Columban when we remember that in it we possess our only extant monastic Rule, in Latin, from an Irish source of this period.[64]

In this Order of the monastic Office the Night Hours were three: at Nightfall (First Nocturn), at Midnight (Second Nocturn), at Morning (Matins). At each of the two former Hours twelve psalms were sung daily. Both services seem, therefore, to have been alike, and the Office at Nightfall did not correspond to that of Compline. The arrangement for the Morning Hour before the Dawn *(ad Matutinam)* was

[62] *PL* XXII, 1080f.
[63] ed. F. E. Warren: *Henry Bradshaw Society,* IV, 1893; X, 1895.
[64] The Rule attributed to St. Columba is in Irish: H. and S. II, pp. 119ff.

more complicated. On five days of the week during the longer darkness of the autumn and winter thirty-six psalms were sung; during the spring and summer, when light broke far sooner, twenty-four were judged sufficient. Two nights, those ushering in Saturday and Sunday, were held in special reverence as "holy." During the winter, from November 1 till March 25, seventy-five psalms were sung at this Office on those nights. From March 25 till June 24 a small number of these were dropped each week till at midsummer only thirty-six psalms remained. For some time this number remained constant, but with the increasing of the hours of darkness the number of psalms increased each week, till by the beginning of November the full quota of seventy-five was again reached. At all Offices the singing of the Psalms was accompanied by antiphons.

The Day-Hours prescribed by Columban may fairly be inferred from those laid down in the *Antiphonary of Bangor*, on the ground of other correspondences between the parent and the daughter foundations. At Bangor five were observed: Of the Second Hour (Prime), of the Third (Terce), of the Sixth (Sext), of the Ninth (None), and Vespers. At each of these three Psalms were sung, with the exception of Vespers, for which twelve were prescribed.[65] Prayers of intercession were recited in versicles after the psalms at the Hours; the list which Columban gives of these intercessions corresponds very nearly to actual prayers given in the book of Bangor. They include supplication "on account of our sins," "for all Christian people," "for priests and other sacred ministers," "for benefactors," "for the peace of rulers" and "for our enemies."[66]

---

[65] ed. Warren, II, pp. XVIf.
[66] *ibid.* The "preces" at Bangor are given here for *ad Matutinam*: pp. 22f. See also Gougaud, pp. 330ff.; *Dict. d'arch. chrét. s.v. Celtiques (Liturgies),* col. 3017; W. C. Bishop, *Church Quarterly Review,* XXXVII, 1894, pp. 337ff.

Closely connected with his Rule was another prescription made by Columban for his monks, known as the *Regula Coenobialis*.[67] This dealt with sins and failings, in an assessment of penalties for different offences. The introduction counsels frequent confession of error, according to the Irish tradition: "before meals, before bed time, and whenever convenient." Neither are small sins to be neglected in confession: "for he who neglects little sins gradually lapses from good." Much of this ruling on monastic penance is occupied with these small faults, and frequently corporal punishment is prescribed in atonement. Such minor frailties as lack of attention to grace at table, failure to say "Amen" at the end, or to make the sign of the Cross over one's drinking-bowl, unnecessary speaking at table, coughing when beginning to sing a psalm in Office, smiling during Office, speaking of a thing as "mine," brought on the offender six strokes of discipline. To strike the table with one's knife, presumably in anger, meant ten blows; forgetting to offer prayer on leaving or entering the monastery brought twelve; contradiction of one brother by another, save of a junior by a senior, as many as fifty. The proper thing for the one corrected to say was: "I hope that you are right. I'm sorry I was so forgetful."

Sometimes the penalty imposed extra prayer in Chapel, as for those who wasted food in cooking or in serving, or were guilty of sins of the tongue, or of sloth. To speak wrongly of a layman brought imposition of twelve psalms; of a fellow-monk, twenty-four psalms. The same number fell to the monk who presumed to choose a task on his own initiative after completing a prescribed piece of work, and to him who spoke with a layman unbidden. Falling asleep during Office brought six psalms if a rare offence, double the number if of frequent occurrence. Extra fasting and unbroken silence were

[67] ed. O. Seebass, *Zeit. f. Kircheng.*, XVII, 1897, pp. 215ff. See for criticism of the text, his *Ueber Columban von Luxeuils Klosterregel und Bussbuch*, pp. 33ff.

frequently inflicted for more serious faults; such as speaking evil of the Abbot, telling details of past sins, deliberate lying, breaking fast, disobedience, discontent. Attempt to excuse oneself always aggravated the offence, just as prompt confession and contrition lightened the penalty, sometimes by as much as one half.

Special instructions are given here, also, for the punishment of those guilty of carelessness with regard to the Blessed Sacrament, which the monks, as was the custom of this time, were allowed to carry with them in journeying. Loss of the Host involved penitence of a year, irreverence by neglect, of six months. Penitence involved strict fasting. Other ordinances bade the monk whose Host had suffered injury to burn It with fire, to hide the ashes under the altar and practise special repentance forty days. Should the monk fall into water from a boat or a bridge or from his horse while carrying the holy Viaticum, he was to repent one day, if his fall was caused by accident. If, however, he did not take immediate thought for his precious burden, consuming It immediately with any water which had entered Its vessel, he was to fast the period of a Lent. The holy vessel was called a *chrismal*, the name also given to a vessel containing the blessed oil for anointing. A story is told of Saint Comgall that once he and certain of his brethren were attacked by pirates on the shore of Britain. The robbers seized his companions, but let the Father alone in their terror of the *chrismal* which he wore on his habit. For, says the legend, they thought he was carrying his God. Very probably it was, indeed, the Blessed Sacrament which Comgall bore for the comfort and aid of the travellers.[68]

Not only monks, but a vast general company came to the monasteries of Columban for penance; and we have from his hands another Penitential which shows evident kinship with

[68] *Via secunda S. Comgalli, Boll. Acta SS.* May II, p. 585.

that ascribed to Finnian of Clonard.[69] This document of Columban undoubtedly also represents the early discipline of Ireland.

We find here the monastic life assigned to the sinner as penance for the crime of perjury committed through greed. Such a one shall shave his head and serve God all his remaining days in a cloister. Secondly, the office of the priest as judge and confessor is prominently recognized.[70] After due penance for grievous sins of homicide or fornication the penitent may "be joined to the altar" by decision of the priest, in other words, be again allowed to make his communion. A layman guilty of habitual theft, in cases where restitution is not possible, must observe strict fast for a year and three Lents, promise never to commit the sin again, give alms to the poor and "a banquet to the priest who is judge of his penitence." A layman who has indulged impure desire without fruit in action is to confess his fault to the priest and fast forty days on bread and water. At the end there is appended some counsel to monks, including the recommending of a diligent habit of confession in preparation for Communion: "especially when the mind is agitated, lest one should go to the altar with unclean heart. For it is better to wait till the heart is whole and free from offence and ill-feeling, than to go boldly to the judgment-seat of the altar, where the Body and Blood of Christ condemn those who approach unworthily." This would be more interesting if we could be sure that it is not a later addition to Columban's own text.

From this discipline introduced from Ireland by Columban the practice of private confession with its assigned penance spread through Gaul in the many continental monasteries of

[69] ed. Wasserschleben, pp. 353ff.; and O. Seebass, *Zeit. f. Kirscheng.* XIV, 1894, pp. 430ff. For the authenticity of the text see *ibid.* and McNeill, *Revue Celtique,* XXXIX, pp. 277ff.

[70] Watkins, p. 617.

the seventh century patterned after the model of Luxeuil. That it was welcome is seen by the multitude of penitents who, as Jonas tells us, flocked to seek Columban's aid. Other Penitentials followed in due course, drawn up by other confessors; in one of them, composed before the end of the eighth century, we find detailed directions for the priest.[71] Another tradition, apparently a genuine one of the eighth century, tells of private confession regularly practised in England by clergy, monks, and lay people since the time of Theodore of Tarsus, Archbishop of Canterbury shortly before the seventh century closed.[72]

In the seventh and the eighth centuries, then, Penitentials were in constant use. The ninth century disputed long and fiercely as to their worth, and in two of its Councils they were condemned, though not extinguished. But their use was always rather Celtic than Roman.[73]

Columban, however, had other aspects of his character than those of Father Abbot and Father Confessor, though in all his busy work within he had scant leisure for thought of the very real Church outside his walls. Apparently he conceived the function of Abbot in Gaul to be similar to that in Ireland; at any rate, we do not read of any episcopal Visitor for his various houses or of any formal permission from the diocesan for their establishing. Yet both had been repeatedly required in ecclesiastical Councils, and the bishops of Gaul and of Italy in this sixth century were so keen to enforce their

[71] For this *"Poenitentiale Pseudo-Romanum"* and others related to that of Columban see Wasserschleben, pp. 360ff. He includes the *Penitential* of Columban among the Frankish ones, of which it was the predecessor, on account of its suitability for Frankish sinners, especially in the inclusion of Frankish idolatry (see p. 13, p. 56, p. 353). But see Watkins, pp. 618f.; McNeill, *Revue Celtique,* p. 320.

[72] Watkins, pp. 654f.; *Dialogue of Egbert,* H. and S. III, p. 413.

[73] For their later history see Watkins and Le Bras, cited above. For the theory of Schmitz (not generally accepted by scholars) that penitentials came originally from Rome, see his *Die Bussbücher und die Bussdisciplin der Kirche,* I, 1883; II, 1898.

authority over the monks in their spheres of control that we hear of many cases of monastic protest.[74]

The bishops of Burgundy had further cause for indignation against Columban. He and his followers were keeping Easter according to the older reckoning practised in the Celtic Churches, while Gaul at this time was observing the canon of Victorius of Aquitaine. It was certainly a scandal that Easter should be observed at different times within one See, and Columban's diocesan Bishop naturally considered this a matter for his jurisdiction. But in vain, and so sharp became the dispute that we find Columban writing both to a Council of bishops assembled to judge of the matter and to the Pope himself. The letter to the Pope, Gregory the Great, came first, dated some time between 595 and 600.[75] Its tone is immensely vigorous, evidently coming from a spirit whose Irish zeal and eagerness were only tempered by its piety toward the Catholic Church. "Do you bid us, Holy Father, to keep a Victorian Easter on the twenty-first or twenty-second day of the moon?[76] But the moon rises at this time of the month after midnight, and the night's darkness is greater at this season than its light. Why do you keep a *dark* Easter, you, the diffuser of light throughout the world? Surely you know that Anatolius, that most learned man, who was praised by Jerome himself, declared this to be wrong, saying that the Resurrection of the Lord is a Feast of light, not of darkness. Please spare us the scandal of seeing you, our Father, at variance with Saint Jerome. For anyone in the Western Church who disagrees with *him* must be banned as a heretic, no matter who it be."

[74] See Dudden, *Gregory the Great*, II, pp. 185ff.
[75] For text and dates of these letters see W. Gundlach, *M.G.H. Epist.* Tom. III, pp. 156ff, and in *Neues Archiv d. Gesell. f. ält. deutsche Gesch.* XV, 1890, pp. 506ff.
[76] According to the cycle of Victorius, Easter might fall between the sixteenth and the twenty-second day of the moon inclusive.

Unfortunately for Columban, though Anatolius, Bishop of Laodicea (d. 283), had indeed composed a paper on the Paschal controversy, its argument differed entirely from that urged here, and it was a forged pamphlet published under the name of Anatolius that was now misleading him. It misled also both Colman of Northumbria and Saint Wilfrid in their debate on this very question of Easter at the Synod of Whitby in 664.[77]

Columban continues that the canon of Victorius was scorned by the wisest men of Ireland in olden times as deserving laughter and pity rather than obedience. Would the Pope please either defend it or condemn it, and of his grace soon calm this tempest raging around the Abbey of Luxeuil? For the Bishops of Gaul were saying that its monks did not scruple to keep Easter on the fourteenth day of the lunar month, as did the Jews, and were therefore really Quartodecimans and schismatics![78]

The letter then asks counsel of Gregory regarding bishops who have obtained Holy Orders by payment of monies, "and there are many such in this province." What was Columban to do, as their confessor, now that the bishops had revealed their troubled consciences to him? What about those who had been elected as bishops with sins against chastity on their secret minds? Could such serve as bishops? Or should they be banished even from the communion of the Church till their penance had been fulfilled? Again, what of those monks whose fiery desire for perfection was driving them against the will of their Superiors to run loose in civilized places or even in the desert? "Finnian asked Gildas about them and he wrote back a splendid letter, but I am so worried that I wish

[77] Bede, *H.E.* III, 25. See Gougaud, pp. 189f., and Kenney, p. 217.
[78] The old 84-year cycle retained by the Celtic Church of Ireland and Britain allowed Easter between the fourteenth and the twentieth day of the moon inclusive.

you would tell me what to do." The reference is probably to Finnian of Clonard.[79]

"I would ask you all these things more humbly in your presence and many more, too long a list for a letter, if ill-health and the care of my fellow-foreigners here did not keep me at home. I do want to see you, that I might drink in that spiritual stream of living water of knowledge. I would seek you, not Rome—may the ashes of the blessed Saints forgive me!—if only my body could follow my spirit and I were free.

"I have read your *Pastoral Rule,* so concise, yet so full of instruction and marvellous learning. It was a work sweeter to me in my need than honey. . . . I beg you, for Christ's sake, assuage my thirst by sending me your commentaries on Eze-kiel, for I hear they are wonderful. . . . And send part of the *Song of songs,* . . . and please explain the obscurity of Zachariah, that our blindness in the West may give thanks to you. I know I am a worry and that I am asking a great deal. But you have so much to give! . . . Forgive me my bold-ness, and pray for me, meanest of sinners." [80]

There is something that calls for our sympathy in the thought of Columban, trained in the best of Irish scholarship, struggling to study in the midst of building up houses and harvests and monastic discipline and the characters of men and women in troubled Gaul.

The Council of Bishops, whom he also addressed by letter, had met, probably at Chalon-sur-Saône in 603,[81] to debate on his conduct with regard to this matter of Easter. He writes to them with even greater confidence: "I thank God that on account of me so many holy men are gathered together to

---

[79] Gundlach, *Epp.* III, p. 159, note 2. The Latin words here, *Vennianus auctor,* are generally thought to mean "Finnian."

[80] This letter, as other passages in this book, I have represented by a curtailed substance, not by a literal translation.

[81] Kenney, p. 191.

treat of the truth of faith and good works and to judge with just judgment. Would that such Synods were assembled more often! Thank God, I say, that even the way I keep Easter has provoked one. . . ." Here follow some counsels to the Lord Bishops of the Burgundian realms on the humble and sincere character needful for the Pastors of Christ's flock. Differences and variety of traditions, Columban declares, have harmed and still are greatly harming the peace of the Church. Let vainglory and contention be set aside and let all seek simply the truth in peace and love. "Forgive my presumption in writing to you. I have not dared to come myself in person, lest I should show myself too contentious. *I* am not the author of this strife. For the sake of Christ our Saviour and the Lord God Whom we acknowledge in common, I came forth to these foreign lands from my home. Therefore, in the Name of Him Who shall judge us all, the living and the dead, I beseech you, if you be worthy to be received by Him who shall say to many: 'Verily I say unto you, I never knew you,' suffer me of your peace and charity to live quietly in these forests near the graves of the seventeen of our brethren who have departed hence, to live as it has been permitted me and mine to live among you for now these twelve years.[82] Let us pray here for you as we have done hitherto, and as we ought to do. Let Gaul hold us together with you as fellow-dwellers, even as we shall be, if we merit it, in the Kingdom of Heaven. We have come forth as strangers to keep and to hold the biddings of our Lord and His apostles. Take care, holy fathers, take care what you do to these poor and foreign old men in your midst. For, I think, it will be better for you to uphold than to upset them. I admit that I follow my 84-year cycle, the tradition of my native land, rather than the dubious and modern way of

---

[82] If, as seems the case, this letter was written to the Council in 603, we reach a date of c. 591 for the arrival of Columban in Burgundy.

Victorius. You do as you like. If you drive me out hence from my monastery, the responsibility will be yours. But let us rather go our respective ways. Bishops and monks have different vocations; let us all strive to make up together the perfection of the Body of Christ our Head in love and in peace. For we are all fellow-members of one Body, whether we be Gallic, or Britons, or Irish, or whatsoever our nation may be."

Unhappily we know nothing of the proceedings of this Council. But once again Columban appealed to a Pope, probably Sabinian, who held the Holy See till 606,[83] approaching him directly after the same Council had issued its pronouncements. These could not have been favourable, for the Father and his monks are still much distressed. Satan, he affirms, prevented his messengers from reaching Gregory. He now forwards them to Gregory's successor and prays him with his authority to stay the turmoil of these worrying Burgundian bishops. Also, would the Holy Father in his prayers for Columban from that resting-place of the Saints please remember this—that a certain Council of Constantinople *did* once enact that the Churches of God established in foreign countries should be permitted to follow their own laws?[84]

Other conflict engaged Columban against the secular power of Burgundy: in the person of Brunhild, now living with her docile grandson, Theodoric, its King, after she had been driven from Austrasia by Theodebert and his nobles. Jonas tells us that Theodoric was glad to have so holy a man living within his dominion and that he often visited Luxeuil. He had a great reverence, it seems, for Columban: a strange attraction, for his living was of the worst; as a youth of twenty he already had four sons born of various mistresses.[85] Colum-

---

[83] Gundlach, *Neues Archiv,* XV, p. 511.
[84] In 367: Mansi, III, 559.   [85] "Fredegarius," IV, 21, 24, 29.

ban's courage, here as ever, flinched at nothing, and he demanded plainly why the young man did not marry and beget
children of honourable wedlock? Theodoric decided to repent and obey. But the prospect of a lawful Queen of Burgundy did not appeal in the slightest to Brunhild, and her
anger was roused against this dangerous man of God. Even
after Theodoric had wedded a Visigothic princess called
Ermenberga, daughter of Witteric, King of Spain, the evil
cunning of his grandmother so worked on him that he refused
to treat the girl as his wife and after a year sent her back to
her home in Spain. But he kept the riches she had brought
him as dowry! [86]

The Lady Brunhild also, however, had the reverence for
the Church held by all, saints and sinners, in this time, and
was rash enough to bring two of her unlawfully begotten
relatives to Columban's notice when he came to see her one
day at the royal house of Bruyères-le-Châtel.[87] The man of
God looked at them and said, "What do you want?" "They
are the King's sons," she replied, "protect them with your
blessing." "No indeed," said Columban, "you may be sure
that they will never receive the royal sceptre, these children
of a brothel." The Queen was furious, and never forgave the
words. Theodoric still continued his evil ways till Columban
"sent him a letter full of blows and threatened him with
excommunication if he did not amend." This gave Brunhild
her opportunity, and she stirred up the King, his nobles, and
the bishops of the realm against this offending monk. We may
imagine that the bishops were not overly reluctant, though
Jonas, of course, neglects to lay stress on this.[88] The story
goes on that Theodoric went to Columban at Luxeuil and
complained that in his monastery the Abbot had secret rooms

[86] *ibid.* 30.
[87] dép. Seine-et-Oise: Krusch, *Script. rer. Merov.* IV, p. 87.
[88] *ibid.* p. 88, note 1.

into which entrance was not granted to all Christians; where-upon Columban replied that he was not in the habit of open-ing the privacy of monasteries to seculars and to enemies of religion. All the same, he *did* have reception-rooms where all guests could be seen! Then the King threatened to cut off his alms, which threat brought from the Abbot a quick retort that he did not desire alms from people who violated the rules of the Church, and that if the object of Theodoric was to destroy monasteries and upset religious discipline, without any doubt his kingdom would soon fall and he himself would perish with all his royal family. When Columban did not cease his shower of rebukes: "You think," cried Theodoric, "that you are going to win through me the crown of martyrdom! I'm not such a fool as to commit a crime like that. But beware! I have better devices in store."

It took, however, two ejections to banish the Saint perma-nently from Luxeuil. We are told that when soldiers were sent to drive him into exile, they found him sitting at the entrance to the church, reading a book. When they ap-proached to seize him, blindness came upon them all. It was a lovely sight, Jonas declares, to see Columban enjoying him-self while all the King's men were groping about around him. Only their tribune was allowed to catch sight of the Abbot, because he had come against his will, and with all speed he gave the order to retreat. Another company was then des-patched to the monastery and found the brethren saying their Office. This time the Abbot did consent to go, when the cap-tain declared that he and his men would be put to death if they failed to seize him.

So in the twentieth year after he had come to Luxeuil Columban went out from it into banishment, about the year 610. Only those who were not natives of Gaul were allowed to accompany him. The story of his adventures describes his journey through Besançon and Autun to Avallon, and on past the River Cure to Auxerre. There he said to the officer of Theodoric who was escorting him and his monks into exile: "Remember, Ragamund, that within three years Chlotar, whom you despise, will be your Lord," which prophecy, as we know, did come to pass. From Auxerre they travelled to Nevers and thence to Orleans and Tours by boat on the Loire. When the officer would not allow Columban to land to pray at the shrine of Martin, the boat, so we read, suddenly whirled round and sailed into the harbour! At any rate, we are to picture Columban spending a whole night in his devotions at the church and breakfasting afterward with its Bishop. When he was asked at the table why he was leaving his monastery, he replied cheerfully: "That dog Theodoric has driven me away." On returning to his boat he found his disciples much agitated because their common purse had been stolen. Columban, however, was a man of prayer. He hurried back to Saint Martin in the church and told him emphatically that he had not spent a whole night in supplication before his shrine in order to lose the Community purse! Martin was also equal to the occasion and revealed through grace of the Lord the name of the thief.

Finally, Nantes was reached at the mouth of the Loire, and here the little company were to be put on a boat sailing for Ireland. We have a letter which Columban addressed, just before embarking, to the dejected brethren he had left behind at Luxeuil.[89] A few of its words will show the Abbot at his best.

"To my most sweet sons and dear disciples, brethren of poverty, and to all my monks, I, Columban, a sinner, send greeting in Christ. . . . Peace to you, and do ye live together in love. Remember that strife concerns only things that perish, and that not men, but devils in men, pursue you for

[89] *Epp. III*, pp. 165ff.

evil. Let Attala rule over you now, or Waldolen, if Attala would rather follow me into banishment. Stay at Luxeuil if you possibly can and only leave if strife makes it necessary. I am afraid the dispute about Easter may trouble you through those who want to bring you over to their side, and I think you are the weaker without my presence among you." Then follow some special words for Attala, left in charge as Abbot: "The effort to help so many, I admit, has broken me down. Do you be more careful, and do not take on yourself all the burden of my toil. Different men need different handling, and it is a vast undertaking to which I call you, I who myself am running away. Manage them all differently, each in the way he needs, and beware of their love, for it means danger to you. Dangers, dear one, there will be in any case: danger if they dislike you, danger if they love you. Hatred is the destroyer of peace for men; love, of their integrity. Keep then to that one keen desire which you know my heart craves. You know that I yearn for the salvation of many, and for myself, solitude in retreat: the one for the glory of God and His Church, the other, from the longing of my own heart. But these things have been mine in wish rather than in reality; let them be perfected in you, I pray."

Even, however, in his gloomy hour the Irishman in the Father Abbot cannot be wholly sad: "I wanted to write a mournful letter, but I know how hard things are for you all, and I have written otherwise. A brave soldier should not weep on the field of battle. . . . As I write, a ship is being prepared to take me back to my own country against my will. But no one is keeping watch to see I don't run away; they seem to want me to do it. If I am hurled out into the sea, like Jonah" (a reference to the Hebrew form of "Columba"), "do pray that I don't meet a whale, but some good stout boatman to carry your Jonah back to the land where he would be. . . .

Now I must end. My letter isn't very orderly, but love does not cling to order. I wanted to say everything quite shortly, and I could not. There was so much to say. Look to your consciences that they be cleaner and holier, even though I be absent from you. And do not seek me for your love of me, but only leave Luxeuil if you must. . . . If God build with you and you love your home, grow and increase there with His blessing to thousand thousands, and pray for me, my own children, that I may live to God."

But the Lord did not will that Columban should return to Ireland, and the ship which was to take the brethren thither was nearly wrecked by a great wave before it left the river for the high seas. This was held a mark of Divine displeasure by Columban's enemies, and all their captives were finally allowed to go where they would. Columban then went to Chlotar the second, who had heard how Brunhild and Theodoric had acted, and now begged him to make Neustria his home. But he would only stay long enough to reprove his host for errors which Jonas himself thought of very ordinary occurrence in the courts of Kings. Then he asked for an escort, with the hope of reaching Italy, and journeyed to Paris and Meaux; in Meaux he dedicated to God the baby girl, Burgundofara, who was afterwards to be famous as the Abbess of Faremoutiers, one of the "double monasteries" of the sixth and the following century. But all along the way the steps of his passage were sown by him with seeds of monastic living which were to come to maturity in future years. At another resting-place, Ussy on the Marne,[90] he gave the blessing of the Church to two little boys, "seeing the faith of their mother" who offered them. It is an interesting contrast to the story of the little sons of Theodoric the second. These children of Ussy also grew up to preside over monasteries: one at Jouarre, the other at Rebais.

[90] *Script. rer. Merov.* IV, p. 100.

Both abbeys, with that of Faremoutiers, were situated in the district of La Brie, and belonged to the numerous company that followed the Rule of Columban.

And now the exile arrived at Metz and was most hospitably received by Theodebert, still possessed at this time of his throne of Austrasia. He, also, was eager to keep Columban with him and held out the temptation of plenty of heathen to instruct. With this fair prospect in view Columban decided to stay a while and journeyed along the Rhine to Mainz, from which by way of the Lake of Zurich he reached Bregenz on Lake Constance. Here he found a rich harvest of idol-worshippers awaiting him and set to work with the aid of his companion Gallus, afterward famous as Saint Gall. But when the heathen raged wildly at this interference with their worship, and Columban, deciding that Italy would be more amenable, prepared to depart, an attack of quartan fever kept back Gall. The leader thought that his disciple was feigning an excuse because he was tired of wanderings, and laid a bitter penance on him: "I know, brother, that it is troublesome for you to be wearied with so great labours on my account. But this shall be my last word to you: that you never presume to say Mass as long as I am alive." [91]

And so Columban pressed on to the Alps, entered Lombardy, and was welcomed by its King Agilulf, whose wife, we remember, was a Catholic, while he himself was still held by the Arian error of his ancestors. Here was another promising field of combat, and the apostle, with a small band of followers, took possession of a solitary but fertile spot in the Apennines near the River Trebbia. Ancient tradition named the place from the stream of Bobbio flowing hard by, and here Columban established the monastery which made the name known for holiness and learning throughout mediaeval times.

[91] Walahfrid, *Vita Galli,* ed. Krusch, *Script. rer. Merov.* IV, p. 291.

His arrival was welcome to many sons of the Catholic Church; for he came into Northern Italy just when the dispute of Aquileia was raging; and another letter, perhaps the last still extant in prose from his pen, appeals once more to a Pope. It lacks nothing of his old vehemence, though its object is a personal one, to clear Columban's name from suspicion of erroneous doctrine before a Synod of the Church.

This breach in the Church of Northern Italy, known as the Schism of Aquileia, resulted from the yielding of Pope Vigilius to the intense desire of Constantinople that the "Three Chapters" should be condemned. We have seen already that these "Chapters," the writings of Theodore of Mopsuestia, of Theodoret of Cyrus, and of Ibas of Nessa, Bishops of the fifth century, had been seized upon by Justinian, that emperor so devoted to theological research, as containing dangerous Nestorian doctrine, and that Pope Vigilius had been invited by him and his fiery Empress Theodora to consent to their anathematizing at the Fifth General Council of the Church held in Constantinople in 553. The invitation had been of the nature of an Imperial command, and a great outcry arose in Western countries at what these deemed the timid submission of the Holy Father. Especially in Northern Italy feeling ran high, and some of its Bishops, with Milan and Aquileia at their head, refused to partake further of fellowship in the Church of Rome so inadequately shepherded, as they held. The division that thus came about was still yawning in Aquileia early in the seventh century. Boniface the fourth was on the Papal throne, and both Agilulf, the Arian King of the Lombards, and his Catholic wife Theodelinda were in sympathy with the schismatics.

At their request, therefore, Columban addressed about 612 an impetuous letter to the Holy Father at Rome.[92] He is writing, he declares, at the bidding of Agilulf the Arian.

[92] Gundlach (*M.G.H.* Epp. III, p. 170) dates the letter 612-615.

Surely this is a miracle due to the special grace of the Lord. How dreadful if cause of offence should come from the Catholic side! The King and his Queen are eager that all should be one in one flock with all speed. May the Church follow the Pope, the King of Kings, even as the Pope follows Saint Peter. What is sweeter than peace after war? What more delightful than the union of brethren long separated?

The letter is really an argument in defence of those who blamed Vigilius for condemning the "Three Chapters" at the behest of Constantinople. But it goes far further in daring to beseech the Holy Father to defend the very Papal Chair from aspersions of erroneous doctrine cast against it. "I write not of presumption, but of necessity, for the edification of the Church. Please consider, not who is speaking, but what is said. For, I confess, I am grieved at the thought of a blot on the name of the See of holy Peter. If I be heard, then, it shall be for the common good; if rejected, it shall be gain to me. And so, timid sailor that I am on the mystical ship of the Church now tossed by storm, I dare to cry to you: Watch, for the ship you guide is in danger! I dare, because I and mine are the followers of holy Peter and Paul and of all the disciples who wrote the divine canon of scripture by the grace of the Holy Spirit: Irishmen, all of us, dwellers in the uttermost part of the world, holding nothing true but the doctrine of the Gospel and the Apostles. Not one of us has ever been a heretic, not one a Jew, not one a schismatic! The Catholic Faith is still held unbroken by us, even as it was given to us first by the Bishops of Rome, successors of the Apostles. In the strength of this faith I have dared, as if driven forward, to rouse you against those who blaspheme you, and cry against you 'receiver of heretics!' and 'schismatic!', that the joyous pride and zeal of my answering for you may not be in vain. I have promised them in your name that the Church of Rome would defend no heretic against the Catholic Faith. Am I not your disciple and are you not my teacher. . . ?

"Watch, then, for the peace of the Church, sound your Shepherd's call and come to the rescue of your sheep in this terror of wolves. Guard the faith of the Apostles by your witness, confirm it by your writing, protect it by a Synod. The times are waxing late. The Chief of Shepherds is at the door; see to it that He find you not heedless of your charge. And so, I beseech you, Holy Father, watch, and again I say, watch. For it may be that Vigilius did not prove loyal to his name of vigilance. Indeed, they call him the source of offence, those who cast blame on you. . . . Summon, then, an assembly for the purging of your faith from all accusation. It is no light matter which is brought against you. They declare that you have conversation with heretics, as Vigilius, they say, received Eutyches and Nestor. . . .

"Forgive me for treating of matters so delicate. Liberty was the tradition of my fathers, and among us in Ireland no person avails, but rather reason. As I have said, we are bound to the Chair of holy Peter, and, whatever the greatness and the renown of Rome, she is only great and glorious to us through that Chair. From the time of Peter and Paul the Bishops of Rome have been great and glorious; for their sakes you are almost of the company of Heaven itself, and Rome is Head of the Churches of the world, save only for the special privilege of the place of the Lord's Resurrection. . . . Yet your power shall last but as long as right reason shall remain. Judge, then, of my feelings when almost as soon as I entered Lombardy, some one warned me in a letter that I must beware of you as of one fallen into the sect of Nestor! And so I have appealed to you, for I do believe that the pillar of the Church stands firm in Rome."

No one can doubt Columban's enthusiastic and whole-hearted loyalty to the Church; it was this very eagerness which drove him to write thus impetuously to her Pope. It is sad that his devotion should have been so ill-directed; that all this fire, levied thus passionately at the Holy Father by one who was himself a reverend Lord Abbot and an experienced guide of souls, should have been kindled by a vague rumour concerning a matter of which Columban himself had scarcely any knowledge. The whole document is filled with words tumbling out thick and fast, based on hearsay and hint and vague report. Its very title itself is so unusual in its Irish insouciance that it is worth translating in full: "To the most beautiful Head of all the Churches of Europe, so sweet Father, so high President, Shepherd of shepherds, most revered Guardian: the most humble to the most high, the least to the greatest, the rustic to the cultured, one of small speech to one most eloquent, the last to the first, the foreign-born to the native, the poor to the most powerful: A marvellous, a strange thing! A rare bird, (Columban) the Dove, dares to write to the Father, Boniface." Let us hope, for Columban's love of the Church and her Chief See of Rome, that the holy Father forgave this tilting at shadows in the dark.[93]

Subsequent tradition tells that Columban spent his last days in a cave near Bobbio.[94] The monastery was too comfortable for him, and his joy in the hard and perilous life was constant to the end, which came on November 21, 615, a day honoured by the Church in his name.

A word may be added on his love of poets. He knew well his Vergil, his Horace, his Ovid, and later men: Ausonius,

[93] The letter No. 6, which Gundlach was induced by Krusch to include in his edition, as written to the same Pope Boniface IV concerning solemn Feast-days and the keeping of Easter, was afterward held by Krusch to be of other authorship: see his note 1, *Script. rer. Merov.* IV, p. 20. For criticism of the letter 5 discussed above see Hodgkin, *Italy and her Invaders,* VI, pp. 138ff.; Horace K. Mann, *Lives of the Popes in the early Middle Ages,* I, pp. 273ff.

[94] For memories of Columban still traceable in Bobbio and its district, including the Church of St. Columban, see Margaret Stokes, *Six Months in the Apennines,* pp. 154ff.

Prudentius, Juvencus, Sedulius, Dracontius, Venantius Fortunatus.[95] The severe simplicity of Luxeuil and Bobbio did nor forbid the planting of their future renown as treasuries of books. When and whence did this renown take its beginning, in the manuscripts which have spread the fame of Bobbio? Columban must have done much. But to him fell neither that peculiar mission of sacred study nor that devoted labour of gathering books for its advance which we have seen as the special vocation of the latter years of Cassiodorus. It has been suggested that the riches of Vivarium travelled north to Bobbio, a thought which might be of great comfort in one's reflection on the comparatively short life of that southern home of tranquil learning and fruitful production.[96]

But also Columban himself tried his hand at verse in his scant leisure hours, and has left a number of lines composed in correct Latin metre. Most of them are not very exciting, and nearly all are little sermons warning one or another friend to flee the vanities of this wicked world and to anchor his soul in the hope of things eternal. The greater number are written in hexameters, running smoothly enough without any claim to original thought. By far the best is a letter of one hundred and fifty-nine adonics, sent to Fidolius, "my brother," when Columban was over seventy years of age. The pleasant little verses trip merrily along, telling, first, of the joy of correspondence with this old friend:

> Nam velut aestu
> Flantibus austris
> Arida gaudent
> Imbribus arva;
> Sic tua nostras
> Missa frequenter
> Laetificabat
> Pagina mentes.

[95] See the notes of Gundlach, *M.G.H.* Epp. III, *passim*.
[96] For the theory see Rudolf Beer, *Anz. d. Kais. Akad. d. Wiss., Wien, Phil. hist. Kl.* XLVIII, 1911, pp. 78ff.

Such joys are vastly to be preferred to the deceits of riches, the writer then declares, and illustrates his point by a whole *catena* of legends; the Golden Fleece, the Judgment of Paris, Polydorus, Amphiaraus, Danae and so on, all yield their moral for Fidolius.

Toward the end rhythmic instructions are given on the art of composing poems in this metre, "in which Sappho used to sing," and the whole closes with six lines in hexameter verse:

> Haec tibi dictaram morbis oppressus acerbis
> Corpore quos fragili patior tristique senecta.
> Nam dum praecipiti labuntur tempora cursu,
> Nunc ad Olympiadis ter senos venimus annos.
> Omnia praetereunt, fugit irreparabile tempus;
> Vive, vale, laetus tristisque memento senectae.

The composition shows a thorough training in secular classics, and is of interest for the picture it gives of an old Irish monk, steeped in the strictest practice of mortification, yet daring to turn for recreation to the old pagan poets at a time when most of his continental brethren of the cloister were fleeing such frivolities and snares as offspring of the devil's own mind.

In one poem of our collection the author leaves classical metre for rhyme and alliteration; if, indeed, its hundred and twenty verses be really his work. The rudeness of the rhyme suggests an early date,[97] and the subject is the one so often chosen by Columban, the pomps and vanities of worldly life. Another composition of interest, though the authorship again is not certain, is a boating-song. Strange theme for a monk, perhaps, but it came of a joyful and courageous heart, and after Columban's own spirit would be its speeding from rolling lines of encouragement for the boat's crew to lines carolled out in heartening of the Christian athlete. The refrain of the

[97] Kenney, p. 195.

first and secular part is taken from an earlier boating-song. It is a lively production, and we should like to think that Columban wrote it, as Krusch suggests, in 611 when he was journeying along the Rhine after his ejection from the lands of Theodoric. He needed something to enliven him! [98]

The prose of Columban is simple, as his verse. It is not so easy to read, largely because it is poured out in such a bubbling stream of ill-ordered sentences. But it is classically correct, unlike the mediaeval pages of Gregory of Tours. And, for all its fullness of words, it savours of the more direct fervour born of plain living in the solitude of forest lands, a thing refreshing after the sophistries that besprinkle so abundantly the writings of Christians of courts and palaces in this time.

[98] The song was discovered by Wilhelm Meyer and first published by E. Dümmler in *Neues Archiv,* VI, 1881, pp. 190f. Of the author's name in the MS. only *–banus* remains, and the *b* is not quite clear. In the MS. containing the older song (ed. R. Peiper, *Rh. Mus.* XXXII, p. 523), this little boating-chant immediately precedes it. Columban did write vigorously of the sea in his stirring appeal to Boniface IV to aid the labouring ship of the Church, and Jonas in his *Life* says that the Saint "composed much that was worthy of song." See Krusch, *Script. rer. Merov.* IV, p. 69. W. Gundlach (*Neues Archiv,* XV, p. 514) agreed in thinking Columban the author; Dümmler preferred to assign the lines to a later Irish Columban, probably of the Carolingian age. For other poems of more doubtful authenticity attributed to Columban, see Kenney, pp. 195f. Writings of Columban now lost to us are: letters of rebuke to Theodoric and Chlotar; a letter against Agrippinus on the condemnation of the "Three Chapters"; a pamphlet against the Arians: see Krusch, *ibid.* p. 20.

CHAPTER III

SAINT BENEDICT OF NURSIA

OF THE monastic foundations which we have noticed none remained permanent. None was sufficiently clear and comprehensive to form a Rule by which men of differing centuries, nationalities and characters should fashion the mould of their lives all down the ages. All were unsuited for training the endless varieties of soul, mind and body called to fulfil their differing perfection in one school of the cloister. Cassiodorus had written for the monastic student of Holy Scripture, to whom sacred science was the most lovely road to God. The Rules of Caesarius and of Columban persisted for some time. Yet the view of Caesarius was too narrow; it did not deal broadly and deeply with the problems and possibilities of monastic life in general, and it left its mark upon that life for women rather than for men. Columban had held out a life too austere in its Celtic asceticism, too formidable in its myriad penalties of the lash, of black fasting and of banishment, to attract a multitude of men of other races than his own, living under other climates and conditions.

Moreover, by the time of this sixth century the vocation to poverty, chastity, and obedience had been known in monastic practice for two hundred years. It had borne a marvellous harvest of holy living and dying. As in the case of other less excellent things, enthusiasm had, nevertheless, outrun its bounds and familiarity had lost its former zeal. Monks there were now in plenty who confessed allegiance to no Abbot, to no monastery, who roamed from place to place at their own will, distinguished by fanatical excess, uncontrolled. Others, like many secular Christians of this age, had no fiery enthusiasm for leading a life of peril and mortification. The first fine careless rapture of the primitive Church had subsided; unconsciously or consciously, earnest souls were now longing for a firm yet reasonable Rule which should uphold in a stable and permanent conversion within the cloister all classes of men, high and low, learned and unlettered, priest and lay, saint and sinner, provided always that their purpose did not fail. "To pass from the influence of St. Columban to that of St. Benedict was a transition from the uncertain and the vague to the reign of law. In fact, neither the code of St. Caesarius nor that of St. Columban is really a rule of life at all, the whole direction depending upon a discretion which might or might not be wisely exercised. That St. Benedict's legislation should have superseded all others was in the very nature of things inevitable." [1]

That Rule was given in the fullness of time. Toward the end of the fifth century, about the year 480, Benedict, "Father of Monks," was born in the little town of Nursia among the Sabine hills. About this same time Boethius first entered the troubled world of Rome and Cassiodorus was lying in his cradle far south in the land of the Bruttii. A little while before, Odovacar had been set up as King in Italy by rebellious barbarian soldiers, and the rightful ruler, Nepos, was assassinated almost as these three children first saw life. Their early years progressed during the struggle between Odovacar and Theodoric and ended with Theodoric securely established in Ravenna as their King. Nor was the Church of their infancy more peaceful in external matters than the State. Hardly could they walk when the Emperor Zeno sent out from Constantinople the *Henoticon* of lasting memory,

---

[1] Cardinal Gasquet, *Monastic Life in the Middle Ages,* p. 210.

followed shortly by the rupture of schism which for thirty-five years was to divide Christians of the East from their brethren in the West. As lads they thrilled with excitement in hearing of the baptism of the barbarian Clovis at Reims in 496, and attained ripeness of youth amid the turmoil caused by the struggle for the Papal See between Symmachus and Laurentius.

Our knowledge of Benedict is drawn from two sources alone: from the second book of the *Dialogues* of Pope Gregory the Great and from Benedict's own *Rule for Monks*. The first is of extraordinary interest, as written by the greatest of Popes concerning the greatest of monks.[2] It, therefore, in itself belongs to our writings of the sixth century, and we can enjoy its details tranquilly here without scruple of digression. Of the second, Gregory shall speak in his own narrative: "The reverend Father wrote a Rule for monks, excelling in discretion, radiant and clear in its wording. If any one desires to know intimately of his character and life, all the manner of his work as Abbot is set forth in the precepts of this same Rule. For this holy man's teaching exactly followed his life."

Unfortunately, however, Gregory was concerned to show forth the Father's virtues, not to satisfy the reverent curiosity of future centuries, and our knowledge of Benedict's early years is scant. We learn that his parents were well-born, and that he had a sister named Scholastica who was also dedicated to religion. At Nursia he gained, no doubt, his earlier training in Holy Scripture and sacred writings, in grammar and pagan literature, and in elementary mathematics. We find him later on at Rome studying in the regular University course of the seven liberal arts. Like other future Saints of

[2] Hodgkin, *Italy and her Invaders*, IV, p. 411. For the *Dialogues* see c. XI, pp. 599ff. below; for the *Rule* Delatte, with text, trans. and commentary.

the day, and probably many sinners, his spirit revolted against its quips and sophistries and pedantic *minutiae* of rhetoric and artificial philosophies, grown dull and dingy at this late time save when illuminated by the mind of a Boethius. At any rate, Gregory tells us that after seeing many falling down the steep way of evil through these same studies, Benedict drew back the foot he had placed on the threshold of the world, lest he, too, might be hurled over that same fearful precipice. We can imagine him absorbed in the *Lives of the Fathers* when he should have been deep in his Aristotle and his Martianus Capella, afire with zeal to try for himself the rocky path that leads up the mountain of contemplation. At last he could bear it no longer, and left his studies, his home and his family, to seek the Lord in some place of solitude, "full of ignorant learning," as Gregory tersely describes him, "and wise where he was not taught."

The story now becomes more detailed; Gregory obtained it from four Abbots, who knew Benedict intimately in the cloister as their own Father in God. The desired peace in the wilderness was not immediately forthcoming; for his old nurse, who loved him devotedly, could not be shaken off. They wandered out, this strange pair, as far as Enfide, now Affile, a lonely village among the mountains about forty miles from Rome. There they settled down among the earnest Christian congregation of the Church of St. Peter, he to learn of the difficult art of prayer, she to take care of him and his bodily needs. But even in this far-off place he could not avoid the thing he would escape at any price, fame among men. One day he came back to their little home and found his housekeeper in floods of tears over a broken sieve. Alas! it had been borrowed to sift the grain for his bread, and something had to be done about it at once. So prayer, and, lo! a miracle, and Benedict fled alone from the talk of the village.

Doubtless the old lady was fully occupied in the happy praisings of her boy!

This time he set to work more carefully and hunted till he came upon a really secret retreat: a cave in the valley of the Anio, at Sublaqueum, now famous as Subiaco, where the river swelled into the lake that gave the place its name. Pilgrims from Affile, some few miles along the course of the river, find now in Subiaco great conventual shrines dedicated in the names of Saint Benedict and Saint Scholastica. Two Churches, the Upper and the Lower, magnified with chapels and grottoes cut from the rock of the mountainside, stand in the spot where Benedict lived in his cave, and tell his story in their painted frescoes. For three years he held there his communing with the Lord, aided by a monk called Romanus who had met him on his way. Romanus lived not far off in a monastery ruled by Abbot Deodatus, from whom, however, he hid all knowledge of this kindly work of his. He sympathized keenly with the young man's longing, helped him in his search, witnessed his solemn vow to enter monastic life and promised to bring him his daily loaf of bread.

The deed was one of sincere charity, if somewhat irregular. No path led to the cave, for it was perched on the side of a precipice, and Romanus could only lean over the summit and peer into those yawning depths to which Benedict by the grace of God had managed to scramble down. Every day the friendly brother would fasten a loaf to a rope and lower it along the side of the cliff, with a bell attached also, so that the hermit might know when his dinner was arriving. It proved too much for the devil's patience in the long run, and he dislodged a great piece of rock which silenced the bell forever. Romanus was too familiar with Satan's ways to be easily daunted, and it was the Lord who in His wisdom exchanged this providing for other means of succour. He appeared at this time, Gregory tells us, to a certain priest who lived at a considerable distance from the lonely cave. It was the Feast of Easter, and the good Father, having piously kept his Lent, was about to sit down to a succulent dinner. He had cooked it himself and was rejoicing in the day which the Lord had made. Just at this moment the voice of the Lord interrupted his joy: "You are preparing to feast deliciously, and my servant is starving to death over there!" The Father rose at once from his knees, caught up his Easter dinner, and plodded sturdily up mountains and down valleys, through ditches and across streams, till by the guidance of Heaven he found Benedict in his retreat. They fell at once to prayer, and then the visitor exclaimed: "Up and let us eat! Today is Easter Day!" And Benedict answered: "Surely it is Easter to me in this visit of yours." But the priest cried again: "But really this is the Paschal Feast of the Lord's Resurrection, and it is by no means proper for you to fast. And I, too, have been sent to partake with you of the gifts of the Almighty Lord." Then they said grace and shared together the priest's Easter banquet before he returned to his own home.

Soon afterward shepherds discovered Benedict. They had seen him moving about in his shaggy dress of hides among the bushes and had thought some strange beast must be prowling round. When they understood that here was a servant of the most high God they listened to his words, and many were brought to accept the Faith who had been but little better than the beasts themselves before. While he fed their souls they brought him food for the body, and so he continued his years of preparation for the work of God.

Solitude brought its own sharp temptations, to melancholy, to dissatisfaction, to restless cravings for change, all those evils so well described by Cassian under the name of *accidie*.

Gregory pictures the source of such trials as a little black bird, which at times would fly about Benedict's face and worry him by lighting on his head. It might have stayed permanently with him, if the young man had been willing to capture it. But he never did; he merely crossed himself and paid as little attention as he could. Then the little black bird would fly away. It was harder to shake off another worry sent by the devil, the persistent image in his mind's eye of a beautiful woman who had once attracted him. This picture pursued him so eagerly that once he nearly left his cave to go in search of human love and its delights. In his hour of conflict he suddenly threw off his coat of skins and flung himself into a thicket of briars and nettles growing near, that by sharp burning of his flesh he might drive away the fire that tormented his soul within. The sudden impulse was not in vain, and never from that time, as he used to tell his disciples in after days, did temptation of this kind trouble his life.

Tradition has it that long afterward Francis of Assisi came to visit the Sacred Cave, and that while he was deep in contemplation of the holiness of Benedict the briars and nettles disappeared and roses took their place. And thus the roses, fruit of the virtue of two Saints, blossomed down the years for the healing of sick pilgrims.[3]

But Benedict's time of purgation was now ended, and he was ready to teach and to train others. The retreat grew in fame as the shepherds told of all they had heard and seen, and soon many people of all kinds were finding their way there in search of light and help among the problems of a weary and disillusioned world. After a while he was led to a change of dwelling, when a community of monks, established, it is thought, where Vicovaro now lies about twelve miles from the Sacred Cave, came to beg him to be their head

[3] Luke Wadding: *Annales Minorum,* II, ann. 1222, sect. V.

in the place of their abbot who had lately died. Benedict seems to have heard of these brethren. For he long refused them, saying that his ways were not theirs, till at last he could no longer hold out against the pressure and went to preside over their house. His fears were well grounded; little by little the strictness of his governing so vexed these soft-souled disciples that finally they plotted his death. The best way seemed to put poison in the cup presented to him as Abbot for blessing at the beginning of the monastic meal. Benedict bent low to make over the cup the sacred sign, and at once it broke into pieces. Quite calmly he rose, gathered all the Community around him and said: "The Lord Almighty have mercy on you, my brothers! Why have you willed to do thus? Go ye all and seek for a Father after your own heart, for no longer can you retain me."

He returned to his old place of refuge; but his solitude had departed. So many desired to learn the way of religion under him that he and his first disciples built a monastery near his cave. Soon other like houses were needed, and at length there were twelve of these in the valley of the Anio: each ruled by its own Abbot under the visitation of the Father General and engaged in the training of men and boys of noble birth as well as the peasants of the countryside.

Fame, as Gregory observes, usually arouses envy, and envy in this case kindled fierce flames in the heart of one Florentius, priest, sad to relate, of a church near the monastery where the Father Abbot ruled in person. From his presbytery this minister of God could see very well the constant stream of people coming to consult Benedict on spiritual matters or to beg admission to the cloister. No evil words of his could stop them, try as he would, and at last the devil worked through him in a second attempt to bring death to the Father, this time by means of poisoned bread. It was customary in those days to send gifts of blessed bread from the Church to devout Catholics, and Benedict received the seeming token of courtesy with thanks. But he was not caught unawares. It was the hour for dinner, and among the guests of the monastery was a raven, which used to come every day at this moment to receive its portion from the hands of the Father. As it waited expectantly, Benedict threw out the priest's gift and commanded: "In the Name of Christ our Lord take up this bread and carry it to some hidden place which none shall know." The bird opened wide its beak, flapped its wings and flew distractedly round and round with great croakings, as though trying to say it did want to obey, but this task was really impossible. The man of God quietly repeated his order, adding: "Do not be afraid; it won't hurt you." Then the raven picked up the bread and flew off. After three hours it returned with a satisfied croak and received its belated dinner.

But the priest was not satisfied. As he could not succeed in killing the body of the master, he turned to try to murder the souls of Benedict's disciples. One day their horrified eyes looked out from the cells of the monastery upon seven dancing girls, displaying all the allurements of the world, the flesh and the devil right in front of their windows. Henceforth all their zealous efforts to attend to work sacred and secular were fruitless; in spite of all their resolves their eyes *would* seek the windows, and at last the Father decided that he himself, the target of all this rage of jealousy, must leave Subiaco for another retreat. With his usual tranquillity he packed up his belongings and started out, accompanied by some of his monastic sons. We are told that the priest Florentius watched him go, but that his smile of triumph quickly faded when suddenly his room fell in ruins about him and he was killed. Benedict placed under stern penance the monk Maurus, whom he loved dearly, for the unseemly joy with which he ran after his departing Abbot to relate this news.

It was too late. The Abbot had started out and would not now turn back. He continued his journey in search of a new home until he reached the foot of the great mountain of Casinum, half way between Rome and Naples; from the point where he stood the rough trail led up two thousand feet of rocky cliff to an ancient fortress, still dedicated even at that time to pagan worship.⁴ We can imagine the brethren toiling up. Once at the summit, they hurled down the images of the heathen and the altar of their rites; then more slowly they changed the pagan sanctuary into a Chapel of Saint Martin of Tours, that the thought of Martin's monastery at Marmoutier might inspire the dwellers in this Christian retreat. At the very top of the mountain, where the altar of idolatry had stood, Benedict built a place of prayer dedicated under the name of Saint John the Baptist, in the desire that simple austerity might also be the hallmark of his own solitude.

Here, then, at Monte Cassino, was rooted and grounded the great Benedictine Order. Here little by little with immense toil and difficulty the brethren built their first cloister, adding, as the years went by, the different portions needed for their life and work. Here Benedict preached continually to the peasants of the mountain and of the settlement at its foot, striving hard, not only to train himself and his followers in their appointed way, but also to teach the ignorant and the wicked of the things that make for goodly and peaceful living. Here, as the house on the mountain became known, many pilgrims were welcomed, if only they came in sincere desire and need.

Once more the good work roused the wrath of the old

⁴ Gregory says it was a shrine of Apollo, Herwegen (*St. Benedict,* trans. Nugent, pp. 58f.) emends to Jupiter.

enemy, and Satan, having found that terrible visions sent to Benedict on his bed by night were of no avail, frequently, so Gregory tells, appeared in the Abbot's cell by day. His shouts and protests became so loud that the brethren outside all heard the noise. "Maledict, not Benedict," he screamed, "what have you to do with me? why do you vex me so?" The devil also did his best to delay the work of building. One day, we read, he sat on a stone which the monks were trying to lift into place, tugging in vain; on another, he deluded their eyes by imaginary flames; on another, he overthrew a wall and actually killed a young monk, the son of some middle-class official. But Benedict conquered all these difficulties, even death, by his availing prayer. There were giants on the earth in those days, and the spirit of Gregory was no more daunted by disbelief than that of this Father Abbot!

The buildings at Monte Cassino were far more permanent, we may think, than the very simple ones that Subiaco had known, since here the Father laid the secure foundations of the many sides of Benedictine life as it is now lived and wrought all over the world. The Rule which he wrote and realized here needed an assembling of structures, big and little, huts and sheds, fields and granaries, for its fulfilment. No wonder that the heavy labour seemed to the monks in their lack of experience and skill to be aggravated by diabolical spite. It is, rather, a very marvel that Benedict should have been able to see and direct with his imagination and practical sense all the operations, from the laying of the first stone to the day of thanksgiving for the completed work,[5] when the brethren found themselves housed in one great House prepared with its necessary annexes for the full life in community.

It was about 529 when Benedict climbed the height of

[5] See Herwegen, pp. 61ff.

Monte Cassino for the first time, and here he died about 543,
if we accept the traditional dating.[6] Some fifteen years, possibly more, were his for the fostering of his monks according
to the plan he slowly conceived. One other house he also
planned and established on an estate by the seashore near
Tarracina, forty miles away. The owner was a pious Christian and begged of him this boon. But the Abbot did not
leave his cloister even for this holy work; he dwelt among
his disciples of the spiritual life in the Mother House both
day and night.

Let us visit in imagination the cloister in these years of the
sixth century when Benedict himself presided over all, and
see something of the life of the brethren according to his
Rule.[7] It will be well, perhaps, to suppose ourselves entering
Monte Cassino during the night, that we may begin at the
beginning of the monastic round of work. The brethren are
asleep in various dormitories, each arranged to hold ten
monks and a "senior," or "dean," on beds formed of thick
mats of straw or rushes woven together. We will imagine that
it is winter-time, and therefore each outstretched figure is
wrapped in two blankets, one a light covering of wool, the
other a heavy outer rug of sheep or goat skin. Each brother
has a pillow, too, for his head, and is sleeping in much the
same kind of clothing he will wear during the day, a long
tunic gathered in by a girdle of leather or cord, and a cowl,
or hooded cloak. As we look around in the light of the candle

[6] Butler, *Downside Review,* 48, 1930, p. 182, dates the migration to
Monte Cassino c. 525 and Benedict's death c. 550, in round numbers. For
the date c. 550 see Chapman, *St. Benedict and the Sixth Century,* p. 145.

[7] The sources of the following pages are the Rule itself, the second book
of the *Dialogues* of Gregory the Great, the various books mentioned in my
notes, especially Cuthbert Butler, *Benedictine Monachism*[2], c. XVII, and
Morin, *La Journée du Moine, d'après la règle et la tradition bénédictine,
Revue bénédictine,* VI, 1889, in eight instalments. I have left many
details out of the picture rather than introduce them from sources which
belong to later centuries.

which always burns all night, we see that on some of the beds boys are asleep, and of tender years. They have been entrusted to the Father Abbot for training, dedicated to the cloistered life in childhood by pious parents who would save them from the miseries of this present world. There is no furniture in the rooms save the beds. By the side of each monk lies the rest of the outfit allowed him by the Rule: a second tunic and cowl for use by day, and at times when the set he is at this moment wearing is being washed; a scapular or smaller cowl for wearing at work; a pair of light but durable socks; a pair of heavy shoes for work out-of-doors; and a stout girdle with pockets for the articles he must have for the day's needs: a handkerchief, a knife, a pen, and some writing-tablets. Nothing else may be his, and it is the duty of the Father Abbot now and again to examine the bed, the monk's only possible storehouse, lest some brother be tempted to hide away something for his own possession.

But now it is about half-past two in the morning,[8] and the monks have been in bed since darkness fell last evening. That means about half-past five in the winter of southern Italy, and their monastic night has therefore lasted some nine hours. For a long time already the brother whose present duty it is to awaken the Community has been saying his prayers in the cold. The other day he was late, and the Abbot had to shorten the holy Office in the Chapel. It happened on a Sunday, of all days, and he still remembers the penance done by him in that same Chapel in sight of his brother monks. The Father often takes upon himself the duty of waking the brethren; he has a habit of rising before the Night Office begins, to pray alone in his own private cell near the

[8] It must be remembered that hours of time were reckoned as in the Roman calendar, according to the sun, not by an artificially regulated clock. Thus in winter each hour of the twelve between sunrise and sunset would be considerably shorter than in summer.

places reserved for the guests, turning from time to time toward the starlit night as he thinks upon God. But tonight Benedict has bidden this brother call the rest, and it is rather difficult. The sky is covered with clouds whenever he looks out to tell the hour by the stars, and he has to judge it by the waning of the candle. At last he thinks the time has come, and the brethren rise quickly at his touch. At least, most of them! Human nature is human, even on the summit of a monastic mountain in the sixth century, and occasionally a novice rolls over for another last precious moment of sleep. He is gently but firmly encouraged to get up by one of the older monks, with a little shake, or perhaps a word in the ear.

Now they pass in the darkness to the Chapel, not running, yet not laggard; for they are bound for the "work of God," as Holy Office was called by these first framers of monastic Rules.[9] They have not stayed to change their clothing or to "dress"; any change of clothing and business of "dressing" is left till the Night Office has been chanted to the end. The watcher of the night is already lighting the candles as they file in and take severally their appointed places in the choir.

At the head stands the Abbot; just now he is intent on the big manuscript which holds the script of the Office Psalms. His face is grave and stern, as one who remembers that on him rests the burden of all these souls called of God to be trained for Heaven under his single and absolute direction and charge. He looks ever to the Rule which the Lord has inspired in him, as Mistress of himself and his brethren alike, and he diligently teaches his disciples to follow it alone. Yet he must always interpret it to them, especially in these first days. His words must rebuke the sensitive and the docile if they err; his chastisements and stripes must bend the way-

---

[9] So St. Caesarius, Holstenius, *Codex,* I, p. 356, X, and, of course, St. Benedict's *Rule: e.g.* cc. 22, 43, 47; cf. c. 19.

ward and the stubborn. None, he knows, must be especially cherished as born of high rank in the world, or unduly flattered for a brilliant brain; none must be despised by any of the brethren for humble birth or for a mind slow of working and ignorant of culture. Goodness, stability and obedience; these are the virtues accounted great in Benedict's school. And yet his face is tender, for he never forgets his name of "Abbot," "Abbas," "Father of his monks." If gentle and encouraging words will help the brethren to fulfil the precepts of the Rule, he will never be slow to give them, happy to be able to govern after this milder sort. Above all, he knows that his life must show in practice the working of every word he utters, in consolation, in warning, in rebuke. To his monastery he must hold up the mirror of perfection so far as mortal man may do, and to his ways and manners his sons look to learn of the Lord Christ Himself. For this reason he alone is addressed as *Dominus;* he stands as supreme ruler, not of his own power, but of the power of Heaven.

Nearest to him stand those appointed by his own choice to hold authority under him in the cloister. His chief assistant in the holy work is not here, but at the monastery of Tarracina; where he has been established by the Father as Prior, substitute for himself in the government of this daughter house. Later on, when Benedictine congregations became larger and more numerous, both Abbot and Prior were found in the same monastery. But the Rule enacted that the Prior should always be chosen by the Father Abbot and be subject to his authority without appeal, as were all the brethren, lest strife of divided governing should arise among them. If possible, the Rule would be content to dispense with the office of Prior for this very reason, relying on the aid given the Abbot by the "Deans."

These come next in order, masters each of ten monks in

the Community, chosen by the Abbot for their outstanding merit and their ripe knowledge of men and affairs. Age and birth have nothing to do with their election; the Abbot singles out as his assistants in ruling those whom he deems most fitted for the work, with no other consideration whatsoever. Serious fault, such as arrogance or disobedience to the Rule, will bring sharp rebuke even upon such as these, high in office, and if rebuke prove useless, their responsibilities will pass to others better fitted to bear them.

In a special place, just beside the Abbot himself, the Priest of the monastery is standing, charged by Benedict with the duties of saying Mass and of giving the blessing of the Church during Office and in the Refectory. Priests are received into this House if they are willing and able to pass through its customary discipline as prescribed by the Rule for lay novices. Reverence, indeed, is given to their sacred calling, but no special privileges are accorded them as brethren of the Order. If the Community finds itself faced with the need of a priest, the Abbot will choose from among the brethren one well fitted for this honour and present him to the Bishop for ordination. But Benedict will be very careful that none be ordained unless he be worthy. We read that once he healed a cleric in minor orders who was vexed by an evil spirit, and sent him away with the warning that henceforth he should never eat meat and should never presume to desire ordination as priest. He disobeyed the command at the price of long suffering and, at last, of a miserable death.[10]

The rank and file of the brethren stand after those placed in authority. As we have seen, they vary greatly in age, in station, even in race. Romans of noble blood, fitted by birth to take high place in intellectual matters, stand with hardy peasants of the soil, with tall and muscular Goths who delight to give of their strength in union with those who have taught

[10] Gregory, *Dial.* II, 16.

them of God, Three in One. There is no division into monks of the Choir and lay-brethren in this House of the sixth century. Whatever their standing in the world, whatever their age, with the exception of those reverenced for special dignity, all stand to chant the psalms, all approach the altar to receive the kiss of peace and the Body and Blood of the Lord in the order given by their first entry into its gates.

And now "Vigils," the Office of the Night, begins as prescribed by the Rule, and soon, after the first prayer for the help of the Lord, we hear the joyful words of the third Psalm: *Ego dormivi et soporatus sum, et exsurrexi quia Dominus suscepit me,* followed by the Psalm of invitation, *Venite, exsultemus Domino.* During the chanting two or three late comers, perhaps, have crept into their places, just in time to escape the penalty of tardiness. For this reason the Abbot has mercifully prescribed that the *Venite* be sung very slowly! After a hymn, taken from the hymnary of Saint Ambrose of Milan, the main part of the Office progresses. It is divided into two Nocturns and contains, during the winter, its twelve psalms, intercepted between verses by refrains; its three lessons from the Bible or from the writings of the Fathers, read by chosen monks from the lectern while the rest sit to listen, rising at the end for the solemn *Gloria* in honour of the Holy Trinity; its lesson from the Apostle Paul; its last versicle and *Kyrie Eleison.* In summer the three lessons are shortened to one on account of the brief time of darkness. On Sundays, on the other hand, the Community rise earlier than usual to attend faithfully upon three Nocturns, including twelve psalms, twelve lessons, and three canticles from the Prophets. At the end of the third Nocturn comes the *Te Deum,* begun by the Abbot, who afterwards reads a last lesson from the Gospel while all stand; the ritual then ends with the hymn *Te decet laus* and the blessing. So, too, will the Office be said on the Feast Days of Saints, except that psalms and lessons proper for the Day will be chanted and read.

When the Night Office is over, there remain nearly two hours before the dawn of the winter day. Many of the monks spend this interval in study, especially those who find it hard to learn psalms and lessons by heart, those accustomed to dig and delve rather than read. There are no Office books easy to handle and to carry in these early days. Manuscripts are heavy; they are also rare and therefore precious. They cannot be carried on journeys when need arises or taken out into the mud of the fields or garden. There are also other difficulties. The light in the Chapel is necessarily dim for those who must bend over candles or oil lamps, and much-used manuscripts get the worse for wear; [11] and so, even when books are at hand, reading is laborious and requires familiarity with the text. Moreover, monks bidden by the Abbot to intone the psalms and refrains or to read the lessons, generally in turn according to seniority, are bound to do so without stumbling or other irreverence, "with gravity and rightful fear," and this fluency needs preparation.

Others of the brethren already know their Office. These now turn to the pages of the Fathers of the Church or of other writers on the spiritual life. Reading, even in these first days of the Benedictine Order, occupies a goodly portion of a monk's day, and is ranked only next to the more special "work of God" in the Chapel. The monastery has its own library, well furnished with books. A special clause of the Rule bids that each monk shall obtain from it at the beginning of Lent a book which he shall read without skipping straight through from beginning to end.

Others, again, are eager to continue the work of prayer. These, says the Rule, are not to be hindered whenever they desire to pray by themselves. Only let them do it quietly and

[11] Delatte, p. 142.

with simplicity, not making any loud outcry about the business. Prayer, according to the wisdom here laid down, should be "short and pure, except if it be prolonged by inspiration of Divine grace."

Saint Benedict made no provision for any set time of private prayer as a necessary duty of his monks. Furthermore, the practice of mental prayer which forms so great a part of modern devotion was not yet at this time a formal ingredient in the monastic life. But that during the life of Benedict his monks did regularly devote a portion of their day to private prayer seems to be shown from a story of a brother in one of the twelve monasteries near Subiaco. This monk, we are told, could never stay in the chapel when the others remained behind to pray after the Office had ended, but always went outside to think of earthly and passing things. The admonition of his Abbot had only temporary effect, and at last Benedict himself was called to intervene. The holy Father promptly saw that the devil in the shape of a little black boy was pulling the deluded man outside, and as promptly healed him with chastisement for his blindness of heart. A monk, so the Rule bade, must ever pray for grace and lean on its support. Benedict was heart and soul in union with the teaching of the Second Council of Orange, held just about the time he founded his house upon the Mount.[12]

But now dawn is beginning to break in our monastery, and the summons comes to all to gather again in the Chapel for the first Office of the monastic day: "Matins," now known as Lauds. While the brethren pray, we may look for a moment at the Office Book of Saint Benedict.[13] For, though much had been done before his time, it is to him that monks and nuns throughout the world owe the form in which they

[12] *Dial.* II, 4; Cabrol, *St. Benedict,* pp. 113f.
[13] For the history of the Breviary see Bäumer, *Geschichte des Breviers* (French trans. by Biron, 1905); *Dict. d'arch. chrét. et de lit. s.v. Bréviaire* (H. Leclercq).

offer now their round of prayer by night and by day. In Palestine of the fourth century six Hours were recited by monks of the Church, and were then named and arranged thus: Matins, the Office of the Night; Lauds, the Office of the Dawn; Tierce, Sext, None, the Offices of the Day; Vespers, the Office of the evening. In the fifth century of the West these same Hours were observed in the monasteries founded by Cassian at Marseilles, fruit of experience gained under Eastern discipline,[14] with the addition of a seventh Hour, the Hour of sunrise, established late in the fourth century at Bethlehem between Lauds and Tierce and practiced by Cassian's monks under the name of Prime. This practice became general, in accordance with the words of the Psalmist: *Septies in die laudem dixi tibi,* and was observed in the Churches of Rome and Milan in Italy; from them we know that Benedict drew details of his Rule.

He bade his monks, moreover, to follow another saying of the Psalmist: *Media nocte surgebam ad confitendum tibi.* But this was already fulfilled by the Office of the Night, and thus the Seven Hours were completed in this Monte Cassino as the Proper of the Day by the addition of Compline: an Office introduced by Benedict into Western use, though there is good evidence for its observance in the East during the fourth century. The Benedictine Rule differed, however, from the East in saying the Evening Office, Vespers, by daylight; in the East the Evening Office was *Lucernarium,* the "Office of the Lamps." Benedict also ordered that Compline should be recited while it was yet day, so that his monks could go to bed before darkness set in, both winter and summer.[15]

[14] Cf. the *Peregrinatio Etheriae,* written c. 385.
[15] See Delatte, pp. 171f.; Baudot, *The Roman Breviary,* pp. 24ff.; Leclercq, *Bréviaire,* 1306; St. Basil, *Longer Rule, PG* XXXI, 1016. Cf. also the custom of Severinus, introduced from his training in the East; above, page 362.

Each of the four "Little Hours" under him followed regular tradition, in its three Psalms, its Lesson, and its proper Hymn. The Office of Vespers at Monte Cassino was much shorter than that of the Irish School of Columban; for the twelve Psalms of Columban's Rule corresponded here to only four. Lauds under Benedict had its *Benedictus,* "the Canticle from the Gospel," and Vespers had its *Magnificat,* destined for all time to be the traditional glory of the evening sacrifice. Scholars have attributed the introduction of each of these canticles into its Office to Benedict himself, though this theory is not held as certain, or even probable, by all.[16] Each week saw the whole Psalter chanted from beginning to end, in his careful arranging of a series beginning anew at the Night Office on Sunday.

We return now to the Chapel. Those monks who arrive after the beginning psalm of any one of the Day Hours, as also those arriving late for the Night Office, must take a place at the lowest end and perform penance afterward. "Matins," or Lauds, we will imagine, is just ending on this winter morning, and the Chapel has seen already some two hours of common prayer. If it be a Sunday, an interesting ceremony is now carried out in accordance with the Rule. Those of the brethren who have done duty in the kitchen as cooks and in the refectory as servers during the past week come forward to give thanks to God and to receive a blessing in the presence of all the Community. After they retire, the monks appointed for the present week are blessed in their turn and pray for aid in their labours. Some of them, no doubt, are as inexperienced and unskilful as was Brother Juniper in days yet to come! On Sunday, too, the monk chosen by the Abbot to read aloud during the week in the refectory receives his

[16] Cf. for example, Bäumer, p. 177, Leclercq, *ibid.* with the doubt of Cabrol, *s.v. Cantiques évangéliques,* in the same *Dict. d'arch. chrét. et de lit.* 1996, 1998.

blessing and begs the prayers of all that he may be kept free from pride. Not every one in this varied gathering of the sixth century is able to read at all, to say nothing of reading correctly his Latin, though it be his mother's tongue. This blessing of the reader takes place after Mass, celebrated, it would seem, only on Sunday and solemn Feast Days, when all the brethren make their communions. Benedict tells us nothing of a daily Mass.

But we will suppose that this is a week day and picture the brethren quietly leaving the Chapel after Lauds. It is about six o'clock. The next three hours are given to reading and study, with one short interval at sunrise for Prime. All now bend silently over their long rolls of manuscript: not only older men and youths, but the children of the monastery as well. These attend Offices with their elders and are carefully trained in knowledge of the Bible that they may understand what they hear. One or two of the senior monks walk quietly around from time to time, to make sure that no lazy brother is passing the tedious hours in a little nap, or even whispering in idle gossip with his neighbour, to the disturbance of the monastic peace and profit.

At nine o'clock the Community meet again in the Chapel for Tierce and then disperse to the various lesser duties of the monastery. We will try to visit them in their appointed places. First, the Abbot's cell, up his stairway on the second floor. Thither climb many of the brethren, either called by his voice, or led by conscience or other urgency. Some are summoned for rebuke and admonition in the hope that they may turn from their faults before graver measures are needed. The Abbot is a wise physician and draws from his store all manner of medicaments for sick souls: the soothing ointments of his own kindly counsel, the stimulating draughts of words from sacred writings, or, when these fail, the sharp

cautery of the lash or of banishment from the fellowship of
the refectory, of the Chapel, even of the monastery itself.
Hard and obstinate characters are brought to obedience by
physical stripes or by severe fasting; sensitive souls find banishment from their brethren a sufficiently painful remedy. Before meting out severe sentences, however, the Abbot will
consult the dean who has charge of this erring monk, or call
a conference of the whole Community. As we pass through
the building, we may meet one who walks alone spiritually
as well as socially, to whom no one gives the accustomed
greeting of "Benedicite" as he passes silently by, who does not
eat in common of the food blessed in the refectory nor meet
his fellows in the Chapel at the Hours. Yet even such a one
is visited by the kindness of the Father Abbot, who sends to
him frequently some older brother for his speedier return
to grace.

Many come, as the Rule bids them, to confess their faults
of their own accord directly they find themselves guilty. The
chanters and readers who have carelessly stumbled over their
part in the Chapel through lack of preparation and have thus
disturbed the whole Community, the cooks who have wasted
its property in the kitchen, the servers at table who have
broken its crockery and glass, the labourers outside and inside
who have spoiled their tools, all seek the Abbot or his representative to ask forgiveness for their careless work and receive
due penance. The story is well known of the Goth, powerful
in body but humble in spirit, whom the Father gladly
received among his monks and set to work at clearing away
briars from the monastery's ground. He began with immense
energy just above a deep pool, when suddenly his billhook
snapped in two and the iron blade gave a leap into the
water. The postulant was terribly troubled and frightened.
But he knew his Rule and rushed at once to his appointed

senior, confessed his loss, and submitted to penalty. The
senior reported the matter to the Father Abbot and roused
his sympathy for this giant in distress. Benedict promptly left
his cell, found the Goth by the pool still holding the empty
wooden handle of his hook, took it from him and threw it
into the water. Then the iron shaft rose slowly from the bottom
of the pool, joined its wooden half, and swam tranquilly to
the bank. The Father handed it back to his barbarian son
with an encouraging word which we are glad to have in our
records: "There! now go on with your work and don't be
sad!" [17]

A word may be said here on sacramental confession. This
is never directly prescribed in this Rule of Benedict, so different from the penitential codes of Celtic origin. The monks
confess their sins against the Rule to Benedict as their Father;
they are also bidden to acknowledge to him their secret
thoughts or deeds of evil, for the profiting of their souls by
humility and for the gaining of wise counsel from his
experience. There is no certainty that Benedict was a priest.
In one passage, however, the monk is directed to confess his
secret faults to the Abbot or to one of the "spiritual seniors,
who know how to cure sins." Here we may have a reference
to confession before a priest: a matter left, it would seem, by
Benedict to prescription for individual needs. [18]

Benedict oftentimes had a strange power of reading the
thoughts of his spiritual sons. Once he was visited by a servant who brought from his master a flagon of wine for the
monastery. He had set out with two, and Benedict knew it.
"Take care, my son," he said, "be sure you do not drink of
that flagon you have hidden. Turn it over very carefully and
you will see what is inside." The boy was much embarrassed,
but curious enough to do as he was told. He did tilt the

[17] *Dial.* II, 6.   [18] See *Rule,* cc. 4, 7, and 46.

bottle, very gingerly, and out glided a deadly serpent. Some time afterward he became a novice under Benedict.

On another occasion Benedict was having supper in the light of a candle held for him by one of his monks. Both, of course, were engaged in silent thought, but the meditations of the disciple were not those of the Father. He came of a noble family, and at the moment he was angrily wondering why on earth he should have to play slave to Benedict? Who was he, anyway, that a Roman aristocrat should hold a candle for him? At this point Benedict quietly broke in: "Put down the light, my son, and go off by yourself a little while to think the matter out." The story illustrates the Abbot's watchful care of the souls in his charge.[19] He always remembered that his was the work of a spiritual physician, not exercise of tyranny over the whole and well.[20] Whenever any very important matter relating to the Community had to be decided, he called a general assembly of all the brethren; and all, even the youngest, were permitted to offer counsel to aid him in making his decision. "For the Lord gives wisdom where He wills."

Very often Benedict would sit in front of the monastery as he read and meditated. It was here one day that he looked up and saw the Gothic King Totila approaching. The date was probably 542, soon after the Goths in Italy had made Totila their leader for the better resisting of the Roman Emperor in Constantinople; Ravenna had just been taken before the assault of Belisarius, but the Goths were proceeding in the south toward the capture of Naples in the next year. Totila had sent word that he desired to visit Benedict and had been told to come. But he wanted to find out whether the Abbot really did possess the spirit of prophecy which was said to direct this place. Accordingly he ordered

[19] *Dial.* II, 20.   [20] *Rule,* c. 27.

one of his bodyguard, a man named Riccho, to borrow his shoes and royal dress and attendants and in this disguise of Totila himself to try out the Abbot's power. Benedict, now over sixty years of age, but as keen and vigorous in spirit as ever, did not wait till the impostor should formally present himself. As soon as he came within hearing, there struck on his ear a voice, crying: "Take off, my son, take off those things you are wearing, they are not yours!" The man retreated in a panic, and Totila decided it would be well worth while to learn of this magical monk.

He was, indeed, so impressed by what he had heard from his soldier that he did not dare to greet the Abbot with any common courtesy, but remained some distance away, bowing low to the ground in reverence, and Benedict had to rise to make his visitor stand upright. The words of the Father were not at all what Totila had hoped to hear: "Many evil deeds you are doing, many you have already done. It is time at last that you refrain from iniquity. Of a truth you shall enter Rome, you shall cross the sea, nine years you shall reign, and in the tenth you shall die." Gregory relates that the King was much perturbed, and begged Benedict to pray for him. "Henceforth," the narrative goes on, "he was less cruel. Not long afterward he entered Rome and went on to Sicily. In the tenth year of his reign by the judgment of Almighty God he lost both his kingdom and his life." [21]

From the Abbot's cell we pass to the great Gate of the monastery. Here sits the porter, a monk old both in years and in knowledge of men. His duties are many and keep him constantly at his post, though sometimes he is relieved for a few moments by a younger monk appointed to assist him. A stream of visitors knock at the outer door, and to each one the porter immediately cries "Deo gratias," if the arrival be

[21] *Dial.* II, 14f.

known to him, or prays "God bless you" for a stranger. Pilgrim monks arrive to see the Abbot; they are welcomed and bidden to remain as long as they desire. Sometimes in these days of easy transference they may wish to offer a new allegiance to this house of Monte Cassino; and their wish may be granted if Benedict and his monks, as well as the abbot of the monastery whence they first came, think well of them and their prayer. But they will promise to stay steadfastly in Monte Cassino for the future if they are admitted there as monks of Benedict. Penitents arrive to consult the Father Abbot in their distress. These are escorted courteously to his cell, as are the many visitors who wish to confer with him on matters of religion: bishops, priests, and laymen. Many knock who are eager to be admitted as postulants of the Community; these, when they do not come as members of another Order, must be severely tried and tested. The porter is instructed to offer all sorts of objections to their petitions and to send them away to call again and again. If, however, the stranger perseveres humbly in his knocking and receives patiently all the reluctance of the gate to let him in, he may be admitted for a short stay in the Guest House. The Guest Master has been chosen from among the brethren; he welcomes each guest, once safely inside, with a lowly bowing of the head, trusting that the Community is reverencing in this Christian the advent of the Lord Christ Himself. Yet he, too, is cautious and first bids the new arrival pray with him, to make quite sure that the devil in disguise has not managed to get past the porter's eye. Then, if all be well, he gives the kiss of peace.

In addition to human beings, letters and parcels arrive in plenty from relatives, friends, and benefactors. These are all taken directly to the Abbot's cell to await his decision; no monk may write or receive letters, send or accept gifts, unless the Abbot give him leave. Presents are bestowed where the Abbot considers they are most needed, if received at all.

We pass now outside the Gate, and walk around the building. There is a garden which supplies fruit and vegetables in their seasons, and there are fields for the harvest of grain which shall provide the daily bread. We will suppose that we are visitors in the spirit, to whom the secrets of the Rule are free, and that we are for the moment in charge of a young brother to whom the Father has given special permission to show us its workings. He tells us that in summer the monks will be busy in this garden and in the fields. They will rise for the Night Office at midsummer about one in the morning and go out-of-doors after Prime, said when the sun rises over an horizon that has already seen two hours of light. Four hours will be given to labour on the monastery land, followed by Tierce, which may be recited from memory where the monks happen to be standing; then two hours of study in the house; then will come Sext in the Chapel, and then a midday dinner. After dinner in summer-time the monks will rest on their beds, sleeping or reading, as they will. None will be said at two o'clock, and then all will be occupied with the work needed inside the monastery till Vespers. After this Office a light supper will be shared, then reading in assembly, followed by Compline, and finally bed about eight o'clock while the daylight still lasts. This, our young brother informs us, is the monastic day from Easter till Holy Cross Day, the fourteenth of September. From Pentecost onward on Wednesdays and Fridays and all Fast Days the monks will take only one meal, dinner, served three hours after midday, unless their work on the soil is very hard or the weather is very hot. "Our holy Father," we are told, "does not wish any to do more than his strength allows. In outward matters, such as food or sleep or manual labour, our

lives here are very much like those of the humbler people who
work with their hands outside our monastery. We are indeed
poor here; for our house and buildings are very new and
have cost us much to put up, even with our own toil. So we
try, so far as we can, to till our own land and gather in our
own harvest. But the Father teaches us that all work which
may rightly be offered to God is fitting for us, his spiritual
sons, whether it comes from the head or from the hands. It
all depends on what we have to offer. There are some every
year whom he keeps at their books and writing inside the
cloister, even during spring and harvest time. Yet he himself
regularly shares our work in the fields whenever his many
other calls give him time." Our young monk is so patient in
his courtesy that we are tempted to ask him what happens
on Holy Cross Day? The reply comes with a smile: "That is
the day, the Father tells us, on which all monks should
begin their Lent; and so we are now keeping our time of
'Lenten' Rule from September the fourteenth till Easter."

We remember that this is mid-winter and that he has been
fasting since he rose, before three in the morning. So we ask
no more questions, but move on to see the various workers in
this hive of the Spirit. Some of the brethren are busy drawing water from the spring, others are employed in the bakery,
others at the various arts and crafts in which they were skilled
before they came here. "What is done with the things they
make?" we ask, thinking of the story of Abbot Paul in Cassian's *Institutes:* a solitary who lived far from any market
where he might sell his handiwork and found no profit in his
wares except to keep busy and cheat the devil of joy in human
idleness. "Most of the script," replies our guide, "done by
those who copy the Psalms and Lessons of the Office, is
needed to replace old and torn copies in our Chapel, and to
provide new ones for new brethren. This is, indeed, my own

special joy, the making of books, when our Rule permits. But, as you see, our art is very simple at present. Who knows? Perhaps some day other sons of our Father Benedict will limn beautiful paintings in their scripts and will write great works. Already the Father is eager that we read and copy well. Other produce of our House, such as the fruits of the earth or of weaving or carpentry, he is willing that we should sell, if only we do so for the glory of God in the supplying of what we need for His service. Benedict desires that we should support ourselves and furnish our own necessities so far as we can for ourselves, but he allows no thought of vain profiting through our work."

By this time we are again in the House. Sext, the midday Office, has been said while we were outside. As we enter, we catch sight of two of the brethren going out on a journey. They are better clothed than those whom we have seen hitherto in the various parts of the monastery; indeed, they have received special dress for their travels from the room set aside for the keeping of the clothes of the monks. Shortly afterward we pass this room and give it a curious glance. It holds a neat pile of cowls and tunics, stout woollen ones for winter, thin ones for summer, and special underclothing for those who must make long pilgrimages. All are very much the same as those worn by poor people in the surrounding district; and, indeed, the monks seem to us to differ principally from the peasants outside by always wearing the same kinds of garments and by always choosing those of some coarse stuff and some quiet colour. All we see in our round are of black or nondescript brown or white or grey. Our guide tells us that the monastery buys them at as low a price as possible, though the Father himself sees that each cowl and tunic fits with comfort the monk who is to wear them so constantly.

At this point we are greeted by a pleasant smell and think

about bodily refreshment, a thought apparently far from our guide. He is far more interested in the sudden sight of an older monk coming along the passage. As they meet he bends his head and murmurs: *"Benedic, Nonne!"* "Your blessing, reverend Father!" The monk bows slightly to his junior, and with a smile, though no unnecessary word, receives us into his care, while the other with a courteous gesture bids us farewell in silence. We warm at once to our new friend, who turns out to be the cellarer, sent by the Father to show us the kitchen and refectories. He looks wise and sympathetic, and has a fatherly way about him, as though the monks to him are one big family which he is to feed and care for in sickness and in health. We notice that he tends all the things in the kitchen and offices with a kind of reverence; in his eyes surely all the kettles and pans and plates and dishes in this House of God are blessed as truly as if they rested on the altar itself.

It is nearly two o'clock in the afternoon, and the cooks for the week are busy in the kitchen preparing dinner. The cellarer informs us that this will be served in about an hour's time, directly after the Office of None has been said in the Chapel. No one may eat or drink except at the hours assigned in the Rule, and no one may come in late for grace at meals without penance, either of rebuke or of banishment from the refectory if the fault be frequent. The amount of food, we learn from him, is the same whether the monastic day of the year prescribes two meals or only one. One pound of bread is allowed each monk a day and two courses of cooked food, mostly vegetables. Sometimes eggs or fish or cheese form these dishes, sometimes even wild fowl or the meat of other birds not costly or luxurious. "The Father considers this," our guide observes, "in keeping with that part of our Rule which forbids all flesh of four-footed beasts at any time to the brethren, except the very infirm and the sick." The cellarer's view of the reasonableness of the Abbot Benedict appears to agree entirely with that of our previous informant, the young junior. "We are allowed two dishes," he continues, "because the Father understands the infirmities of our different tastes and digestions! When we have fresh fruit and tender young vegetables in our garden, he allows us even a third, and we may eat of all three if we will, provided always that we do not fall to greediness. We are allowed, also, about half a pint of wine each day, and sometimes, when it is very hot and we are thirsty, or when we have been working very hard, the Abbot tells me to serve an extra allowance. In all this he is trying, he says, to treat us as the ordinary men we are and have been all our lives. Most of the brethren would find it terribly difficult to give up their daily cup of wine. Sometimes, as in Lent, the Abbot is glad that we should give it up for a while, in the sacrifice which the Rule bids us make at that time, of food or drink or sleep or speech. But he always requires that we tell him beforehand of our individual plans for observing the Great Fast, and always reminds us that we should offer our resolutions, each of us, to God "with joy of the Holy Spirit, looking for a blessed Easter with the gladness of spiritual longing."

Other little things show us the thoughtfulness of the Father Founder. As we pass to the Refectory, we see a number of monks quietly refreshing themselves with a piece of bread and a cup of wine. "The Rule," we are informed here, "allows these to break their fast because, as cooks and servers, they will not have their regular meal till after all the others have finished and that would keep them too long without food in the midst of hard work. The same comfort is allowed to the monk who reads in the Refectory during dinner. Only, on all Sundays and other solemn Feasts, they wait till after they have made their communions at Mass." We express our content at these considerations, and the monk adds with a little smile: "But, for all this, the Rule is strict. Not one of us is allowed to eat outside the monastery, even in the houses of our holy and devoted friends, if he can possibly get back in time for a meal. And no one ever speaks during a meal, except sometimes the monk placed in charge. All listen intently to the reader, just remembering to pass to the brother next at hand what he needs, or perhaps making a little sign if he wants something himself. At some other times during the day the Rule allows us to talk a little, if we keep strict silence when we are praying or entering or leaving the Chapel, or studying or resting. The Father does not expect complete silence. But he never allows any unseemly and foolish laughter or frivolity in his monks."

At this moment the first signal sounds for None and directly afterward we see the brethren on their way to the Chapel. They are walking with eyes on the ground and hands clasped within their habit, apparently heedless of the fact that they have worked without eating for some twelve hours. It is true, of course, that their life is designed in material matters to resemble that of peasants accustomed to meagre fare, and that they live in southern Italy, not in a northern land. Yet we gladly bow our heads in reverence as they pass out of sight, and follow, full of thought, to share with them the Office when the second signal bids that it begin.

When it is over, all assemble for dinner in the common Refectory just before the sun reaches three o'clock. We ourselves are bound for another dining-room, the Refectory of the Abbot, where he refreshes the guests who have come to confer with him. A separate room is needed, partly because the silence of the brethren in the common Refectory must not be interrupted, partly because the duty of charity and hospitality sometimes bids the Abbot break the fast imposed by the Rule. He will not break fasts imposed by the whole Church; occasionally, however, he will eat of his courtesy as host to some guest, perhaps one in sore need of food. At times in these strenuous years of the sixth century the famine prevailing throughout Italy taxed heavily the slender resources of Monte Cassino, especially as the Abbot would give of its substance to hungry men till scarcely anything was left in the larder. A story is told that once, when all the surrounding land of Campania was in great distress, a certain subdeacon came to the monastery and begged for some oil. As it happened, the monastic cupboard did hold on that day a little oil in a flask and practically nothing else. Benedict commanded that this should be given; the cellarer heard and understood, but did not obey. When Benedict learned this, he was so angry that he ordered the flask, oil and all, to be thrown out of the window. "Nothing," he declared, "shall remain in this House of God through an act of disobedience." Beneath the window fell the great precipice on which Monte Cassino was built, and the flask was dashed against its rocks; miraculously it was not broken and its oil was not spilt. Therefore the Father gave fresh command that it should be rescued and that the gift should be made to the deacon, as he had said before. But the cellarer of the time was severely rebuked in full assembly of the brethren for his pride and lack of faith.

During dinner we ask the Abbot how the remaining hours of the day are arranged in this winter-time, and learn that directly. after this meal the monks will have another period for reading and study. We are much impressed by the importance given to sacred science by this Father, in no sense a pedantic scholar, especially when we learn that in the narrower Lent of the whole Church reading goes on here for an extra hour in the morning, and that on Sundays it is the usual occupation of all who can profit by it, except when they are attending Mass or Holy Office or are engaged in private prayer or in the necessary domestic work of the house. No work is done on Sundays in the fields, but if any of the less educated monks simply cannot attend so long to his books, he is allowed by the Rule to busy himself with some handiwork appropriate to his powers, that he may not sin through idleness. Here, again, the Rule proves the reasonableness of its Father. The mention of the Church's Lent prompts us to ask whether it brings much difference in the daily routine; and we are told that, with the extra hour for reading, the brethren study four hours instead of three in the morning, then work at their various duties in and outside the house, till the hour of Vespers, about half-past four. After Vespers dinner is served, the only meal, as throughout the winter. The food is the same, the only difference being that it comes more than two hours later than at this present time of December. "But, of course," the Abbot adds with a smile, "the Rule does not forbid us to keep our own resolutions for abstinence in details!"

On other days, however, of the longer monastic "Lent" of autumn and winter, Vespers comes after dinner and after the reading which follows that meal. When the monks leave the Chapel at the end of this Office, they have a short interval for necessary household duties, and then all assemble to hear a brief reading of perhaps four or five pages from some profitable book, very often from the manual of Cassian on the monastic life called *Conferences with Abbots in the Egyptian Desert,* or from the *Lives* of these Abbots, or from the Bible. But not from the historical books! These, with their stirring tales of adventure, might excite youthful spirits unduly just before bed-time. The children of this monastery have no boyish yarns of perils and pranks, and therefore the adventures of Joshua and of the Kings of Israel would be very thrilling to ears unaccustomed to the like. Then comes Compline, then the Great Silence falls, and all go to rest about five o'clock, before darkness has set in.

While we have been talking, the time of after-dinner reading has arrived, and we take leave of the Father, who gives us special permission to visit the Infirmary for a moment. Here it is clear that the sick receive the same honour as the guests of the monastery from those who see the Lord Himself in their patients. The most careful watch is kept over them by their Infirmarian, a monk specially chosen for his diligence and skill. Hot baths, a rare luxury for the young and the strong in this house, are allowed to the sick as often as seems needful. Meat, too, is given them, in the sense of the flesh of four-footed creatures, for their quick recovery and strengthening. We learn also that the aged and the children of the monastery are not obliged to keep the long hours of fasting required of the general Community. All these individual cases, as every other matter in which the Rule allows some exception, are left to the discretion and wisdom of the Abbot.

From the Infirmary we return once more to the Chapel and sit at the back a little while before the signal comes for Vespers. It is very still, and we seem to be alone, till suddenly we catch sight of a kneeling figure in the shadow of one corner. No doubt it is the novice who, as the Abbot has told us, is to be professed at the solemn Mass of tomorrow's Feast Day. We try as we sit there to imagine for ourselves, from what we have heard, the thoughts that must be in his mind and memory as he kneels and gives thanks to God Who has brought him to the haven where he would be. Perhaps he can recall all the rebuffs cast at him by the good old porter when first he timidly knocked for admission? "Too young,

my son," or, "Too delicate you seem for the hard life here,"
or "Surely you have lived over-daintily to settle in this poor
place." How glad he is that he persevered, till one day with a
curt, "Then have your way and the Lord go with you," the
porter sent him to the Guest House. He stayed there, he
remembers, for a few days and then was allowed to live in
the Community as a novice. It was hard at first, that
inexorable round of prayer and reading and toil; hard, even,
to have to eat and sleep and awake just when the brethren
did, not as his own wishes would have it. Always he was
conscious that he was on his trial, and the monk in whose
special charge he was made no illusions of the difficulties and
temptations of the life under Benedict's Rule. Perhaps, we
think as we watch him, he is rich and now has nothing of
his own? Or is he highly cultivated, and must now be
content to dwell happily with rustics as well as with those
congenial to himself? The Rule encourages silence; what of
those thrilling debates on matters of philosophy and scholarship that were the very breath of life to him in the world?
Or, again, he may be poor with little education, and cannot
help wondering whether he will ever be prepared to play his
part in the Chapel of the monks and in their common life?

For two months, as we have learned, he must have
struggled on, promising to persevere, and then at last the
Rule was read to him in all its provision. He remembers
vividly the words of the Novice-Master when the great code
had reached its end: "This, my son, is the law under which
you ask to fight the battle of God. Can you keep it? Then
enter upon it. If you cannot, then freely depart." Twice
afterward he heard again the reading of the Rule, at the end
of his eighth month and at the end of the year, and three
times he promised to obey and to persevere in all commanded
him.

He is meditating now, of course, on the pledge he will give tomorrow in the presence of all the brethren assembled for Mass. Of *stability:* that he will remain faithfully unto death a member of the monastery to which he has bound himself, unless the Abbot command otherwise; of *conversion of way of life:* that he will henceforth live and grow in grace by God's help in accordance with the holy Rule of Benedict; of *obedience:* that henceforth the Rule, as interpreted by the Father Founder and those whom he shall elect to bear authority under him, shall be his to follow in all things, whether he himself deem the order wise or no. "Let no one in the monastery follow the will of his own heart," the Rule reads, and the obedience must be as ready as it is full, unquestioning and glad. It is a great Profession, and he prays earnestly that, if God will, he may be able to meet its requirements. Stability will be hard; in other monasteries of Italy and Gaul monks are permitted to come and go.[22] Can he hope, also, to ascend, slowly and painfully, the twelve rungs of the ladder of humility of which the Rule has told him, and "arrive thereafter at that love of God which casteth out fear," no longer driven to obey by the thought of punishment here and in eternity, but constrained by the love of Christ and goodly custom and the joy of virtues? Will he ever possess for his perfecting that long list of seventy-two spiritual tools by which the Benedictine artist of the spiritual life is bidden to accomplish his work on earth? No wonder, he must be reflecting, that it ends with the solemn word of hope: "And never to despair of the mercy of God."

Our thoughts are interrupted here by the entrance of the Community, and our eyes, not trained in the guarding prescribed to monks, light immediately upon a tall grave man who leads by the hand a little boy. Both attend reverently to

---

[22] Benedictine "stability" was a marked contrast to the wandering of Celtic monks.

the psalms and prayers which follow, though now and again the man lays his hand upon the boy, no doubt his son, as if he would protect him ever from all ill and distress. Occasionally, too, one of the children living in the monastery looks up from his book and across toward the little stranger and, if he gaze too long, is gently recalled to the work in hand by the monk who sits beside him. We wonder what the new arrivals desire.

Next morning we understand. First of all, at the time of the Offertory during Mass the young novice makes his promise and his petition in the Chapel: before God, before the saints, whose relics are there, in the presence of the Abbot to whom henceforth he shall be a newborn son. With his own hand he writes his petition for reception within this monastery and places it upon the altar with the prayer of the Psalmist: *Suscipe me, Domine, secundum eloquium tuum, et vivam: et non confundas me ab exspectatione mea.* Thrice the brethren answer him, with the cry of *Gloria Patri.* Then they take him as one of themselves while he lies at their feet silently asking their prayers.

Henceforth he belongs to this monastery and has nothing of his own, not even his own body and its powers. All his property will be given either to the poor or to this Community which he has entered, according to his choice. In token of his complete surrender his secular dress is now taken from him, and he is clothed in the tunic and cowl of the Order. His old clothes are kept, however, in the room set apart for the monastic wardrobe, so that if ever he should so persist in rebellion that he must be dismissed he may go again to the world in its own array. But the paper of his petition has been received by the Abbot before God on the altar; it is never blotted out or allowed to leave the place where it was signed.

When at last he has retired in the fullness of his joy, we see the stranger of yesterday come forward, leading once again his little son. In the clearer light of day we discern that they are of noble rank, richly dressed and evidently of refined and cultured family. Just such a petition as we have here seen offered is now again presented on the altar. But this time the father offers it with and for his son, and in it he promises that he will not reserve the hope of any income in the future for his boy. Thus the committal of the child is made the more solemn, and his stability the easier, if he have no reserve on which to lean in the world without. As we gaze intently on the two, we see the father take in his hands the paper of all this writing, together with the bread and wine for the Holy Sacrifice; then in sight of the Abbot and the brethren he takes his child's hand and wraps it, with the paper and the bread and wine, in the altar-cloth, and thus offers all together at the altar in one great and permanent oblation to God. We learn afterward that all is done in the same way if the child accepted come of poor parents, save that the promise to leave nothing to the child is omitted, in that for him poverty is already assured.

Such, in a rough picture, is a very little of the richness spread out in the Rule of Saint Benedict, the greatest work of this sixth century. He himself writes of it in his conclusion: "We have drawn up this Rule that by its keeping in monasteries we may show that we have to some degree uprightness of conduct and the beginning of religious life." And thus he sums up all its exhortations: "Whosoever thou art who dost hasten toward the heavenly fatherland, keep faithfully with the help of Christ this very little Rule of beginning here shown forth; and then at length under the protection of God thou shalt arrive at the greater things which we have described above, the very heights of doctrine and of virtues."

In thinking of the work of Benedict as compared with that of Columban two questions arise. First, what was the relation of Benedict to the Bishop of his diocese? There is brief mention of the Bishop's function twice in the Rule, and the Abbot's position seems to be one of monastic independence, without, however, any of the strife indicated in the case of Columban. It is the Abbot himself, Benedict prescribes, who is to choose from among his monks one worthy to be ordained priest or deacon if it seem to him desirable. Here lies the seed of the "monastic exemption" of the future.[23] If the monk thus ordained priest should in future days prove rebellious against the Abbot and refuse to change his evil ways, in spite of continued rebuke, then, in the words of the Rule, "let even the Bishop be called in as witness." What that exactly means we do not know; but very probably the Bishop was to confirm by his authority *ex officio* as diocesan and approve by his presence the sentence declared by the Abbot against the offending priest as a member of the Community subject to his rule. For the Rule never bids that the Bishop be called in should the Abbot judge it necessary to expel a monk who is a layman, even though he be Dean or Prior.[24]

It would seem, moreover, that the election of the Abbot was to be confirmed by the diocesan Bishop or by neighbouring Abbots. It is true that no express order is given for this in the instructions of Benedict; but it may be inferred from the wording of the Rule. At the same time, the monks were to be free to choose whom they would to present to high authority for such confirming in office, and from the time of Gregory the Great it was already customary that the choice of the monks should be accepted.[25] Such supervision of a

[23] See Delatte, p. 426.   [24] *ibid.* p. 429.
[25] I am following here Dom J. Chapman, *Downside Review*, 1919, p. 85, and Dom C. Butler, *ibid.* 1930, p. 183; cf. Butler, *Bened. Mon.*[2], p. 408.

monastic Community by its diocesan was, indeed, in accordance with the practice of the Roman Churches, in distinction from the Celtic, in this age.

Lastly, the Rule provides that if the Community should ever fall into wickedness, should unite in electing an Abbot of such character that he would consent to their wicked ways (which may God forbid!), and these wicked doings should come to the knowledge of the Bishop of the diocese, or of Abbots or of Christian people dwelling in the neighbourhood; then these are to frustrate such evil agreement and appoint an administrator, worthy of this House of God, to rule its erring brethren. Delatte in his *Commentary* explains this as meaning, in all probability, that such neighbouring Abbots were to work under their Bishop in this matter, supported by the practical strength of the devout laymen living near.[26]

Secondly, what of the surrounding district? Did Benedict feel it incumbent upon Monte Cassino to shepherd the people dwelling outside? Undoubtedly. Two narratives in the second book of Gregory's *Dialogues* tell of Benedict's care for the souls of women in his neighbourhood. In one we read that he frequently sent his monks to give spiritual counsel to a community of nuns established not far away. Perhaps this was a convent over which his sister Scholastica presided.[27] The other gives a story of interesting detail. Near Monte Cassino there lived two women of gentle birth, dedicated under religious vows, but resident in their own private house, where their domestic needs were served by a steward, a man of high character and Christian life. But, as Gregory says, "noble birth sometimes brings forth an ignoble mind"; and these pious ladies had not yet learned to control their hasty tongues and tempers, of which the poor steward constantly enjoyed full benefit. He exercised patience for a long time and

[26] p. 447.   [27] Mittermüller, ed. *Dial.* 1880, p. 45.

then could bear it no more. Both he, it seems, and his mistresses were under the spiritual direction of Benedict. For the steward told Benedict of his distress, and the Father warned his catty daughters that he would forbid them to make their communions if they did not cease worrying their steward with cross words. Shortly afterward they both died, before, indeed, the words of excommunication had been spoken, but without any sign of penitence, and were buried in the church where they had worshipped. A little while later, at the moment when the deacon cried out during Mass that those who were not to make their communions should now depart, their nurse, who used to make offerings to the Lord on their behalf, saw them come out from their tombs and leave the church. This happened again and again. Then the nurse remembered the words of Benedict, evidently related to her by the offenders themselves. With her offering in her hand she went quickly to the Abbot, and, holding it out to him: "Offer this," she begged, "to the Lord for them, and they will no longer be outcast." So when the oblation had duly been made, the sisters no longer left the church with the penitents and catechumens during Mass, but received their communions from the priest with the rest of their brethren.

Other stories, also, show that Benedict was constantly aiding souls and bodies, both of pilgrims who came to the cloister and of those outside to whom he went for their relief. We read in Gregory's *Dialogues* of a neighbouring village converted by his preaching; of the peasant who declared he had given all his belongings to "Father Benedict" lest he should be robbed of them; of the farmer who carried the body of his dead son to the Abbey Gate, requiring earnestly that the Abbot should give the boy back again to him. In his dealings with sinners, many and varied, Benedict was like Columban, yet unlike him. For Monte Cassino possessed no detailed and formal list of sins and of punishments to match each crime. Its monks and its penitents lived by love rather than by fear, as its Abbot himself bade them.

It was a woman that he loved above all on earth, his sister Scholastica.[28] Yet he loved God in his Rule even more than he loved her, and Gregory tells how once she prevailed with the Lord against the monk and his strict obedience to the cloister. The story is, of course, widely known, but no account of Benedict is complete without it. We read in the *Dialogues*[29] that Scholastica, who had been vowed to the monastic life since she was a child, lived in a cell near Monte Cassino. Once a year each went out to meet the other soon after the sun rose, to spend the day together in prayer and talk on holy things. Probably they sat in one of the huts built for workers on the grounds of Benedict's monastery, while the brethren and nuns who had accompanied them waited at a little distance out of hearing. Benedict was director of Scholastica in spiritual matters as well as her brother, though they so rarely met, and there were always many things she wanted to ask for the guidance of her companions and herself. Talking was so much more satisfactory than writing, and there was only this one day a year for talk! So on one occasion, when the time was nearly over and they were taking their evening meal together before returning to their separate cloisters, Scholastica suddenly said: "Please do not leave me tonight, but let us talk till morning of the joys of heaven." Benedict was very naturally shocked. "Sister," he declared, "what are you saying? Of course I cannot stay outside my cell." It was a beautiful evening, cloudless and tranquil. But Scholastica, bitterly disappointed when she heard that decided "No," laid her head down on the table and burst into tears. For a long time she stayed so, growing gradually

[28] Later tradition held that they were twins.   [29] II, 33f.

quieter, till Benedict hoped at last that she was content. Then all at once she looked out at the sky with a smile of triumphant happiness, and her brother, following her glance, was horrified to see that it was rapidly growing dark. In a moment a terrific thunderstorm burst over their heads with vivid flashes of lightning and torrents of rain. The little company waited and waited, but the tempest raged on lustily, with no sign of abating, till Benedict saw he could not let his followers risk their lives by trying to get home that night. Nothing but most necessary business allowed the monks to stay all night outside their enclosure, and the Abbot made energetic protests. "May God forgive you, sister!" he cried, "what *have* you done?" Then Scholastica answered merrily: "I asked you and you wouldn't listen. I asked my Lord and He *did!* Now, then, go if you can and leave me for your monastery!" So Benedict had to stay against his will. We like to imagine that he did not really regret the hours as they passed; for the narrator pictures them eagerly telling each other all night the secrets of their life in God. And for Gregory there is a glad moral in the ending. "No wonder," he observes, "that the woman's larger love won victory over the brother's lawful judgment of what was fitting. For God is love." And Peter, the young deacon to whom Gregory is telling this for his instruction, remarks: "That really *is* a delightful story!"

At dawn, Gregory goes on, Scholastica went back to her cloister and Benedict to his. On the third day afterward, as he was sitting in his cell, he looked up and saw the soul of his sister as a dove flying beyond his sight into the clouds that hide Heaven. That, then, told clearly why she had craved a long, last talk, and he rejoiced, giving thanks to God. Some of the brethren went at once at his bidding to bring her body to Monte Cassino, where they placed it in the tomb which he had made ready for himself. "Thus it came about that their bodies were not separated in death, even as they had always been of one mind in God."

Another vision which Gregory describes as given to the eyes of Benedict holds yet further marvel.[30] Servandus, a deacon, was Abbot of a monastery not far from Monte Cassino, built by the Liberius of whom we have read as Prefect of the Goths in Gaul under Theodoric the Great. He came to visit the Father and was given a cell just underneath that of Benedict, connected with it by a little stairway. That night the Father rose in the darkness toward the hour of Vigils and stood at the window absorbed in prayer. Suddenly in the deep quiet a great splendour flooded the black depths of the sky and lighted up all from east to west; as he watched spellbound, it seemed to him as if all the world stood revealed to him under one single ray of the sun. A moment he gazed as at a quivering sea of flame, and then he saw the soul of Germanus, Bishop of Capua, borne by angels in a ball of fire to Heaven. Benedict at first could not believe his eyes, and called loudly two or three times to Servandus to come up quickly. No more, certainly, could Servandus believe his ears, when he heard these extraordinary sounds breaking the Great Silence from the mouth of the Abbot himself, always a pattern of unruffled calm and obedience to the Rule. He rushed up with great perturbation, just in time to catch a glimpse of the waning glory. Soon after it was heard that Germanus had in truth departed this life at that very hour.

As we shall find from other narrative of Gregory, records of such visions were not rare in these days among those whose inward eyes were strong through the prayer of faith.[31] Concerning this revelation to the Father Founder, Gregory explains to Peter that Benedict could see all the world thus

[30] *Dial.* II, 35.   [31] IV, 7.

in a ray of light because to him that sees by the light of God all creation is a very little thing. The soul that sees by this radiance is lifted up above itself to see what in its own little-ness it could not see, to look upon all created things lying for this one moment below it, as it gazes forth from its rest in God.

Other visions were sad. We learn, also from Gregory, that Benedict prophesied to the Bishop of Canosa, the Canusium of ancient history in Apulia: "Rome shall not be destroyed by the barbarians; for by dint of thunderstorms and whirl-winds and earthquakes she is perishing within herself." Gregory then goes on: "The mysteries of this prophecy are now clear to us as the daylight. We behold in this city walls shattered, houses overthrown, churches destroyed by hurri-cane; we see her buildings perishing by long decay, falling in ruin that increases more and more." [32]

The prophecy, then, had already been fulfilled when Gregory wrote, so far as his time was concerned. The same is true of another prediction of Benedict, equally a matter of accomplished fact when Gregory was writing of it in his *Dialogues*. A nobleman named Theopropus, a convert and spiritual son of Benedict, found him one day in his cell with tears of distress in his eyes. The disciple waited till the tears should turn to prayers, as he confidently expected. But they continued to flow. Then he asked the reason of this trouble and was answered at once: "All this monastery which I have built and made ready for the brethren has been given over to the barbarians by the judgment of Almighty God. Scarcely have I prevailed that the lives of all in this place should be granted me." Gregory then describes the descent of the Lombards upon the monastery between 580 and 589. All its monks did, indeed, escape safely to Rome.

[32] II, 15.

The same second book of the *Dialogues* tells of the passing of Benedict. It happened shortly after Totila went to see him at Monte Cassino, and he was, therefore, it would seem, somewhat over sixty years old. Six days before his death he gave order that his tomb should be opened, and in a few hours he was lying in the grip of acute fever. On the sixth day he told his brethren to carry him to the Chapel. There he fortified himself against his approaching departure by his last communion, and at the end stood held by the arms of his spiritual sons, with hands stretched out toward heaven to breathe out his last breath in prayer.

On that day two of his brethren, one in his monastery, the other far away, had one and the same vision. They seemed to see a path strewn with material woven in many colours and radiant with innumerable lamps, stretching from Benedict's cell eastward straight up into the sky. Then there appeared near it a man clothed in bright apparel, who declared to them: "This is the way by which Benedict, beloved of the Lord, ascended into Heaven."

Monte Cassino, restored in the eighth century, became famous throughout Europe. In the ninth century its monks were again forced to flee, this time before the Saracens, and once again in 949 they returned to their own home. The eleventh century saw its glory supreme, when in 1071 under the Abbot Desiderius the work of rebuilding and beautifying its Church was hallowed by consecration at the hands of Pope Alexander the second. One of the chronicles of Monte Cassino describes the scene: "News of the event spread abroad far and wide. So great a multitude flocked thither for the appointed day: bishops from well-nigh the whole of Italy, abbots, monks, clergy, leading laymen, nobles and burghers, men and women of divers sorts and conditions—it were easier to count the stars in heaven than the vast number of them all. On all the secular buildings of the monastery and the very roofs of these buildings, on all the paths of the Mount from foot to summit, on all the houses of this City, if I may term it so, in all its open spaces, in all the level ground available far and near around it people swarmed and pressed, packed fast in solid wedges that they might gain a glimpse of these most solemn rites. For the three days before and after the great event such an abundant array of bread and of wine, of various meats and plenitude of fish were set forth in public that scarce one in so innumerable a gathering could be found who did not declare himself well satisfied."

There follows an awe-inspiring list of ten archbishops who were present, forty-four bishops, three princes, two dukes, no small gathering of counts, and of other potentates and nobles from North and South, a number impossible to estimate. The chronicler finally borrows from the verses in which Saint Paulinus of Nola praised his dear Saint Felix words wherein to depict the throngs that assembled at Monte Cassino in the week of this solemnity.[33]

The records of the monastery never afterward recaptured in things external the high standing of that day. Its subsequent history shows constant struggle and strife. In the fourteenth century Monte Cassino was made by Rome a diocese in itself, under authority of its Priest-Abbot for its governing; but this tended to cut it off in practice from the Catholic world outside, and its importance steadily waned. Later on, renewed efforts were made to revive its growth, without permanent success. In 1866 the order for the suppression of all Italian monasteries included Monte Cassino in its action, and it is at this present time a national monument owned by the Italian Government. But it does not stand desolate. It still holds an Abbot and a Community of the Order of Saint Benedict, who keep there the rule of their

[33] *Leonis Marsicani chronica monast. Casinensis,* lib. III: Pertz, VII, pp. 719ff.

Founder and preside over a large school for boys. The Abbot still holds pontifical authority over the diocese of Monte Cassino, aided by his monks, who form the Chapter of his Church, a Cathedral and an Abbey at one and the same time. He still exercises pontifical functions, save only those reserved exclusively to one who has been consecrated bishop by conferring of Holy Order.

If we turn back once again from this point to the onset of the Dark Ages, we find that Monte Cassino held high a torch of learning and scholarship which was to lighten the shadows of the world when culture entered eclipse. The wise and practical ritual with which Benedict wrought the marriage of faith and intellect, of things contemplative and things practical in one sacrament of daily life within the cloister, bore its fruit steadily, through all the years of barbarian terror, through all the succeeding vicissitudes of invasion and recovery. It still bears its fruit wherever the sap of the branch of science rises day by day within the Tree of Life.

The study of the *ipsissima verba* of the Rule has occupied Benedictine scholars in modern times, trying to recover the original wording from the mass of extraneous matter due to the constant recitation and reading of centuries. Saint Benedict wrote the original in simple Latin words and in a style that would be as easily understood by peasants in southern Italy as by cultured noblemen from Rome. The language was that of the sixth century and, therefore, dipped in the deepening colour of mediaeval Latin; the words were not only those of the period, but those commonly spoken among the people of Campania. Yet this original text was dignified and noble in its deliberate simplicity, as meet both for the high matter of which it spoke and for the various people it would instruct. Of Holy Scripture it was naturally full. Among writers of the Catholic Church it revealed, especially, study of the *Institutes* and the *Conferences* of Cassian; of the

Lives and *Rules* of the Fathers, particularly of the Latin version of the *Rule* of Pachomius by Jerome, and of that of Basil by Rufinus; of the writings of Augustine, especially the *Letters* and the *Commentary on the Psalms;* of the writings of Jerome, in particular, of his *Letters;* of both the *Rules* of Caesarius, for monks and for nuns. Benedict knew, moreover, his Cyprian, his Ambrose, his Leo, his Sulpicius Severus on holy Martin. But his training in pagan classics can also be traced: in Terence, in Sallust, in Vergil.[34] These were all introduced for use and for illustration, not for ornament. All was as brief, in consideration of the unlettered as well as of the cultured, as might be in the exposition of so great detail of thought.

Those who would study its clauses and the changes introduced into them, largely for practical reasons, may read of them and of authorities which describe them in the works of Dom Cuthbert Butler, who has made a special study of the form of his Rule. In 1912 he published a "critical-practical" edition, a text, as he explains in his preface, "drawn from the best manuscripts, examined with the most scrupulous judgment of critical art, differing in nothing from the words of Benedict himself save for certain words of uncultured and unclassical Latin, intended by him for the convenience of his monks when reading the Rule in choir or in chapter or in their cells, but deemed inappropriate here." His labour has wrought a text both scholarly and genuine, and at the same time satisfactory for modern Benedictine use in the practice of every-day routine.[35]

Of commentaries there have been many, dating from that

[34] See the *Index Scriptorum* in the critical edition of Dom Cuthbert Butler, 1912, pp. 176ff.

[35] This edition, published by Herder, is well furnished with the history of the text and contains in footnotes passages of Latin writings on which it draws. The text itself, with the permission of the publisher, was beautifully reproduced by the Stanbrook Press in 1930. See also *Benedictine Monachism*[2], pp. 170ff.

of Paul Warnefrid (Paulus Diaconus), who wrote the *History of the Lombards* after he had become a novice in Monte Cassino at the end of the eighth century. Among others mention may be made here of the learned works in French by Dom Mège and Dom Martène, published in 1687 and in 1690 respectively, and that of Calmet, published in 1732. The best modern commentary, by Dom Paul Delatte, published in the translation of Dom Justin McCann in 1921, is not only learned in historical knowledge, but illuminating in its spiritual content.[36]

We have seen sundry facts that point toward Cassiodorus as moulding his discipline on these lines. There is no such attractive evidence for Caesarius, and as Caesarius became Bishop of Arles nearly thirty years before Benedict established his Rule, it is easier to forego the theory of any influence of Monte Cassino on the monasteries founded by the Bishop in that city.[37] The convent of Holy Cross in Poitiers and many others in Gaul followed the example of Arles and kept alive in the seventh century the discipline of Caesarius. More wide-spread in Gaul was the Rule of Columban, mother of many daughter houses scattered through the land. The final victory of Benedict's monastic way of life was inevitable in its supreme wisdom and practicability: the outcome, as, indeed, were all these Rules, of a life lived in obedience to the counsel: *non velle dici sanctum antequam sit, sed prius esse quod verius dicatur.*[38]

[36] On these commentaries see *Benedictine Monachism*[2], pp. 177ff. That by Martène is reproduced in Migne, *PL* LXVI.

[37] Cf. Butler, *Bened. Mon.*, p. 165 with Chapman, *St. B. and the Sixth Century*, pp. 75ff. The words *opus Dei* used by Caesarius of the monastic office (*Rule for Nuns*, 10) can be traced to Lérins (*Bened. Mon.*, p. 30, note). Against the theory of Dom John Chapman (p. 204) that Benedict deliberately wrote a Rule for all monasteries of the West at the bidding of the Pope, probably Hormisdas, see Dom Cuthbert Butler, *Downside Review*, 48, 1930, pp. 186ff.; and Dom Fernand Cabrol, *Dublin Review*, July, 1930, pp. 126ff.

[38] *Rule of Benedict*, c. 4. For the gradual victory of the Benedictine life see Zöckler, *Askese und Mönchtum*, II, pp. 371ff.

CHAPTER IV

SAINT GREGORY THE GREAT

FROM the greatest of monks we come last of all to the greatest of the Popes, a Pope himself a monk, called from the contemplation of the cloister to struggle day and night in active labours: for the Church in Rome, for the last remnants of the Roman Empire, for strangers and barbarians throughout the known world. In temporal matters his own genius for practical affairs, his energy and his experience gained in civil government stood ready for Italy's need; the failure of the Imperial throne in Constantinople and of its representative in Ravenna gave over to him as Pope the burden of her administration and of her defence from enemies, already possessed of her lands, marching on to threaten Rome. Herein lay the seed, as yet unripened, which developed after his time into the temporal power of the mediaeval Papacy. In matters of the spirit he spread far and wide the influence of Rome as the Metropolitan Church of all the world and held high her Bishop's claim as Chief Pastor and Father of both East and West. Herein lay the spiritual foundation of the See of Rome in the Middle Ages. Yet his keen sense of justice protected the rights of each individual Church as zealously as his loyalty to the See of Peter demanded allegiance from all; his humility saw and acknowledged his own shortcomings as eagerly as his sense of Papal dignity bade him exact honour from all his subjects in religion; his grasp of detail and quick ability in affairs directed matters great and small throughout the world which he held his diocese; his compassion and charity extended from the inner organization of Rome in an ever-widening sweep, embracing missionaries, monks, nuns, layfolk, wherever poverty and sickness reached his ears and his heart. In matters of intellect he presented a curious contrast. Possessed of the ablest mind in Rome, and trained in the best education his time could give, he fiercely subjected thought to faith in a subordination which admitted of little fellowship. Intellect for its own sake was nothing to him. The world, he firmly believed, was drawing to its end, an end already foretold by dread signs and portents. Let none, therefore, waste precious time in vain studies of secular things. The Bible and the Fathers of the Church, Ambrose and Augustine in particular, gave ample light upon the path of penitence and charity, and happy those who found before too late their way therein. Even the pastors and leaders of the flock, he judged, should heed learned writings only so far as they might use them to direct and defend the Faith and its children. Was not the scourge of God visiting the present world in wrath for men's offences in His sight? All the Church's ministry was needed to call men to repentance before the hour of salvation was over, to warn, to counsel, to encourage souls, to feed and tend the bodies of the naked, the hungry and the sick. Miracles, therefore, he welcomed gladly on scantiest evidence, as meat and drink for the brethren's faith in hour of peril and temptation, as beacons for those still sitting in the night of pagan idolatry. His eager credence in marvel wrought by holy men during life and after death, in all kinds of supernatural workings, stands out sharply distinct from the sound and shrewd workings of his brain in practical matters both mundane and ecclesiastical. Herein his influence paved the road to the superstition and easy credulity rife in the mediaeval Church.

The year 540, according to the best evidence available, saw his birth in Rome of a family renowned in annals of Church and State.[1] The names of senators were found among them; his mother Silvia and two of his aunts, Tarsilla and Aemiliana, are honoured by Feast Days in the Calendar of Saints;[2] a Pope, Felix, probably the fourth, was his ancestor. His father, Gordianus, was an official of wealth and of standing in religious and administrative circles; his title *Regionarius* seems to show that he transacted secular business for the Church.[3] The son's devotion presented his family house at a later day with portraits in painting of his parents, and his biographer, John the Deacon, who saw them in the ninth century, describes the tall figure of Gordianus, slightly bearded, grave of countenance, clad in chestnut-coloured mantle, while Silvia appears with round fair face, now wrinkled, but still showing traces of great beauty. Her large blue-gray eyes twinkle with merriment, and her hand points to the words of the Psalter she holds: "My soul lives and shall praise Thee." After her husband's death she sought the retirement of a monastic cell in Rome, near the Church of St. Paul.

Gregory himself tells us of his two aunts, who lived under strict religious rule in their own home. A third sister, Gordiana, also lived with them. But she, sad to relate, though she had bound herself by the same vow, was fatally attracted

---

[1] Much of our knowledge of Gregory the Great comes from his own writings. Other documents of importance are: (1) From the 6th century itself: the short account in the *Liber Pontificalis* (ed. Duchesne, p. 312), used by later authorities, and the *History of the Franks* by Gregory of Tours; (2) From the 7th century: Isidore of Seville (*De vir. ill.* 40) and Ildefonsus of Toledo (*De vir. ill.* 1); (3) From the 8th century: *Life of Gregory*, by an unknown monk of Whitby, ed. Gasquet, 1904; Bede, *Ecclesiastical History;* Paul the Deacon, *Life of Gregory* (PL LXXV), and *History of the Lombards;* (4) From the 9th century: John the Deacon, *Life of Gregory* (PL LXXV). The best modern authority in English is F. Homes Dudden, *Gregory the Great,* vols. 1 and 2, 1905.

[2] December 24; January 5.   [3] Dudden, I, p. 6.

by the world she had forsaken and loved to talk with visitors from without. Meanwhile the eldest sister, Tarsilla, waxed keener and holier day by day, till in the darkness of one Advent the Pope Felix who adorned their family appeared to her in a vision and bade her come to him in the dwelling of light. Just before Christmas Day she was seized with fever and died; those who prepared her body for burial found her knees rough and hard as a camel's through her long hours of prayer. In a few days her sister Aemiliana had a like visitation. In the night Tarsilla stood near her. "Come," she cried, "I spent the Lord's Birthday without thee, but together we will keep the Feast of the Epiphany." So Aemiliana also departed. Then Gordiana threw aside all restraint and ended by marrying her steward; "forgetful," as Gregory puts it, "of the fear of the Lord, of decent feeling and modesty, and of her consecrated life." [4]

The family mansion of Gordianus stood in the centre of Rome on the Caelian Mount. It looked out on the *Clivus Scauri*, the "slope of Scaurus," built where now the modern pilgrim finds the Church of Saint Gregory facing the Via di Santi Giovanni e Paolo. From it Gregory as he grew up looked out upon a Rome far different from that in which Theodoric and Cassiodorus had gloried at the beginning of our century and our tale. Rome's great buildings still stood, but in ruins; her theatres could still be seen, but the races and spectacles that had entranced her people in the time of Cassiodorus had long been dead; her magistrates and generals still held office, but robbed of much of their power and life. The hand of war had brought the substance of the

---

[4] *Hom. in Evang.* II, 38, 15; *Dial.* IV, 16. The works of Gregory the Great are found in *PL* LXVI; LXXV–LXXIX. For the *Dialogues* see the edition of Umberto Moricca, 1924, and the trans. of 1608, ed. E. G. Gardner, 1911. The Letters have been edited in *M.G.H.* Epist. Tom. I (ed. Ewald) and II (ed. Hartmann).

Eternal City to a mere shadow of its former self. Four times during Gregory's childhood Rome changed hands; now captured by Totila, now recaptured by Belisarius; and we may picture him carried by his parents to the rich lands in Sicily which formed part of his father's estate, far from the suffering of siege after siege, of famine and slaughter and disease. When he was fourteen, Narses entered upon his governorship of Italy, and in the less troubled years that follower Gordianus, again busy in work at Rome, superintended his son's preparation for public life and office.

The boy received the training that Rome's impoverished schools could offer after barbarians had worked havoc and distraction to buildings and books and regular courses of study. He learned what the sixth century could still teach of literature and rhetoric, of dialectic and law, more especially of law, as more practical in those difficult days. Of Greek he tells us he knew nothing all his life. At the best he could not be expected to pursue calmly in Rome all that Cassiodorus was at this time prescribing for his monks in the peace of Vivarium.

In 568, as he neared the end of his twenties, the Lombards descended upon Italy under their King Alboin, and from that time he lived in the lengthening shadow of their advance. The story of his early manhood is not clearly told us, but his family's record, his own ability and serious purpose, his popularity and his circle of friends must have carried him further year by year in public notice and regard. And so, not long after his thirtieth year we find him honoured by the chief administrative office in his city, the Prefecture of Rome.[5]

---

[5] The "praetorship" mentioned by the authorities (Joh. Diac. *Vita*, I, 4; Greg. *Epp*. IV, 2) is unsatisfactory, since it seems at this time to have gone out of use, and *praefecturam* has been thought a better reading: see Dudden, I, p. 101; Hodgkin, V, p. 288, note 1.

We have seen the efforts of Theodoric and his loyal secretary Cassiodorus to honour and illuminate the various civil ministries of Rome. In this year of Gregory's office, 573,[6] her Prefect still impressed the crowd as he rode past in his chariot, splendid in robes of State. But his actual responsibility was no longer inspired by the keen vision of Theodoric. Narses, recalled to Constantinople in 567, had now been replaced by the Imperial legate Longinus, governing in Italy for the Emperor in Constantinople; and although Longinus and his successors, excepting only Smaragdus, did little to aid the wretched state of Italy during the last quarter of this century, yet they were her supreme rulers, under the Emperor's control alone. Under the legate's general pre-eminence the Prefect of Rome still superintended the financial accounts and the provision of food for the City, regulated her police and judged her criminals, cared for her buildings and their protection, presided over her Senate. But now her Senate was a body in name rather than in authority, her people were worn out by sufferings, her civil exchequer was depleted.

Moreover, the menace of the Lombards was throwing more and more power into the hands of the military, as distinct from the civil administration. In 572 they had taken Pavia, and when Gregory was Prefect already held in their control most of northern and central Italy. Imperial Italy still guarded some of the more important cities in these parts, among them Padua, Cremona, Genoa; Ravenna and her five neighbouring towns; Rome and the adjacent lands in Latium. Further south her best surviving possessions were Naples and the territories of Calabria, the Bruttii and Sicily. But already at this date the great Lombard dukedoms of Spoleto and Benevento were being formed for the terror of Italy both north and south of Rome.

[6] Ewald, ed. Greg. *Epp.* I, p. 234, note 7.

The situation was depressing in the extreme. With all his initiative and energy Gregory could hope to accomplish very little for his people while he remained a civil magistrate. It is not surprising, then, that other thoughts began more and more insistently to make themselves heard in his mind. His training in a Christian home, his childhood and youth spent among the ravages of wars past and rumors of wars to come, his own serious spirit, looking ever above the present and the visible to things beyond—all these had combined for years to foster discontent with empty or, at least, ineffectual workings in the secular world. He was about thirty-three and a Prefect of but short standing when his ponderings came suddenly to decision. His father was now dead, his mother had withdrawn to her solitude of prayer, and he was possessed of all they had left. With part of his inheritance he built and endowed six monasteries in Sicily on his paternal estates; the rest he gave to the poor, leaving just sufficient to furnish and support in decent poverty a monastic retreat in his own family house on the Caelian Hill. The eager gossip of Rome received a final shock when the news ran abroad that its wealthy Prefect and most prominent citizen had entered this monastery of St. Andrew, not as its Lord Abbot, but as a humble monk.

Once within its walls Gregory proceeded busily to prepare the physical pains which beset him through all his later years. He had never been strong, and now unceasing prayer and fasting ruined his digestion and played havoc with his heart. We are told that he lived on raw vegetables, sent him by his mother in a silver dish, the one lordly relic she had allowed herself from all the family treasures. Her son, the story goes, in lack of other means of charity, gave it away to a shipwrecked sailor begging alms. But the beggar turned out to be an angel in disguise, and henceforth Gregory's prayers were blessed with marvellous fruit.[7] Another story wit-

[7] Joh. Diac. *Vita*, I, 10.

nesses to the strictness of his zeal as monk. One Holy Saturday he was overcome with anguish because his weakened body could no longer fast, even on this, the most solemn of Vigils. So he called to his aid a fellow-monk named Eleutherius, a man so holy that report credited to his prayers the raising of the dead to life, and begged him to intercede with Heaven on his behalf. Scarcely had Eleutherius risen from his knees when Gregory felt his strength renewed, abstained happily from all food till the evening, and felt perfectly ready to carry on for another twenty-four hours.[8]

Without doubt these years in their service of perfect liberty were the happiest of his life. Whether now and again the thought rose within him that his powers of mind and spirit might again find work for the Church in a more public sphere we do not know. It would be but human. Yet his own words show the craving that never left him throughout his days of active toil in the future: the home-sickness for that absorption in prayer which the cloister offered to its monks.

Neither do we know, in certain fact, whether these monks of St. Andrew looked to Benedict as their first Father. But, if not in all its detail, we may think that much of the Benedictine Rule was followed by Gregory and his brethren in their House, founded some thirty years after Benedict had gone to God.

In 574, about the time that our postulant had entered his monastery, Benedict the first had been elected Pope of Rome. Perhaps to this period we may assign the story, if it be only true, which tells of Gregory's missionary vigour.[9] We read

---

[8] ibid. I, 8; Dial. III, 33.

[9] The earliest Life of Gregory (by the unknown monk of Whitby) names Benedict as the Pope here concerned (ed. Gasquet, cc. ixf.). Bede gives no name for the Pope. John the Deacon (Vita I, 22) follows the Whitby Life; Paul the Deacon (Vita, 19) names Pelagius (II), apparently in error. The Whitby Life speaks of the Angles as visitors to Rome, not as slaves, and represents Gregory conversing directly with them. I have followed here, however, the narrative given by Bede: H.E. II, 1.

that as the young monk passed through the Forum one day his eye fell on some boys stationed there for sale, good to look upon with their blue eyes and clear skin and pleasant, open faces. Gregory was interested, and asked whence they came. From the island of Britain, he was told. "Christians or pagans?" he asked, and the answer came: "Pagans." "Oh! what a pity!" he sighed, "that the Lord of Darkness should possess beings so full of light, and that these fair foreheads should hide minds sick and void of inner happiness! What do they call their race?" "Angles." "Good! for their faces are those of angels, and truly they should be fellow-heirs of the angels in heaven. From what province were they brought?" He was informed that they came from the Deiri, dwellers in Deira of Northumbria. "Good!" he remarked again; " 'Deiri' they are, rescued *de ira,* from wrath, and called to the mercy of Christ. How name you the King of that province?" When he heard that the King was called Alle, he made a merry pun on *Alleluia,* saying that fittingly should the praise of God be sung in those parts.

The story goes on to relate that Gregory went at once to Pope Benedict and begged that missionaries might be sent to Britain, himself among them. Consent was given most reluctantly, after many pleadings, and he set out with the Papal blessing, most careful to hide the news of this sudden departure from the people of Rome. But the fact leaked out, and the Pope was mobbed on his way to St. Peter's by crowds yelling in rage: "Descendant of the Apostles, what hast thou done? Thou hast offended Saint Peter! Thou hast destroyed Rome! Thou hast sent forth Gregory into exile!" Benedict was so perturbed that he sent messengers post-haste to bid the young man come back.

Before they had time to reach him, however, Gregory himself had decided to return. He had travelled already three days, and on the fourth his little band were camping for rest at noon in a meadow. The monk had fallen to his prayers when suddenly a locust settled on the page he was reading in his breviary. It was a calling from God, he told his companions. "Locusta": that meant "Loco sta," "stay in your accustomed place," and obediently he followed the riders who now arrived panting for breath.

It is a pleasant tale, though puns may well seem more suited to our Irish Abbot Columban than to this serious monk of Rome, for all his addiction to mystic allegory.

Gregory's conventual peace was all too short. If not in Britain, then among the poor of Rome, Benedict had active works of mercy for his hand. After four years of retreat he was ordered out from his seclusion to assist the Pope's labours cf charity as Seventh Deacon, administering for this end the business of one of the seven regions of Rome. Shortly afterward Benedict died, and his successor, Pelagius the second, Pope from 579 till 590, saw still further use for the young servant of the Church. The Lombards were pressing now to the gates of Rome; without men and money for their support all would soon be lost; famine was rampant and citizens were terrified. Tiberius the second, since 578 Emperor in Constantinople, had directed little of his enthusiastic spending of the public funds toward his afflicted subjects in the West. Pelagius deemed it his duty to inform and inspire this negligent monarch and despatched a deputation to Constantinople. At its head travelled Gregory, now honoured with the office and responsibility of Papal legate in the Eastern court.[10]

For nearly seven years Gregory lived in the Greek capital of the Empire. It was a dreary change from his cell under Saint Andrew's roof. Of the Greek language, as we have noted, he knew nothing. His duties brought him into daily

[10] *Apocrisarius* or *responsalis* was his official title.

contact with Eastern courtiers, whose fluent insincerities and deep abasement before their sovereign his Roman gravity could neither appreciate nor understand. In wonder, perhaps not untinged by patriotic jealousy, he contrasted the splendour of this "New Rome" with the decaying ruins of that city on the Tiber which for so many ages had been mistress of the world. He saw money poured out by Tiberius: gifts in profusion to soldiers and to men of all kinds of callings, in law, medicine, finance, arts and crafts; he saw soldiers in great numbers recruited for the Eastern armies and abundant provision for their needs. But little answer was given to his repeated pleas for Italy. In 582 Tiberius died, bequeathing to his general, Maurice, his throne, his daughter as wife, and an exhausted Treasury.

The new ruler found awaiting him no money for his own needs, far less for those of a distant part of his Empire, and Pelagius wrote all in vain desperate words to his legate. "Speak with the Emperor," he bade; "discuss with him how you may give us speedy help in our perils. For the State is brought to such stress that unless God put it into the heart of our most pious Lord to bestow that pity which is truly his upon his subjects, unless in our misery he deign to grant us one Master of the Soldiers or one duke, we shall be destitute, encompassed by every danger. Everywhere Roman territories are left defenceless without aid." [11]

Baffled in his attempts to fulfil his mission at Court, Gregory found pleasanter occupation in the retirement of his own privacy. A number of his brethren had accompanied him from the monastery in Rome, and with them he continued to live so far as he could under its rule, looking to their companionship for solace and refreshment in the surging life of Constantinople, "bound to the peaceful shore of prayer as

[11] Pelagii *Epp. PL* LXXII, 704; Joh. Diac. *Vita* I, 32.

by an anchor's rope." [12] He made other friends, also, whose aim for soul and body was akin to his own; especially Leander, afterward Bishop of Seville, who had converted the Visigothic Hermenegild to the Catholic faith and was prudently living in exile after this prince had revolted against his father Leovigild, King of Spain. With Leander and his own monks Gregory would happily discuss various problems of Holy Scripture, and was persuaded at last to enter upon a course of informal lectures on the Book of Job. Other names, first familiar to him during his stay at Constantinople, we shall find in the correspondence he carried on later from his Chair in Rome.

The death of Tiberius took place in the same year as that of Eutychius, Patriarch of Constantinople, whose amicable relations with the Papal legate had been rudely interrupted by a controversy on the nature of the soul.[18] Eutychius maintained that the body of our resurrection would be impalpable to the touch. This Gregory stoutly denied, and the argument grew so fierce that at length Tiberius intervened, listened to the views of each disputant separately in a private conference, and finally decided that the book in which Eutychius had stated his doctrine should be destroyed by fire. At this point both theologians fell seriously ill, Eutychius, indeed, with fatal result. On his deathbed he seems to have changed his mind; for some of Gregory's friends who visited him told afterward that the Patriarch touched his hand and declared to them, "I confess that we shall all rise again in this flesh." Gregory now lived for some years in peace with the next Patriarch, a Bishop of so great abstinence from earthly joys that he is known to history as John "the Faster." His piety evoked sincere admiration from the Papal legate, and the two for long were on very friendly terms.

[12] Paul Diac. *Vita*, 7; Bede, *H.E.* II, 1.   [18] *Moralia*, XIV, 72ff.

But in 585 or 586, to his intense relief, Gregory was re-called to Rome by Pelagius and allowed once again to enter his monastery on the Caelian Hill. During this second sojourn he was installed as Abbot by the voice of his brethren and showed all his old enthusiasm in his ruling of the House. His love for his sons did not spare them, if we may judge from a story told by himself.[14] One of the monks, Justus by name, was skilled in medicine and used to care for Gregory with great devotion in his constant attacks of sickness. At last, however, Justus in his turn fell ill, so gravely that the breth-ren were warned he could not live. On his deathbed he con-fessed to his own brother, who as one of the physicians of Rome was permitted to attend him, that he had hoarded in secret three gold coins. The brother was naturally horrified at this violation of one of the strictest ordinances of the monas-tic Rule, and felt himself in duty bound to reveal the sin to Gregory, as Abbot.

The Father acted at once to save both this son of his from punishment hereafter and others from daring a like offence on earth. He gave orders that not one of the Community should stand by their sinful companion at the hour of his departing, and that when he asked for them as his death approached, his brother in blood was to tell him that for his secret crime he was held in loathing by all his fellow-monks. When he was dead, his body was not to be placed in the brethren's cemetery but thrown into a ditch on some dunghill and his three gold coins cast upon it, while the monks were to cry in chorus: "Thy money perish with thee!" Thus it might be, the Abbot hoped, that punishment in this world might bring redemption in the next.

So it fell. The brother died in misery and abject penitence and was buried as prescribed. All the rest of the Community

[14] *Dial.* IV, 55; Joh. Diac. *Vita*, I, 15f.

were so alarmed by his fate that they came one after another
to Father Abbot to show him even articles they were allowed
by the Rule to keep for their use. A month went by, and
Gregory began to feel uncomfortable at the thought of this
poor soul departed under penance. He commanded, therefore, that the Holy Sacrifice be offered for his intention every
morning for the next thirty days; this done, he returned in
peace to the busy round of his office and lost count of time.
Then one night the physician had a dream. Justus appeared
to his brother and said: "Up till now I have been miserable.
But now all is well, for I received communion to-day." When
he hurried with his news to the monks of Saint Andrew's, it
was found that the thirty days of oblation had just come to
an end.

In the meantime outside the walls of Gregory's peace the
world of Italy was still struggling with despair. Rome, it is
true, had not been taken by the Lombards. But their en-
croachment on Imperial territory steadily advanced, and in
589 to troubles from human source were added fresh miseries
at Nature's hands. The waters of the Tiber rose to a height
almost without precedent, working destruction untold to buildings and to the city's stores of food. Disease followed upon
flood and starvation, and a fearful outbreak of plague laid
citizens low on every side. In the following year Pelagius the
second himself yielded to its attack.

At this crucial hour clergy and people in Rome alike held
the Abbot of St. Andrew's their one salvation and called upon
him to govern its See. The moment had come. Its sudden
advent filled him with terror as it summoned him back to that
life in contact with the world from which he had twice tried
to escape. He wrote off an entreaty to the Emperor Maurice
at Constantinople begging him to refuse his consent. But he
wrote in vain; Germanus, Prefect of Rome, intercepted the

letter and substituted one which declared the desire of the
city that Gregory should be its Pope.[15] Maurice himself was
well pleased. His personal feeling for the former Papal legate
was one of great respect and friendliness, even if he had dis-
regarded his petitions for Rome; and Gregory was godfather
of his eldest son, Theodosius.

It was perhaps happy for the Pope-elect that patriotic compassion for this shepherdless city filled his mind now with
practical thought of the present. Assuming for this moment
of necessity the leadership he hoped eventually to avoid, he
delivered a sermon to the assembled people on the crying need
of penitence in this day of wrath. As a corporate expression
of repentance and faith in God he directed them to gather at
dawn on the following Wednesday, assembled in seven separate companies, of minor clergy, monks, nuns, children, laymen, widows and wives, all led by priests, at the seven prin-
cipal churches of the seven regions of Rome. All were then
to march with solemn procession and chant of *Kyrie eleison*
to the great Cathedral on the Esquiline, now the Church of
S. Maria Maggiore. The well and the sick, the hopeful and
the despairing marched out at the appointed time; but so
heavy was the hand of disease upon the multitude that a
deacon who was present told his Bishop, Gregory of Tours,
that within the space of one hour during their march eighty
persons fell dying to the ground.[16]

Long afterward it was said that Gregory and his vast chorus
of litany proceeded also to St. Peter's to offer their prayers.
As they reached the Bridge of Hadrian on their way, he looked
up suddenly and saw on the highest point of Hadrian's Tomb
the Archangel Michael replacing in its sheath his flaming

[15] Confirmation of episcopal elections, including that of the See of
Rome, by the Emperor at Constantinople dates from the reign of Justinian.
[16] For details see Gregory of Tours, *H.F.* X, 1; Paul. Diac. *Vita*, 1 off.;
Hist. Lang. III, 24.

sword of vengeance: a sign that God had accepted the people's penitence, and that the plague would now be stayed. In the tenth century this tradition had already changed the name of Hadrian's Tomb to the Castle of the Angel, where now the statue of Saint Michael stands to commemorate this tale.[17]

The news now arrived that Maurice delighted in Gregory's election. In panic the Bishop-elect fled from the city. His earliest *Life*, narrated by a monk of Whitby, told that he was carried out in a basket of wares and lay concealed for three days while the people sought him with prayer and fasting. On the third night a brilliant ray shot from heaven to reveal his hiding-place. He was captured, borne in triumph to St. Peter's and consecrated Pope of Rome.

What his holy Ordering meant to Gregory he has revealed in his *Pastoral Rule:* a work that struck home in its simple sincerity and became the standard by which the Church bade her bishops in different lands examine their own consciences. From southern Spain Licinianus, Bishop of Carthagena, wrote in generous admiration. The book, he declared, was a King's court of all virtues, and he felt perfectly foul beside this picture of things that were lovely, and their realization in Gregory's life. "I am bound to say," he went on, "that your teachings don't hold good here. You tell us to consecrate only men well prepared. Well, when we can't find men who are ready for the work of a bishop, what can we do but take the unready, like myself?" [18] We have seen the joy of the Irish Abbot Columban as he read its counsels in Burgundy.[19] In the East the Emperor Maurice requested Anastasius the

[17] Gregorovius, *Hist. of City of Rome in the Middle Ages*[4], trans. Hamilton, II, p. 33.

[18] Greg. *Epp.* I, 41a.

[19] See my page 463. The *Pastoral Rule* has been translated by Barmby, 1874, and, together with Selected Letters of Gregory, in *Nicene and Post-Nicene Fathers*, XII.

second, Patriarch of Antioch, to translate it into Greek and vexed Gregory very much by "taking away the Patriarch's time from better things." [20] In the eighth century the Venerable Bede exhorted Egbert, then Bishop of York, to study it together with the Epistles of Saint Paul to Timothy and Titus.[21] Alcuin wrote to his "dearest son Simeon," Eanbald the second, Archbishop of the same See and once his own pupil, that he should carry it wherever he went, read and re-read it, and learn from its words how he ought to live and teach: "For it is a mirror of the pontifical life, and medicine against all the wounds of the devil's guile." [22] In Gaul of the ninth century Hincmar, Archbishop of Reims, writing a strong letter of rebuke to his assistant bishop and nephew, Hincmar of Laon, reminded him of his consecration: "when, before the altar of Saint Mary, in the presence of all the congregation, I put into your hand the book of the sacred canons and the *Pastoral Rule* of blessed Gregory, calling on you, as God should grant you knowledge and power, so to live and teach and judge as was therein laid down." [23] Similarly, the aristocratic Thegan in his *Life* of Louis, son of Charlemagne, stated as climax to a terrific indictment of the ignoble bishops of his time that "they will not accept the *Pastoral Book* of blessed Gregory." [24] Four Councils of the Church of Gaul, held by order of Charlemagne in 813, were concerned with its instructions. At Mayence it lay on the front benches, ready for reference; at Reims the Fathers in God listened to extracts from its pages; study of its precepts was urged upon those assembled at Chalon-sur-Saône, commanded for those at Tours.[25] In England King Alfred with the help of certain of

[20] *Epp.* XII, 6.   [21] H. and S. III, pp. 314f.
[22] *ibid.* p. 505. Cf. Alcuin's counsels to the bishops Arno and Speratus and to the priest Calvinus: *PL* C, 196, 242, 248.
[23] *PL* CXXVI, 292.
[24] Pertz, II, p. 595.   [25] Mansi, XIV, pp. 64, 78, 93, 84.

his clergy translated it into English, as one of the books "most necessary to be known," and declared that England first knew it when Augustine brought it to her shores.[26]

It is, indeed, a book worthy of a writer whose words earned from the people of Rome the praise of "golden-mouthed." [27] Gregory offered it in the first place to his "fellow-bishop John," probably his friend and fellow-member of the Church of Italy, Bishop of Ravenna.[28] John had reproached Gregory for trying to hide when called to bear the burdens of the Papal See, and now, soon after he had assumed them, the Pope composed this apology. Now he who blamed should understand how heavy Gregory held the responsibility of a bishop to be.

The *Pastoral Rule* begins with the sins and shortcomings which tempt those who are called, or think themselves to be called, to the shepherding of men. First, the sin of rash presumption. No layman ventures on profession of any art in the world unless he has given it long and careful study. Who that does not understand the properties of drugs will dare call himself a doctor? Yet those who have never learned the precepts of the spiritual life are not afraid to declare themselves its physicians, and to practise unashamed without preparation that very art of arts, the direction of souls. In seeking to become bishops of the Church such men are really coveting earthly fame. Of necessity their flocks must sin, seeing that they follow a leader blinded in the ignorance of his pride.

Others truly study their art in theory, but care not to practise it in their own lives. These do but lead their people down

---

[26] ed. H. Sweet, *E.E.T.S.* 1871; see also G. F. Browne, *King Alfred's Books,* 1920.

[27] So, at least, the Whitby *Life*, XXIV.

[28] So the authors of the three *Lives:* Whitby *Life,* c. XXXI; Paul. Diac. 14; Joh. Diac. IV, 73. Isidore of Seville and Ildefonsus of Toledo (see my note 1) state that it was written for John of Constantinople; in favour of this evidence see Schanz, p. 617.

the steeps of evil ways to the precipice of ruin. Far better that such men should remain dragged down by the millstone of secular cares to perish alone in the waves of damnation. At any rate, their punishment in hell might be lighter if they had not drawn into it their people together with themselves. A third peril is the common one of distraction. The Father in God who allows himself to become overburdened by secular cares in his diocese forgets the path he has vowed to tread; he has no time to realize how much he is losing, how great his offence. A bishop, it is true, must heed and administer matters of this world. But before he seek this office let him consider what kind of layman he once made, what kind of priest in lower Order? Those who cannot stand firmly on more level ground should not try to climb a precipice.

Again, what of those who have received from God high gifts of spirit and of mind: chastity, abstinence, learning, patience, authority and so on? Do they remember that their gifts are given them not only for themselves but for others? "A city that is set upon a hill cannot be hid." Do they shut themselves up in the beloved peace of research when they ought to be preaching sermons? Or even remain too long rapt in the joy of solitary prayer?

Here, we imagine, Gregory was thinking of his own temptations. He goes on to describe the danger of false humility. Some there are, he warns, who cry "Nolo episcopari" because they hold themselves unfitted for the work of a bishop in God's Church. Yet he is not truly humble who scorns to heed the voice of God calling him to higher place of obedience.

Let the man who is contemplating the office of a bishop stop, look, and listen ere it be too late. Let him try his character before the judge and jury of his own past life, that he may discover whether the deepest aim of his spirit is in har-

mony with the thoughts he professes to himself and to other
men; whether he has so learned humility in the plains that
he may dare ascend the heights; whether he has so guided
his skiff in quiet waters that he may hope to escape shipwreck
in the storms that await his episcopal man-of-war.

What, then, is Gregory's conception of a true Father in
God? One who fears no adversity, for his desires lie within
his soul; who covets no man's goods, but gives readily of his
meagre store; who of his charity grants quick pardon to sin,
but never against justice, nor forsakes the citadel of his own
uprightness when he bends down to forgive. His own life is
blameless, but he sorrows for the wrong-doings of others as
his own. He tries so to live in practice that he may feed and
refresh by his precepts the parched souls of his charge. He is,
above all, a man of prayer: a strong intercessor for his
people, taught by long years of experience both to discern
aright what he should ask and to hope for his petition at
the hands of the Lord he knows so well and serves so faithfully.

No wonder that Gregory feared the travail which must
bear such fruit. "In such wise," he declares, "should the
bishop excel in his manner of life as a shepherd excels his
sheep." How, indeed, shall this fruit of an ideal Pastorate
attain to ripeness? First, by constant purity of thought. The
hand that desires to cleanse the sores of other men must
itself be clean, or the last state of the soul it touches may be
worse than the first. Secondly, by binding harmony of words
and life; for hearers are better persuaded by example than
by advice. The Chief Priest shall stand before his people in
the ephod of his ministry: glorious with the gold of wisdom,
the blue of heavenly aspiration, the purple of his royal calling, the scarlet of flaming charity, doubled-dyed in colour, as
dipped in the love of God and of man. He shall be clothed

in the fine linen of his chaste life, twined and worked into shape by the labour of discipline.

The Pastor must, moreover, understand due discretion of speech and silence, that he neither lead his flock into error by hasty words nor leave them untaught in their ignorance. Discretion must be his, too, in nicely poised balance of sympathy and reserve: in near approach to all his charge in compassion, in far remoteness above all in contemplation. So Jacob saw angels ascending and descending between heaven and earth; so Moses went in and out the Tabernacle: pondering within on the deep things of God, bearing without its doors the burdens of fleshly men, the stronger to ascend the heights of prayer for the charity which stoops to dull and sordid ugliness. Let the bishop be one to whom his people will not be afraid to tell their temptations and their sins. Let him hold ready at the doors of the Church the laver of cleansing, wherein they may wash and make clean the hands of their thoughts and words. Nor let him fear lest his own mind be sullied, as the water held of old by the oxen before the Temple, by the constant tale of evil suggestion. For God will the more easily rescue him from his own weakness as he bends more readily of his love to listen to his fellow-man. At the same time let him add the stern gravity of a father to a mother's quick understanding, pouring into the wounds of his penitents both wine and oil: sympathetic but not soft, determined, yet in nothing harsh; sharer in worldly business for the sake of others alone.

The same nicety of poise is needed by the Pastor in his personal relations with his flock. Certainly he must strive to gain their affection, or they will not gladly listen to his counsels. Yet of this affection let him make for them the path which shall lead straight to the heart of God.

Such, in a few words, are some of the salient points of the

first two parts of this instruction, stripped of the mass of passages from the Bible and their allegorical interpretation which regularly takes the lion's share of Gregory's written work. The third part is a treatise on the art of preaching, full of advice on the many different needs of a congregation, according to sex, state, rank, age, fortune and endowment. Men, Gregory prescribes, must be exercised by great tasks, women led softly to a better life by light ones; with a similar sagacity bishops-elect are taught by him how to preach to clerics and to laymen, to rich and to poor, to masters and to servants, to the married and to the single, to the successful and to failures, to the wise and to the stupid, and so on. Other distinctions are made on the basis of character. Meat of sound exhortation is provided here for people patient and impatient, generous and envious, lazy and impetuous, crafty and simple, fearful and arrogant, temperant and greedy, with many others of varying degrees of virtue or of vice. A third series of skeleton addresses concerns different classes of sin: of deliberation and of impulse, of thought and of deed, mortal and venial, small and frequent, rare and grievous, repented of in confession but not attacked in daily life. Undue severity must not depress the guilty, while the virtuous are to be warned against the offences that without their knowledge often make supposedly good men their prey. He who preaches before great assemblies must bear in mind the truth *quot homines, tot mores,* and try to sprinkle from his mixed bag seed that will germinate in every heart. Let him be careful not to recommend virtue in such a way as to encourage vice, nor to scourge unduly some of his flock while he allows others to drowse content with their second-best in ways of piety. Sometimes let him pass over slight faults, if he never allows his people to imagine he does not see them; thus his patients will not be utterly cast down as they struggle with heavier sins. Never must he talk above the heads of his audience: "for all deep matters should be kept covered before a large congregation, and scarcely discussed in the presence of few listeners." Finally, as the cock shakes out its wings before it begins to crow, let the preacher of holy works stir up the grace that is within him before he ventures to show to other pilgrims the path wherein they should walk.

And so Gregory leads his brethren of the episcopate to the short sermon on humility which forms the fourth part of this *Rule for Pastors,* and ends with a prayer to John, his friend: "You see, dear Sir, how, driven by necessity of mine own shortcoming, I have laboured to show what a Pastor should truly be, and with my own smirched hands have drawn for you a saintly man; I point out to others the shore of perfection while I myself still toss upon the waves of my sins. But, I beseech you, uphold me in this shipwreck of my life by the plank of your prayer; that, though my own weight drag me down, the hand of your deserts may lift me up again."

It is interesting to compare with these counsels the sermons which Gregory actually preached to his people as Pope in Rome. We have two series composed by him: one of forty homilies on the Gospel for the day, another of twenty-two on the prophet Ezekiel.[20] The sermons on the Gospel are far simpler, as addressed to the ordinary congregation at Mass on Feasts and Fast-days. They are disappointing to the reader who comes to them fresh from the study of either Gregory's own precepts in the *Regula Pastoralis* or the sermons of Caesarius of Arles. For they seem to lack something of that care for individual needs which is so elaborately portrayed in the *Rule's* theory; and they certainly lack the definite and clear instruction with which Caesarius strove to guide the steps of his erring flock in Gaul.

[20] *PL* LXXVI, 1075ff.; 786ff.

The Pope does not deliver here details of teaching on ascetic theology and the doctrine of the Church. His addresses are exhortations to godly life, general in application; interpretations, simple in thought and in language, of the Gospel of the Mass; full of quotations from the Bible, in which he was extraordinarily well informed, packed also with his favourite explanation by allegory. Tears of penitence and solemn, even terrifying, thoughts of the Last Judgment so swiftly coming are their chief aim for their hearers; now and again a story is introduced to heighten the picture of bliss in heaven or of horror in hell. One wishes that their preacher had sometimes chosen to re-tell the stories of the Saints whose Feast-days he was honouring. But any story in a sermon was a novel feature in these days, and witnesses to the common sense and understanding of human needs which Gregory showed in all his dealings with men. He was, indeed, a Father in God, even though his high state and his multiple business with the world kept from his sermons that intimate note which we read in the discourses of Caesarius to his people on the sins and failings he knew so well. The Papal biographer, John the Deacon, tells that the Pope's sermons attracted a multitude of people: "An army of the Lord used to follow Gregory as he went hither and thither in procession, and innumerable troops of both men and women of all ages and professions would flock freely from all quarters to hear him." [30]

This collection of forty sermons at Mass, published in 593, was offered in a brief Preface to Secundinus, Bishop of Taormina in Sicily. The twenty which form the first book had been read to the congregation by Papal notaries; the twenty of the second book Gregory had himself delivered, with great labour of voice, as he confesses, in his precarious health. But the people of Rome naturally preferred this method. Even

[30] *Vita,* II, 19.

before the Pope could put the final touches to his addresses certain brethren of the Church in their pious enthusiasm, he declares, had already published them unedited: "like hungry people who want to eat their food before it is properly cooked." [81]

Emphasis upon the Four Last Things was, of course, suggested by the dire state of Italy. The preacher tells his audience that the prophesied signs and portents on earth and in the heavens are already upon them. And why should Rome dread the end of the world, vexed as she is by miseries, weary of the road through this sad life? It is strange for a tired traveller to be unwilling to reach his journey's end. "Only the day before yesterday, brethren, you saw ancient trees uprooted by a sudden storm, houses overthrown, churches torn from their foundations. How many people of sound life and limb were making plans for the morrow when they were caught that night by death, seized in a noose of destruction? . . . What, then, will the Judge do when He comes Himself and blazes forth in vengeance against sinners, if we cannot endure when He smites us with thin dissolving air? . . . What are these terrors which we behold but the heralds of wrath to come? . . . Think, therefore, beloved brethren, with all your minds upon that Day, amend your lives, change your ways, conquer temptations with resistance, punish your past deeds with weeping. If you hope to look calmly upon the coming of the Eternal Justice, prepare now for His Assize with fear." "Seek Him as witness for your life," Gregory exhorts elsewhere, "Whom you know to be its Judge.". . . "Do not think of what you have, but of what you are.". . . "Endure humbly the scourge of present purgatory that you may appear with greater purity at that Day of reckoning." [82]

[81] Preface to Bk I; Joh. Diac. *Vita*, II, 18.
[82] *Hom. in Evang.* 1; 4; 13; 15.

Stories drive home the point. We hear of the holy Servulus departing this life amid miracle of song and sweet fragrance wafted from heaven; of the pious deathbed of the lady Romula, surrounded by a halo of glory. On the other hand, careless brethren are snatched from a fearful ending only by the petitions of the agonized watchers by the bedside. Thus the gloom of barbarian enemies without and of famine and pestilence within, to say nothing of the approaching Lenten fast, is deepened for the faithful on Septuagesima Sunday by a tale of the experience of a monk in Saint Andrew's House. Gregory declared it befell the very year in which he now told it to his flock. The brother was certainly in need of correction; he hated the Monastery and its life and only stayed on there because he had nowhere else to go and no money. Worse still: he was "frivolous, unstable, conceited, vain and dissipated." "Last July," Gregory continued, while doubtless his hearers hung upon his words, "he caught that plague you all remember so well and became sick unto death. Most of his body was paralyzed, and he lay helpless, though he was still conscious of what was going on and could speak. His Community quickly gathered to aid him at this last hour, so far as by the grace of God their intercessions might still avail. All at once the sufferer uttered a loud cry: 'Oh! I am seized in the jaws of a dragon and he cannot devour me because you are here. Go away! Don't hinder him, he *must* devour me!' In terror those who stood by implored: 'Brother, make, make the holy Sign!' But he burst out with a desperate effort: 'I want to, but I can't, the dragon has me! His foaming mouth is licking my face, he is choking me, my arms are held fast and he has swallowed down my head!' Faster and faster prayed the monks, more and more earnestly they entreated mercy of Heaven. Then suddenly the victim was set free, gasping, 'Thank God! he has gone, he has departed, he has fled from your beseeching of the Lord!' Conversion followed, and partial recovery of bodily health, though in penance the sinner was constantly racked henceforth by fever and divers aches and pains for the purging of his soul's guilt." [33]

Equally impressive must have been Gregory's picture of the last moments of any soul upon earth: "We must seriously lay to heart how awful will be the hour of our dissolution: what terror of mind, what recollection of all our past sins, what forgetfulness of happiness over and gone, what dread and expectation of our coming award! How *can* we take pleasure in this world's joys when they all pass away, but that which awaits us cannot pass, when transient love ends once for all and eternal grief begins? Then malignant spirits get to their work on the departing soul; then they redouble their temptations, eager to drag one more to share their torment.". . . "See how many there are of us present here this morning; the Church is full to the doors. Yet who knows how few of us are numbered among the elect flock of God?" [34]

Yet at all times the preacher painted vividly the wideness of God's mercy to those on earth. To the bishops of the Church, in Gregory's teaching of repentance, is given the authority of binding and loosing the sinner. Confession of sin in itself gives life through the grace of God, even before the words of absolution are spoken. By the word of the Lord Lazarus was already alive in the tomb before the disciples loosed him and set him free. So bishops by their pastoral authority are to loose the penitents who are already alive again in Christ through the confession of their sins. [35]

And perfect shall be the joy of the redeemed in Heaven. No further concern for their lost brethren shall move them; for mercy toward such is now swallowed up in all-pervading jus-

---

[33] *ibid.* 15; 40; 19. [34] *ibid.* 39; 19.
[35] *ibid.* 26; O. D. Watkins, *Hist. of Penance,* II, pp. 568f.

tice and righteousness. Nay, more: in the bright vision of
the Lord the elect shall behold all creation, and the very sight
of the unrighteous in torments shall enhance their own bliss
in contrast, as black in an artist's hands intensifies the vivid-
ness of red or white.[36]

One or two instances will suffice to give some idea of Gregory's passion for allegory. A natural example is the illustration of humanity sitting in spiritual blindness amid the tumult
and noise of temptations which ever distract the heart. Swift
passage is predicated of humanity, stability of the Divine. And
so the Lord as Man hears with pity the cry of those who sit
in penitence by the wayside to await His passing; as God He
illumines their understanding in the eternal power of His
grace. But Gregory often went infinitely further in mystic
parallel than this. One Sunday in Lent, for example, he pondered with his people the meaning of the number of forty
days of fasting? Must it not signify the number of ten Com-
mandments multiplied by the four Gospels, a marriage of the
Old and the New dispensations? Or, perhaps, the four elements of our mortal bodies, multiplied by the ten Command-
ments which they must obey? Moreover, did not the Levitical
ordinances bid the Israelites devote one tenth of their possessions to the Lord? Well, there are six days of fasting in a
week and six weeks of Lent, which makes thirty-six days.
Therefore does the Church bid her children offer in solemn
abstinence the tenth of the year.[37]

Now and again the Pope revealed in these sermons his
heavy sense of responsibility as priest and preacher. The be-
liever, indeed, is brother and sister to Christ; but he who

---

[36] *Hom. in Evang.* 40.
[37] *ibid.* 2; 16. Cf. No. 24, on the 153 fishes: made up of 10 Command-
ments + 7 gifts of the Holy Spirit = 17; × 3 Persons of the Holy Trinity in Whom we work = 51; × 3 Persons of the H. T. in Whom we rest
= 153.

preaches is His mother, if by his words he may bring to birth the Lord in the hearts of men. At the Midnight Mass of Christmas, in a few words on Bethlehem, the House of Living Bread, Gregory explained that the angels appeared to the shepherds in a special vision, merited by the faithful watch which they were keeping over their flocks. So should it be among shepherds of men. On the second Sunday after Easter he upbraided the hirelings who flee the work of consolation and of rebuke by taking refuge in silence. At the end of a sermon delivered to bishops in the Lateran we find his thought in a brief prayer: "God, Who hast willed to call us as shepherds among the people: Grant, we beseech, that we, who are thus known among men, may truly fulfil our calling in Thy sight: through Jesus Christ our Lord." [88]

The twenty sermons on Ezekiel, though preached in public, must have drawn a different and a more select company. They interpret in detail the great vision of the four living creatures at the beginning of the book and the commands to the Prophet in the following three chapters; then pass to the mystic measurings of the House upon the Mountain at the end. Now and again their thought rises to tell of heights of contemplation on which the hearers must have struggled for breath, labouring as they were under fear of invasion from the outer world. Even as Gregory spoke, in the months of 593–594 the Lombards were on their way to Rome, and the words of Ezekiel must have struck with dread meaning within the quiet church of the threatened city, proclaimed once again, as Gregory declared, to a nation now punished for its sin: *Et audiebam sonum alarum, quasi sonum aquarum multarum, quasi sonum sublimis Dei: cum ambularent, quasi sonus erat multitudinis, ut sonitus castrorum:* "And I heard the sound of their wings, as the sound of many waters, as the

[88] *ibid.* 3; 8; 14; 17.

sound of God on high; when they went it was as the sound of a multitude, as the sounding of an armed host." "Put ye on the whole armour of God," the preacher cried; "for our struggle is not against flesh and blood, but against principalities and powers, against the rulers of the darkness of this world." The vision of their savage enemies must have loomed in the thoughts of some of those present as the very devils men so firmly believed did haunt this earth. Against them Gregory pictured the army of the Church Universal marching with its divers cohorts, priests and monks, virgins and married folk: armed with holy deeds and witness of miracles, sounding the praises of Almighty God. No doubt the hearts of many plucked up new courage at his words.[39]

"And they had the hands of a man under their wings." What, the preacher explains, do these hands signify but an active life of good works, these wings but a life of contemplative prayer? There follows much teaching on the Two Lives. The active life comes first in time, lower in merit, Gregory tells. It is the stepping-stone in this world to the contemplation awaiting beyond; the hands lay down their work when the soul at last rises upon its wings. On this earth every soul must lead the active life of virtue as servant of the Lord; the life of contemplation is one of free-will, not of necessity, for all good Christian men. And even those who essay it can rise above the ground of daily works only a little space while yet in this body. For a moment they catch sight of eternal truth as in a mirror reflecting mystery, then sink through their weakness back to the ground once more. Yet must they try. "Let the soul pass from this earth and rise beyond all that God has made. On the light of God alone let it fasten eyes of faith; for God, Who created all things, alone can quicken them into life. Everywhere He is, and everywhere altogether;

[39] *Hom. in Ezek.* I: 8.

infinite and incomprehensible, He may be felt and cannot be seen; nowhere He is wanting, and yet He is far from the thoughts of the wicked. For where He is afar off, there He is not lacking; where He is not of His grace, there He is in vengeance." [40]

If Gregory could thus describe from his own experience the soul's ascent to God, he knew also of its temptations. "Oftentimes," he warns his pupils, "the more a soul is ravished in contemplation, the greater its trials and testings. . . . For if it were raised utterly beyond the reach of temptation, it would fall into pride. And yet if its tempting laid it so low that the vision of God could not raise it, sin would be its fate. But by a marvellous dispensation the soul is held poised as it were in a balance, that it neither waxes proud through good nor yet falls by reason of evil." The meat, however, of mystic truths is for the strong, "the wild deer on the lofty mountains." Most of us, Gregory mourns in his humility, must seek refuge in the rock, "hedgehogs covered with the prickles of our sins." None, it is true, may boast that the heights of prayer are open to him for his high station in the world or his ability; the humblest may fare farthest and best. [41]

And it is the Pastor himself, the watchman unto the house of Israel, who, above all, must bewail his unworthiness. In the eleventh of these homilies Gregory bursts out into a storm of reproaches against his present life: "When I was in the Monastery, I was able to keep my tongue from idle words and to hold my mind almost continuously intent on prayer. But since I have bent the shoulder of my heart to bear a shepherd's load, my mind cannot remain recollected for any length of time, distracted as it is among many things. The

[40] *ibid.* I: 4, *par.* 9ff.; 5, 12; 8, 16. On all this subject see Dom Cuthbert Butler, *Western Mysticism²*.

[41] II: 2, *par.* 3; I: 9, 30f.; II: 1, 17; 2, 12; 5, 8; 5, 19.

different Churches, the monasteries, the lives and doings of individual men, all these I must ponder and discuss; now enter into civic business; now lament the inrushing swords of the barbarians and fear the wolves plotting against the sheep committed to my care; now see to the needs of those who live under religious rule; now suffer robbers submissively, now resist them with studied consideration. When thus my mind is torn and rent among things so many and so great, when *can* it retire into itself and give all its energies to preaching, to the ministry of the word? In my work I must needs associate with laymen, and therefore relax guard upon my tongue. Otherwise, if I keep it strictly under discipline, the weaker brethren avoid me and I lose my hold upon them. So I must listen patiently to needless talk. Yes, but I, too, am weak, and after some time of this idle gossip I begin, myself, to chatter about things I once disliked to hear. So now at last I love to lie where once it vexed me to fall. Who, then, what kind of a watchman, am I, who stand not on the mountain of toil, but lie yet in the valley of my weakness? . . . Think, I beg of you, beloved brethren, how great is the labour of the watchman who must both raise his heart on high and then suddenly recall it to lowest depths; now rarefy his thoughts in innermost communing with Heaven, now quickly, as it were, coarsen them to deal with his neighbour's earthly affairs!" [2]

More and more instantly earthly affairs did raise their threatening heads. Toward the end of his addresses the Pope turns to grieve over the lost state of his country: "Everywhere we see sorrows, everywhere we hear laments. Cities lie destroyed, fortresses overthrown, harvests ravaged; the land is brought to desolation. No peasant in the fields, scarcely a dweller in the cities is now left; yet even these little remnants

[2] I: 11, *par.* 5ff.; *par.* 28.

of the human race are still smitten today unceasingly. The scourges of Heaven's justice have no end; for not even through these scourges are guilty actions turned to right. Some of our people we see led away prisoners, some mutilated, some slain. What, then, is there to please us in this world, my brethren? If even thus we still love it, we love now not its joys, but its wounds. Rome herself, once mistress of the world, how do we see her now? Worn out with mighty griefs, bereft of her citizens, trodden down by enemies, full of ruins. . . . Where now is her Senate? Where her people? Their bones lie rotting, their flesh consumed, all the pride of her worldly glories is dead and gone." [43]

At last Gregory could tarry with Ezekiel no longer; the Lombards were at the gates of Rome. "Let no one blame me that this is my last address. As you all see, our tribulations have increased; we are surrounded on all sides by swords, we look in fear for the peril of death on every hand. . . . And yet He who created us is also made unto us a Father by the Spirit of adoption which He has given." [44]

The story of that busy life as Pope which Gregory constantly deplored, and fulfilled with so great excellence, is told in the fourteen books which still remain to us of his *Letters*. Here, or in one or other of the *Lives* of Gregory, we can read of the vast roll of names of recipients of Papal charity in Rome; of benefactions to bishops and minor clergy, to monks and nuns in extraordinary number, to poor without end: given in money, in clothing, in food. John the Deacon tells a story that when once a poor man was found dead, hidden away in one of Rome's dens of misery, Gregory declared he had died of starvation and was so miserable that he would not allow himself to say Mass for several days afterward, regarding himself as his brother's murderer. [45] Not only did this

[43] II: 6, 22.   [44] II: 10, 24.   [45] *Vita*, II, 29.

hold good of Rome; the heart of Gregory was as large as the lands over which he held influence as Pope.

Minds and souls were tended as eagerly as bodies. Letters of encouragement; letters of instruction; letters of every kind and sort of administrative action sped to one quarter or another of the world. Elections of new bishops must be confirmed or disallowed; established bishops must be rebuked for conduct unworthy their high office; sick clergy must be relieved for a time; special claims to privileges must be judged. Irregularities, crimes, immoralities in monastic, clerical and lay offenders called for prompt penalty and amendment; worship needed formation and guidance; funds required wise spending; heretics and lapsed Catholics stern but just condemnation; individual churches restoration from Arian to Catholic hands. These were matters spiritual, and, as we have remarked, Gregory contended steadfastly in word and in deed for the supremacy of the Pope in spiritual matters throughout this earth. But he had work in plenty among things temporal: especially in the administration of the vast estates of which many men, either through devout piety or through fear of barbarian inroads, had made gift to the Church. These were known as the Papal Patrimony, and entailed an army of governors, overseers, workmen, all controlled with both justice and mercy from the Pope's busy brain in Rome. Gregory did not, indeed, envisage his power in the light of that of a Lord temporal as well as spiritual; but certainly he judged himself called to serve as steward for great earthly possessions of the Church in divers lands.[46] Moreover, in the destitute and forlorn state of Rome her citizens and her soldiers looked to Gregory to save their country, their property and their lives. And therefore the Pope, in

[46] See Edward Spearing, *The Patrimony of the Roman Church in the time of Gregory the Great*, 1918.

this most able holder of the Holy See, became, whether he would or no, a political figure of the first importance, issuing orders to Rome's generals, even daring to parley with her enemy for peace on his own initiative.

In these Letters we find treasure invaluable for the history of the sixth century's end. When, furthermore, it is realized that the Pope, thus buffeted by the cares of all the Church's spiritual and temporal well-being, was always in pain of soul, hungry for the life of prayer from which he had been called, and in pain of body, crippled so badly by indigestion, rheumatism and gout that for years before his glad release he could hardly ever leave his bed, we understand why later generations named him Gregory the Great. Undoubtedly he knew and allowed his power; as undoubtedly he desired it, not for himself, but for the Church he served. The title he was the first to use in these Letters, "Servant of the servants of God," had no empty meaning in his mind.

Of special interest among the Letters relating to Rome is a decree published in 595, containing reforms laid down by this Pope, confirmed by a Synod of twenty-three bishops. Henceforth deacons in the Roman Church were not to sing any part of the Mass except the Gospel. Eagerness to sing well had led them to study music rather than their proper duties of preaching and almsgiving, and to value a goodly voice before a godly life. "So, very often," Gregory declared, "the minister who chants provokes God to anger by his morals while he delights the people by his tones." Next, all officials in personal attendance on the Pope were for the future to be clerics instead of laymen; the reprehensible practice of claiming property unjustly for the Church was to be discontinued; no payments were to be made for the conferring of Holy Order, or for the bestowal by the Pope of the *pallium,* the pontifical vestment allowed from time to time to Metropolitan bishops as a signal honour. Slaves belonging to the Church were to undergo a period of probation before being allowed, if they so desired, to pass as free men into the "stricter service" of monastic vows. No ceremonial pall was to cover the bier at the funeral of any Pope of Rome in years to come; that Rome might no longer see the unedifying spectacle of the crowd tearing it to pieces in their eagerness to obtain a relic pregnant with miraculous power.[47]

From a letter written in 598 we learn more of Gregory's work for the Roman Mass. He is defending himself here from the charge of following the Eastern Church, and in so doing reveals three innovations made by him. Two relate to the Liturgy: The singing of the *Alleluia* after the Gradual Psalm was no longer to be confined to the six weeks between Easter Day and Pentecost, and the Lord's Prayer was to be said directly after the Canon, before, and not, as formerly, after the Fraction of the Bread. "I thought it," he explains, "most unseemly that we should say over the oblation a prayer written by some scholar and not recite over His Body and Blood the prayer which our Redeemer Himself composed for us." [48] A third change, not mentioned in the *Letters,* is related in the *Pontifical Life* of Gregory, as well as by Bede and by John the Deacon: that Gregory added to the prayer *Hanc igitur* in the Canon of the Mass the last three petitions: *diesque nostros in tua pace disponas, atque ab aeterna damnatione nos eripi, et in electorum tuorum iubeas grege numerari.*[49]

Tradition has also claimed for Gregory a revised version of the Liturgy. The book, however, known as the "Gregorian Sacramentary," sent to Charlemagne at his request by Pope

---

[47] *Epp.* V, 57a.
[48] *Epp.* IX, 26. See Duchesne, *Christian Worship*[5], p. 168, p. 184.
[49] *Lib. Pont.* ed. Duchesne, p. 312; Bede, *H.E.* II, 1; Joh. Diac. *Vita* II, 17.

Hadrian the first, though containing alterations made by Gregory in the Roman use, represents the Roman Liturgy as it was in the eighth century. Duchesne prefers to describe it by the name of Hadrian.[50]

The opinions of scholars on Gregory's relation to "Gregorian chant" have been sharply divided. Dudden in his *Gregory the Great* confidently rejects evidence that the Pope left a great compilation of chants, words and music, edited and revised for the Church in a book known as his *Antiphonary*. Frere as confidently concludes that the music of Solesmes runs straight back to its source in Gregory's hand. We will not try to unravel this knot here; ancient music of the Church, whether Mozarabic or Ambrosian or Gregorian, or Ambrosian revised into Gregorian, is a matter too delicate for any but experts to discuss.[51] It seems saner for the amateur to descend to John the Deacon's description of Gregory as he rests his sick body on a couch in the Papal School of Music: with one hand he beats time for the practice, with the other he holds a scourge to whip up the choir-boys. John declares that the couch and the whip were still to be seen in his ninth century. But then, according to him, so was the *Antiphonary*.[52]

Eight hymns are ascribed to Gregory by his Benedictine editors, but unfortunately the ascription is more than doubtful. Nearly all are still familiar in English translations: "O Blest Creator of the light"; "This day the first of days was made"; "Father we praise Thee, now the night is over"; "It is the glory of this Fast," and "The glory of these forty

[50] *Christian Worship*, pp. 120ff.; Dudden, I, pp. 267ff.

[51] Dudden, I, pp. 271ff.; W. H. Frere, in Grove's *Dict. of Music*[3], ed. Colles, *s.v. Gregorian Music*. E. G. P. Wyatt also examined the evidence in his *St. Gregory and the Gregorian Music*, and concluded that this Pope "was the organiser, reformer and to some extent the author of the Antiphoner of the Mass." See for a full discussion also H. Leclercq: *Dict. d'arch. chrét. et de lit.* I, 2, 2443ff.; III, 1, 286ff.

[52] *Vita*, II, 6.

days"; "O Merciful Creator, hear" and "O kind Creator, bow thine ear." [53]

At the other end of Gregory's labours for Rome, her Church and her people, stands a letter to all the citizens in general: "I hear that certain men of corrupt spirit are sowing among you evil seeds, dangerous to our holy faith, forbidding you to engage in any work on the seventh day. . . . It is Antichrist who is driving the people to observe Jewish ways, who wants Saturday to be held in reverence, that he may restore the outer ritual of the Law and subdue the treachery of the Jews for his own end. I have also been informed that wicked men are preaching to you that no one ought to take a bath on Sunday. Truly, if anyone wants a bath for the sake of luxury and his own personal pleasure, I grant that this is not lawful on Sunday or any other day. But if it be of the body's necessity, I do not forbid it even on the Lord's Day. . . . For if it is a sin to wash the body on Sunday, then we ought not even to wash our faces on that day." [54]

The letters regarding the Church in Italy deal largely with the Sees of Ravenna, Milan and Naples, and show that certain of the more prominent dioceses of Italy did not yield with perfect submission to the will of Rome. Indeed, of the three, only Naples was considered directly under Rome's authority; her sway in northern Italy was far less defined.

The Bishop of Ravenna, when Gregory succeeded to the Papal Chair, was his friend John, to whom, as it seems, he dedicated his *Pastoral Rule* in consequence of John's reproof for his lack of courage. In 593 the Pope addressed a letter to

---

[53] (1)*Lucis Creator optime;* (2) *Primo dierum omnium;* (3) *Nocte surgentes vigilemus omnes;* (4) *Clarum decus ieiunii;* (5) *Audi benigne Conditor;* (6) *Ecce iam noctis tenuatur umbra.* The two remaining are *Rex Christe, Factor omnium* and *Magno salutis gaudio.* This last and No. 4 are emphatically rejected by Julian[2], pp. 1668; 1622.

[54] *Epp.* XIII, 3.

him, which the Bishop of Ravenna declared "a mixture of honey and stings," rebuking him roundly for wearing the pallium on unauthorized occasions. Later on, mollified by a courteous answer, Gregory permitted such use, not only at Mass, the ordinary usage, but also in processions on certain Feast-days.[55] Another admonition was even more severe. John had been indulging in vigorous language against the Pope, and Gregory wrote to him of his double tongue, his mocking words, "such as boys articled to lawyers use," his biting ridicule, his false accusations, his utter lack of proper control over the lives of his clergy, and his unlawful pride and presumption in the wearing of the pallium. "From all of which I find that the nonour of the episcopate is for you entirely a matter of outward show, not of your heart. And, indeed, I give thanks to Almighty God that when I heard of this, which had never come to the ears of my predecessors, the Lombards were encamped between me and Ravenna. For perhaps I might have shown to men how stern I can be." [56]

In 595 John was dead, and the Pope wrote to Castorius, legal clerk of the Holy See in Ravenna, that the clergy and people of Ravenna were to elect a successor: "Only let there be no bribery." Five months later another letter reached the city. Two rival parties had each elected a candidate, but neither would do, Gregory declared. One, the archdeacon Donatus, was not of sufficiently holy life; the other, the priest John, was not sufficiently acquainted with the Psalter. At last a third choice, the priest Marinian, was eagerly approved by the Pope as a monk from his own Monastery of St. Andrew, one on whom Gregory was to bestow his *Homilies on Ezekiel*. Under him the matter of the wearing of the pallium was still argued. On another occasion Gregory had to defend against the clergy and laity of the diocese his right

[55] III, 54; 66: V, 11: IX, 167.　　　　[56] V, 15.

as Pope to try a case of complaint made by an Abbot Claudius against this Bishop of Ravenna: "Do not be disturbed by the talk of foolish people," he wrote to Marinian, "or believe that any injury is being done to your church." Later on, severe reprimand was cast upon the same prelate for neglecting care of the monasteries and the poor in his See. In writing to Secundus, a deacon of Ravenna, Gregory urged him to try to wake up his sleepy Bishop, who did not trouble to answer the Pope's letter to him, probably had not even read it. If Marinian did not take care, he would lose all the fruits of his past life by his present negligence.[57]

Yet, when Gregory heard in 601 that Marinian was seriously ill, he was full of concern, invited him to stay in the Papal residence at Rome for his greater comfort, and strictly forbade him to fast. "I myself," he wrote, "am very feeble, and it is greatly to our advantage that either by the grace of God you should return cured to your church, or, if you are to be called hence, that you should receive your call in the hands of your friends. . . . I do not exhort or advise you, I strictly *command* you not to dare to fast. The doctors say it is very bad for this trouble of yours. Only on the most important days do I permit it: five times in the year." This is a striking command from the monk who destroyed his own health by his abstinence.

The same keen sense of charity and her twin sister, justice, is shown in a letter written to the clergy of Milan in 593 concerning their election of a bishop as successor to Laurentius. Milan claimed independent jurisdiction over its own ecclesiastical affairs, and Gregory limits his words to advice: "Weigh carefully the things which are expedient for all, and then to him whom divine grace shall have placed over you yield perfect obedience in all matters. It is not meet that he who has once been preferred over you should after-

[57] V, 24; 51: VI, 31; 24; 28; 63: VII, 40: **IX, 188:** XI, 21: XIII, 30.

ward be judged of you, and therefore your candidate is now the more scrupulously to be examined." While, however, leaving the clergy free to choose their own Bishop, the Pope reserved for the Papal See the right of confirmation of their choice. "We both maintain for individual Churches their own rights and require our own": a remark which formed the text of Gregory's ecclesiastical administration.

The deacon Constantius was duly chosen as Bishop-elect of Milan, approved and consecrated. But neither was the course of his episcopate all smooth sailing. The next year he found fault with a certain Fortunatus, a man prominent in the Church of Milan. The Pope judged that if Fortunatus had incurred grave suspicion, his case should be tried in the Papal Court at Rome. Constantius did not agree, and Gregory wrote to expostulate. "My dearest brother, I was exceedingly surprised by your letter concerning Fortunatus. Either your secretary entirely misrepresented your words, or I do not at all recognize in them my brother the Lord Bishop Constantius." He went on to point out with justice that the case had better be tried away from Milan to avoid suspicion of prejudice. Happier times followed, and Gregory sent the Bishop holy relics of Saints Paul and John and Pancras at his request.[58]

The Church of Naples caused the Pope immense trouble by strife of parties in episcopal elections. In 591 Demetrius its Bishop was deposed for evil living; the "Visitor" appointed by the Pope, a Father in God most reluctantly torn from his own diocese to steer Naples through its time of indecision, was seized and beaten by some of the excited citizens; the subdeacon Florentius, chosen as Bishop after long quarrellings, fled from the prospect. Further vacillation of months, from December 592 till August 593, ended at last in the consecrating of a Bishop, also called Fortunatus. This prelate was

[58] III, 29ff.: IV, 37: V, 18: IX, 183.

rebuked by Gregory for seizing certain revenues of the city, which he was ordered to restore forthwith; for allowing soldiers to be billeted on a convent for nuns; for permitting novices in a monastery to be tonsured before they had been properly tested. The year 600 found Gregory writing again to Naples on the choice of a successor to Fortunatus, now deceased. Feeling was again running high between the supporters of two men, both of whom the Pope rejected outright. John the Deacon had a little daughter as witness to his unsuitable life, and Peter the Deacon, so far as Gregory could gather, was altogether too stupid to deal with Naples. The leading citizens must choose some one else; and Paschasius was eventually elected to the vacant See. Gregory's subsequent strictures in regard to this prelate grew stronger and stronger. "Please exhort this brother for me," he wrote to Anthemius, agent of the Papal Patrimony in Campania, "that he show his vigilance and no longer neglect the discipline of his Church." About the same time he declared to the same Anthemius: "I hear that my brother and fellowbishop Paschasius is so lazy and negligent everywhere that he is not recognized as a Bishop at all; neither his Church nor his monasteries nor his spiritual children nor the harassed poor get any zeal or devotion from him." In fact, the Pope complained, the Bishops of Campania as a body are so slothful and unconscious of their work and calling that Anthemius must assemble them in convocation to remonstrate and point out their pastoral duties! [59]

We note that the agents of the Papal Patrimony were expected to carry out the Pope's instructions in matters of the clergy as well as of the laity. [60]

Much of Gregory's zeal was directed to protecting those he

[59] II, 5; 18: III, 1f.; 15; 60: IX, 47; 76; 207: X, 9; 19: XI, 53: XIII, 29; 31.
[60] They were called *rectores* or *defensores*.

held his sons, especially those under religious rule. He even disputed the proceedings of prelates of the Church, so keen was he to guard the rights of the monks against the bishops who were their spiritual overseers. Two letters remind prelates in Italy of the privileges which monks did and should enjoy. Castorius, Bishop of Ariminum, is requested to confirm, not make, the choice of abbot in the Monastery of St. Thomas in his cathedral city; he may not celebrate public Masses therein, lest in these holy retreats scandal should arise, especially from the attendance of women at such services. Similar injunctions command Marinian, Bishop of Ravenna, that no one steal from the revenues of the Monastery of St. John and St. Stephen at Classis; that its monks choose freely and justly their own abbot, who shall be independent in his own monastery except he render himself liable to the bishop's canonical discipline; that the bishop confine his jurisdiction to fatherly oversight and godly counsel. In these admonitions we trace, though Gregory did not forsee it, the advent of the transference of monks in mediaeval days from the authority of their diocesan bishops to the direct control of the Pope at Rome. Secular clergy, moreover, though they must say Mass for lay monks, were not allowed by Gregory to exercise control within monastic walls; nor, on the other hand, might monks serve as parish priests.[61]

At the same time the Pope kept watchful care for the lawful authority of his bishops. He insisted on their right to try their clergy in their own courts and endeavoured in every way he could to enhance their own dignity and sense of responsibility, as set forth in his *Pastoral Rule*. Even gifts came from the Papal purse for episcopal welfare. Ecclesius, Bishop of Clusium, who was very poor and infirm, was twice comforted: once by the arrival of a horse on which he might ride about his diocese, and

[61] V, 49; VIII, 17; V, 50. On all this subject see Dudden, II, pp. 187ff.

again, when Gregory was so ill that he lay expecting death at
any moment, by a warm tunic to keep out the cold."

From the Italian dioceses we come to Sicily, which held a
considerable share of the Papal estates. Much of its correspondence, therefore, concerns secular matters of administration. Minute instructions are despatched in many pages to Peter
the subdeacon, administrator of the Patrimony in this island.
Alms must be bestowed on the poor and afflicted; slaves who
have fled from their masters to the Church must be restored;
property unjustly seized by Papal overseers must be given back;
unfair exactions from peasants living on the Papal land must be
remedied. More minute details inform the Pope's agent what
to do with cows, bulls, and mares on the Patrimony's farms,
with farming equipment and with the monies raised by agri-
culture. Peter was clearly neither very wise nor very energetic
and had constantly to be admonished to show more zeal. "I
have found out from Abbot Martinian," the Pope writes, "that
not half the work on the Praetorian Monastery has been done
as yet; thanks, no doubt, to the diligence of your Experience!
Now, please, after this warning, get busy and show us what
you *can* do in the matter"; "I have discovered that you are
aware that part, even a good deal, of the property on our estates
belongs to other people, but you hesitate to return it because
of petitions made to you, or your own timidity. If you were
really a Christian, you would be more afraid of the judgment of
God than of the words of men. Now attend to what I say;
for I am everlastingly talking to you about this business." "Once
again. You have sent me a good-for-nothing hack to ride on
and five decent asses. I cannot ride the hack, it is too wretched,
and I cannot ride the decent asses because they *are* asses. If you
want to satisfy me, kindly send me something worthy of my
position." All this in one letter." That tenants of the Papal

____

" VI, 11: XI, 24: XI, 3: XIV, 15.
" I, 39a; 42; 44; 54; 65: II, 38.

land must stay, and their sons must marry, on the estate on which they were born, is part of the instruction sent to an overseer of the Patrimony at Syracuse; another Papal official of the same city receives Gregory's wrath at learning that unjust measure has been used for meting out the corn which the peasant settlers of the Church estates are obliged to contribute as revenue. The agent is at once to estimate the amount of money thus dishonestly obtained, and buy with it live stock as reparation for the poorer tenants.[64]

In spiritual matters Sicily lay under the full authority of the Pope, who directed it in many channels. We may look at a few details. Abbot Eusebius is rebuked because he has refused Holy Communion from the hands of Maximian, Bishop of Syracuse. The rebuke is tempered with kindness; will the pride of Eusebius consent to receive a gift of money to help out his poverty? Maximian is rebuked because in his anger he has excommunicated the said abbot: "I am really astonished that his past life, his advanced age, his long illness did not move you." The Bishops of Sicily may make their *ad limina* visit to Rome henceforth every fifth, instead of every third year. Why does the Bishop of Messina exact fees for burying people, a most reprehensible practice? Why does the Bishop of Syracuse read Gregory's letter aloud to guests at dinner-time? People will think the Pope conceited. Abbot Urbicus must be reprimanded for actually appointing two men as Abbot of the Monastery of Saint Maximus and Saint Agatha in one and the same day, one in the morning, another in the evening; the Abbot of Saint Peter's and the Abbot of Saint Lucy's are censured for disputing about their boundaries. Bishops may only have, so far as the feminine sex is concerned, a mother, sister, aunt or some near relative living in their houses. Subdeacons may not live with their wives if they desire promotion in Holy Order: "No one should approach

[64] IX, 128: XIII, 37.

the ministry of the altar unless his chastity shall have been approved beforehand." Agatho, a married man, wants to enter a monastery. Well, his wife, too, must become a nun, that they who were bound in the flesh may remain bound in the spirit. Why do the deacons of Catana wear shoes of *Roman* ceremonial in processions? In Sicily only the deacons of Messina have been granted this privilege. Manichaeans must be hunted for their conversion; Jews must be gently persuaded by word and by deed, such as mitigation of their rent; fortune-tellers and soothsayers are to be kept under proper restraint.[65]

So in Sicily. Gregory's correspondence was equally active and equally varied elsewhere; as in Sardinia and in Corsica where he also exercised full spiritual control. The letters to Sardinia are largely taken up with the iniquities of old Januarius, Bishop of Cagliari. Had it not been for his gray hairs, Gregory protests, he would have received severe punishment. His clergy are undisciplined, lazy, and immoral; his monasteries are shockingly ruled; his peasants are pagan; his territory lies open without defence to marauding Arian invaders. His personal conduct, too, is scandalous. Did he not one Sunday plough up with his own hands another man's field before celebrating holy Mass?[66]

Both islands were largely tainted by idolatry. The Pope urged on the work of conversion with unremitting energy, and even sent money to pay for baptismal robes.[67]

Further afield, where the Papal power was less well defined, we see Gregory in a prolonged struggle against Salona in Dalmatia. Natalis, Bishop of Salona, was given to attending banquets instead of reading or preaching or administering his diocese. To the Papal remonstrance he retorted that Abraham

[65] II, 31; 35: VII, 19: VIII, 3: X, 4: VII, 9: IX, 20: VII, 36: IX, 110: I, 42: IV, 34: VI, 47: VIII, 27: V, 7: XI, 33.
[66] V, 2: IX, 1.   [67] VIII, 1.

entertained three guests from Heaven, that Isaac blessed his son after a hearty feast, that Saint Paul bids the man who abstains not to judge him who eats, and that, anyway, dinners are often given in the cause of charity. The Pope was not impressed. Neither did such frivolous life commend itself to the archdeacon of Salona, whose name was Honoratus, and his jovial Bishop accordingly deposed him from his office, under pretext of honouring him by advancement to the priesthood. Honoratus appealed to Rome, and the Pope ordered Natalis to re-instate him, under pain of loss of his pallium, or, finally, of excommunication. Later on, when Natalis was dead, Gregory approved the election of this Honoratus as Bishop, accounting him "a man of experience and grave manners," and prescribed sound admonition for any of the clergy of Salona who did not assent. Unfortunately a rival candidate was set up, aided, it was declared, by the will of the Emperor Maurice himself, and Gregory fought a determined battle with this "Pretender," who was consecrated in defiance of the Pope's will. Even excommunication, however, failed; the "Pretender and Apostate" Maximus continued to say Mass. The Pope then ordered him to appear in Rome for trial on the charge of many sins; but nothing would induce the rebel to face the wrath of Gregory's judgment. At last Marinian, the Bishop of Ravenna, was allowed to adjudge the matter, and Maximus for his disobedience soon lay prostrate three hours in the public square of Ravenna, crying, "I have sinned against God and the most blessed Pope Gregory." Then he swore before Ravenna's most sacred shrine that he was guiltless of other crimes laid against him, and finally received from the Pope full pardon and restoration to his See.[68]

[68] II, 20f.; 50: III, 46: IV, 20: V, 29: VI, 3; 25f.: VIII, 24: IX, 176ff.; 234; Joh. Diac. *Vita*, IV, 13.

Africa, since the time of Justinian again included in the Roman Empire, troubled Gregory without cease by reason of the Donatist schism, still flourishing. It troubled him, also, in the opposition of its bishops to his desires. When the Pope directed Gennadius, Governor of Africa,[69] that the Primacy among African bishops should no longer be adjudged by length of episcopal tenure but by merit of life, and should be confined to one city instead of being given to the See held by the bishop of longest standing at the moment, there was so much dissatisfaction that Gregory allowed the Church of Africa to retain all her accustomed practices, with the exception that bishops converted from Donatist error might in no case attain to the Primacy. Dominicus, Bishop of Carthage, receives in these *Letters* of Gregory numerous expressions of congratulation on his love and loyalty toward the Holy See, and the Pope repeats to him his desire for justice to all: "As we defend our own rights, so we preserve their own rights for all the individual Churches." So many Papal epistles reach Columbus, a Bishop of Numidia, though not, in fact, its Primate, that he has to write a respectful plea; jealous people are beginning to take notice! Years before this time Gregory had preferred to act through him rather than through the official leader Adeodatus, who was feeble and old, and was therefore requested to work in all things in union with Columbus. The unsatisfactory state of monastic discipline in Africa appears in a letter to the Bishop of Carthage: "The bearer of this letter, Abbot Cumquodeus, complains that when he disciplines his monks according to their Rule, they leave the monastery forthwith and wander without let wherever they will." [70]

The great event in Spain during Gregory's rule of the Holy

---

[69] "Exarch," is the exact title, as in Italy.
[70] I, 72; 75: II, 52: VII, 2: III, 47f.: VII, 32.

See was, of course, its conversion from Arian heresy. "I cannot declare to you my joy," the Pope writes to his great friend Leander, Bishop of Seville, who has induced this wonderful happening, "in hearing that the son we share together, the most glorious King Recared, has been brought with most pure devotion to the Catholic Faith. When you tell me of him in your letters, you make me love him even though we have never met." This was after the great Council held in Toledo in 589, at which Recared with the Visigothic clergy and nobles had openly acknowledged this new allegiance. There is also a letter of doubtful origin, written in the name of Recared to the Pope to express his gratitude. Gregory, it declares, should have received the King's reverent salutation before, together with gifts offered to the shrine of St. Peter, but his envoys had been wrecked on the cliffs near Marseilles. At last he is sending a message by the hands of a priest, who also bears a golden chalice set with jewels. The Latin of this document is crude, and not wanting in error: a point which is used both for and against its ascription to this King. Those who see forgery here maintain that it was made up from the genuine letter in which the Pope praises Recared for his noble leading of his people: "What shall I myself say to the Judge, Who shall come in that dreadful Assize, if I meet Him empty-handed, when your Excellence draws after him the flocks of the faithful, now converted by his zealous and constant witness?" As a mark of his friendship the Pope sends with the letter "a little key made of iron from the chains of blessed Peter the Apostle, to bring you the blessing of that which has touched his most holy person; a cross containing wood from the Lord's Cross; and some hairs of John the Baptist." [71]

From Spain we come to Gaul, the land of Clovis, the "eldest son of the Church." It had long been Catholic in its

[71] I, 41: IX, 227a; 228.

tradition, though with Gregory the Papacy assumed new meaning throughout its realms: "There was no pope for a long time before or after him whose voice was heard beyond the Alps with so much respect." [72] The Frankish Kings were accustomed, as we have seen, to nominate the bishops of their realm and to convene the Councils of its Church, and only in Sees such as those of Caesarius of Arles, now dead some fifty years, did Rome wield a direct authority over Frankish ecclesiastical destinies.[73]

Four great aims stand out in the dealings of Gregory the Great with this land: that its people should renounce the cult of idols and superstitious rites; that its laymen should not be consecrated bishops without previous admission to lower Order; that bribery should not attend ordinations; that the Church in Gaul should favour and aid his purpose of the conversion of the British across the Channel.

For these ends he called vigorously for aid from the Bishops of Gaul and from the Frankish monarchs: Childebert the second of Austrasia and Chlotar the second of Neustria; Brunhild and her grandsons Theodoric and Theodebert, content to praise their traditional loyalty to the Church and eager to enrol their support in its cause, without enquiring too zealously into their manner of life. This may well explain his fervent laudation of Brunhild, a matter for which further and just apology has been found in the reflection that news travelled slowly in these days; that Gregory may not have heard of the Queen's worst doings; that these doings may have been falsely exaggerated by the hostility of chroniclers, such as Fredegarius; that Brunhild did her worst after Gregory's death. Finally, however guilty she was, Brunhild had still much of good to her credit, as we have seen; Gregory

[72] Dalton, *History of the Franks*, I, p. 272.
[73] Batiffol, *Saint Gregory the Great*[2], trans. Stoddard, pp. 201f.

appealed, no doubt, to the best in her for his missionary labours in Gaul and in Britain. Italy, too, had reason to be grateful to her generosity in ransoming with her own money many prisoners captured on Italian soil by the Franks.[74]

So the Pope "greets her with paternal affection," and extols as well-pleasing in the sight of God her government of Burgundy, her training of her grandsons, her own piety and love of the Church and its clergy, her labours for justice and order. He begs her to work for the summoning of a Synod to deal with ecclesiastical disorders, exhorts her against idolatry in her kingdom, implores her that Christian men shall not be slaves of Jews within its bounds, commends to her his monks on their way to Britain. For that Synod in Gaul, one of the great hopes of Gregory's heart, he wrote letter after letter, though he was never to see its realization in 614, ten years after his death. The episcopate in Gaul caused him unending anxiety; inexperienced laymen, suddenly elevated to a bishopric, often by means of bribery, were, at the best, he said, like timber undried and unseasoned, at the worst, a crying evil. "Many have declared to me," he writes to Brunhild, "what I cannot say without intense sorrow, that certain priests in your lands are so shameless and wicked of life that it is a disgrace for us to hear thereof, and a mournful thing to write. . . . We must rise with burning zeal for vengeance, lest the crime of a few become perdition to many. Evil pastors are the ruin of a people. For who shall stand in the way as intercessor for the sins of the people if the bishop, whose duty it had been to plead, himself commits sins more grievous than theirs!" [75]

Two other letters, to prelates in Gaul, show also Gregory's intense enthusiasm for their vocation and ministry. He writes

[74] Paul. Diac. *H.L.* IV, 1.
[75] *Epp.* VI, 5; 57: IX, 212f.: XI, 46: XIII, 7.

to Aetherius, Bishop of Lyons, concerning a certain bishop who has become insane. It is very, very sad. The poor brother is doing such dreadful things that one may well weep. Of course a temporary substitute must be appointed, lest the devil tear the unprotected flock to pieces with his teeth. Perhaps the bishop may be persuaded to resign? But nothing, save heinous crime, can dispossess a bishop of his place against his will, however insane or ill he may be. Desiderius, Bishop of Vienne, receives a forceful rebuke because he has been giving lectures on secular learning: "It has been reported to me, I am ashamed to say, that your Fraternity is expounding the art of grammar to certain people. This news so vexed and so entirely disgusted me that I turned my previous words concerning you into lament and sorrow. One and the same mouth cannot hold the praise of Jupiter and of Christ. Please do consider how serious, how unutterably *wicked* it is for a bishop to declaim aloud lines of poetry not even meet for a devout layman. . . . If hereafter it be shown that the report is clearly false, and that you are not giving your energies to trifles such as pagan literature, I shall give thanks to God, Who has not allowed your heart to be defiled by blasphemous praises of unmentionable men." [76]

It is clear that Gregory, in this age of bitter contention against enemies temporal and spiritual, had no patience with secular learning for its own sake, even though one need not believe later tradition, voiced by John of Salisbury, that he burned "the writings sheltered by the Palatine Apollo" in order that greater leisure might be given to sacred studies. He tells us himself that pagan literature is that "tongue of the Egyptian sea which the Lord shall utterly destroy," darkened with the evil calculations of astrology. [77]

[76] XIII, 8: XI, 29; 34.
[77] *Policraticus*, ed. Clement Webb, II, 26; VIII, 19. See Webb's notes *ad loc.*; Isaiah, XI, 15; Gregory, *Moralia*, XXXIII, 10.

It is a difficult matter to wait on intellectual thoughts when one is dealing with dioceses filled with problems crying for action. Nevertheless, it might well have been easier for the cultured people of Vienne to listen on Sunday to a Pastor whose secular science they respected in lectures at less holy times. A ship needs ballast, above all, in stormy weather, and Gregory by his attitude toward the reasonings of intellect, especially in his *Dialogues,* did render less steady the piloting of the Church in the later Middle Ages. It is of interest that the name of Cassiodorus nowhere appears in these *Letters.*

On the other hand, idolatry, superstition, crime, rife on every hand in Gaul, may well explain the Pope's impatience in writing to this particular Bishop. And when it was a matter of holy learning, the Pope was keenness itself. As we have noted, he knew the Bible from end to end and expected his congregations to be intimate with it as well; he had read his Augustine thoroughly and knew much of other Fathers in the original and in translation; he expected those who listened to his sermons to be familiar with the lives of the Saints and the traditions of the Church, to be able to follow instruction on the higher science of prayer. The common people he eagerly aided toward sober knowledge of spiritual matters in every way he could. Nowhere is this more evident than in the reproof written to Serenus, Bishop of Marseilles, who in his wrath against superstitious veneration had overthrown and smashed into bits the images of the Saints, cherished by his unlettered flock. Gregory hastened to instruct him: "In truth I praise your zeal that nothing made by hands should be adored, but you should not have broken those images. A likeness made by art is put up in churches in order that the illiterate may read by their gazing on the walls what they cannot read in books. So your Fraternity ought both to preserve these statues and to keep the people from adoring them; so that they may neither sin nor lose the chance of gaining knowledge of history." [78]

' Religion, however, was not to be thrust upon unwilling converts. Admonition from the Pope reached Virgilius, Bishop of Arles, whom Gregory afterward made Metropolitan of Gaul, that Jews were not to be baptized by force: "For when anyone comes to the font of baptism, not through the sweetness of preaching but of necessity, he returns to his former superstition; and therefore in seeming to be re-born, he comes really to a worse death." [79]

In 595 Gregory was busily meditating again on a crusade to Britain, that land in part Christian, as we have seen, but largely sucked back into darkness through the flood of Saxon invasion that had swept it bare. The Pope in this year directed Candidus, a priest starting for Gaul, to purchase there in one of its slave-markets some English boys about seventeen or eighteen years old for training in Roman monasteries, intending, doubtless, to send them eventually as missionaries to their own shores. A priest, Gregory commanded, was to accompany these pagan lads on their way to Italy that baptism might be administered should any one of them fall dangerously sick.

Soon, however, the Pope decided upon prompter measures and prepared a small band of monks for this great work under the leadership of Augustine, Prior of his own Monastery of St. Andrew in Rome. The party finally set out and progressed, it seems, as far as Aix. At any rate, "when they had already travelled some distance on their way, they were seized by a panic of foreboding. Far better, they thought, to return home than to encounter a people barbarous, savage, unbelieving, whose very language they did not understand. And so they held common counsel and decided for safety." Augus-

[78] *Epp.* IX, 208: XI, 10.   [79] I, 45.

tine was despatched back to Rome to beg dispensation from
"this journey so perilous, so toilsome, so uncertain." [80]

But Gregory was made of sterner stuff, and returned Augustine to his companions with a letter bidding them be of good
cheer and courage. He also sent letters of commendation to
the Frankish monarchs and bishops. And thus in 597 the
peaceful invaders, about forty in number, landed on the Kent-
ish island of Thanet, probably at Ebbsfleet, where the Saxons
Hengist and Horsa were said to have first leaped upon British
soil. The Romans, it has been aptly said, had returned to conquer Britain once more.

Their labours are described in the pages of Bede. Here
we may only look in passing at the correspondence of Gregory
with Augustine. The work of conversion in the kingdom of
Kent went on steadily, till on Whitsun Eve, 597, according to
tradition, its ruler Ethelbert was baptized in St. Martin's
Church at Canterbury, drawn not only by the prayers and
preaching of the missionaries, but by the influence of his wife
Bertha, a daughter of Charibert, King of Paris, and already
for some time a devout Christian in a pagan court. The parallel of Clovis and Clotilda occurs to the mind at once. Just a
week later Columba died in his Scottish isle; one wishes that
something more substantial than legend connected Gregory
with his name. "With all the other branches of the Catholic
Church in the West Gregory was brought into contact in the
course of his pontificate; with the Church in Ireland and
Britain alone he held no communication." [81]

Augustine was now consecrated as "Archbishop of the English" by Virgilius [82] in his city of Arles, and shortly afterward

---

[80] VI, 10; Bede, *H.E.* I, 23.

[81] *Epp.* VI, 50a: Bede, *H.E.* I, 25ff.; Dudden, II, pp. 114f. As Dudden
points out, we have here striking evidence of the isolation of the Irish
Church in the sixth century.

[82] On the error of Bede see Dudden, II, p. 120, note 2.

Gregory was able to exult, in a letter to his friend Eulogius, Bishop of Alexandria, that "on the Feast of the Lord's Nativity, 597, more than ten thousand of the English were baptized, we are told, by our brother and fellow-bishop. I have mentioned this that you may know what you effect by your words among the people of Alexandria and in the uttermost parts of the earth by your prayers." Elsewhere he wrote in a cry of triumph: "Lo! the Lord has joined in one faith the East and the West. Lo! the tongue of Britain, which before had known nothing but to make barbarous noise, now at length has begun to chant the Hebrew Alleluia in the Divine praises. Lo! the ocean, once swelling, now lies tranquil at the feet of the saints, and its wild waves, which the sword of earthly chieftains could not tame, the lips of priests now bind with simple words in the fear of God." Letters of thanksgiving and exhortation followed, to Queen Bertha, to King Ethelbert, and to Augustine. In one of these the Pope ordained the future organization of ecclesiastical Britain. The Primacy of all England, as long as Augustine should live, was to be held by him as Bishop of London; he was to consecrate twelve bishops to rule the south under him. In the north, the Primacy was to be held under Augustine by the See of York, whose first Bishop was also to be consecrated and sent forth by him. If the people of the north should follow those of the south in turning to the true Faith, this Primate of York was also to consecrate twelve bishops to rule Sees under himself. All bishops in Britain, including those already in office before the coming of Augustine, were to be subject to Augustine during his life-time; afterward either the Bishop of London or of York was to hold the Primacy of all England, according to priority of consecration.

The plan was excellent in theory and represents, of course, the beginning of England's present administration. But it in no way suited Britain as Augustine viewed things on her actual shores. He judged it better to rule from Canterbury, and he consecrated only two of his twelve bishops. Moreover, the British bishops already established asserted their independence; they clung obstinately to their own monastic ideals of organization and to the customs which we have noted as peculiar to the Celtic Church, in particular, to the dating of Easter and their own manner of tonsure.[88]

It is true that Augustine was not the ideal agent for their reconciliation to Rome. That he lacked the tact and broadmindedness of Gregory is evident from his correspondence with the Pope. Like Gregory he loved the life of strict obedience to rule; but he could not look away from it as readily as did the Pope, in equal love of simple men. A spiritual athlete himself, Augustine was keen on record of spiritual prowess and desired fervently to train his people after the precepts of Saint Andrew's House. He wrote to Gregory rejoicing that the Lord had given it to him to work deeds of marvel, and the Pope answered with counsel of humility. Let Augustine remember Moses and practice much examination of conscience; marvels are granted a priest not for his own glory, but for the conversion of sinners. To Bede we now owe the handing on from some undetermined source of the famous list of Questions addressed by Augustine to his spiritual Father in Rome. How are bishops to behave to their clergy, especially with regard to the offerings of the faithful? Since there is but one Faith, is it right for the Church of Gaul to differ in its use from that of Rome? What punishment should be meted out to a thief who steals from a church? May two brothers marry two sisters of an entirely different family? May a man marry with his stepmother? Is one bishop enough for the valid consecration of another? How should I treat the bishops of Gaul and Britain?

All these interrogations, with others on minute ecclesiastical

[88] *Epp.* VIII, 29; XI, 39.

detail, Gregory answered with careful patience. At last, when confronted by a stream of scrupulous points "all of which," Augustine protested, "must be made clear to the uncouth race of the English," he courteously remarked: "I think I have replied to you on these questions before. But I suppose that you wish me now to confirm the answers which you could have given to them yourself." He then dealt with each one easily, in the light of spiritual common sense. The failure at Augustine's Oak was not altogether the fault of the stubborn British bishops.[84]

The thought of Gregory's relations with the East starts with the work thrust upon him as defender of Italy against the invading Lombards. The Pope remembered only too well his unsuccessful pleadings in Constantinople at the behest of his predecessor Pelagius, and judged that what was to be done in this time of crisis must be promoted by himself. In this the Imperial Governor of Italy, Romanus, was no welcome partner. "The hostility of his Excellency the Patrician Romanus ought not to trouble you," Gregory writes to John, Bishop of Ravenna; "the higher we are above him in place and rank, the more we ought to tolerate any irresponsibility of his with patience and dignity." This was in July, 592. Three years later the Pope's patience had worn somewhat thin, and he wrote to an Illyrian Bishop: "Most reverend brother, I really cannot tell you what I suffer in this land from your friend, the Lord Romanus. In short, I declare that his malice toward us is worse than the swords of the Lombards; the very enemies who slay us seem sympathetic in comparison with the judges of the State, who are trying to make an end of us with their malice and piracy and guile. At one and the same time to look after bishops and clergy, monasteries and people, to keep anxious watch against the

[84] *Epp.* XI, 36; Bede, *H.E.* I, 27.

plots of our foes, to be everlastingly suspicious of the deceits and enmity of the Lombard Dukes—what labour, what pain all this involves, Your Fraternity can the better imagine in proportion as you love me more." [85]

So the Pope issued orders to overseers, citizens, generals: regarding supplies of food, regarding the defence of cities, regarding precautions against the advent of marauding forces. His worry made him ill, but he persevered. It is not possible to trace here the detailed story of this struggle on his part, which culminated in the Papal peace made in 592 with Ariulf, Duke of Spoleto. Romanus would have none of this peace and woke up from his lethargy to wage a campaign against the Lombards on his own account: a step which brought King Agilulf marching to the gates of Rome in 594, and the Pope from his sermons on Ezekiel to concentrate on measures of defence. [86]

But Agilulf marched away once more, though probably not induced, as story has it, by Gregory playing on the steps of St. Peter's the part of Leo pleading with Attila of the Huns. Henceforth the Papal energy was concentrated on the forging of a permanent bond of peace between the Lombard King and Constantinople. For long all efforts seemed in vain, and at last Gregory even dared to contemplate a separate Papal treaty. In 595 he wrote to one of the staff of Romanus: "See to it prudently in your accustomed manner that his Excellency the Governor consent straightway to the making of peace with Agilulf, the Lombard King. . . . For if he will not consent, Agilulf promises to make a special peace with us." [87]

Such a proposal of bond between the invader and the Pope of Italy was entirely illegal, and the Emperor Maurice voiced

[85] *Epp.* II, 45; V, 40.
[86] I, 2: II, 7; 17; 32ff.; 45: Paul. Diac. *H.L.* IV, 8.
[87] *M.G.H. Chron. Min.* I, p. 339; Ewald, ed. Greg. *Epp.* I, p. 319, note 2; *Epp.* V, 34.

his resentment in an indignant letter. Gregory's answer was equally forceful: "In his most Serene efforts to convict me my Most Pious Lord spares me, yet spares me not. For under the polite word 'simplicity' he calls me a fool. . . . Indeed if I had been a fool I should never have come to endure the things I suffer here among the swords of the Lombards." The letter goes on to suggest energetically that respect is due from temporal lords to spiritual ones; that Maurice would do well to believe in real facts rather than vain rumours. Among the facts are Romans slain, carried off with ropes round their necks to be sold as slaves, starved through lack of corn. "In short I tell you," the Pope ends, "that I, sinner and unworthy as I am, place more trust in the mercy of Jesus at His coming than in the justice of your Piety. There are many things of which men are ignorant concerning His judgment; perhaps what you praise He will blame, and what you blame He will praise." [88]

These were bold words to the Emperor of Constantinople, whose consent was sought before the very Pope of Rome was consecrated, who appointed the bishops of the Eastern Church, to whom Gregory himself was accustomed to defer. At last in 598-599 terms of a peace which was to last two years were confirmed by Agilulf, and, on behalf of Maurice, ruler of the Roman Empire, by the Governor Callinicus, who had by this time replaced Romanus. As Hodgkin remarks, permanent possession of Italian soil by the Lombards was now for the first time officially recognized by Constantinople. It was the first step toward their throne. Gregory wrote a letter of congratulation to King Agilulf and of gratitude to his Queen Theodelinda, to whose toil the treaty owed so much: "Be sure, most Excellent daughter, that you have gained no little reward on account of bloodshed spared on either side. But

[88] Hodgkin, V, pp. 382ff.; Greg. *Epp.* V, 36.

with this our greeting we also exhort that you move your most Excellent husband to desire his part within the Christian state."

In 601 the savage action of the Governor Callinicus in seizing the daughter of Agilulf and carrying her off into captivity with her husband Gottschalk caused a renewal of the war. Not for long, however. A treaty, covenanted in 603 for eighteen months between King Agilulf and the Romans, this time in the person of another Governor of Italy, Smaragdus, acting for another Emperor of Constantinople, Phocas, allowed Gregory to depart this world in the temporal peace for which as Chief Pastor of Christendom he had dared so much and laboured so long.[89]

He did indeed dare greatly in his spiritual relations with the political powers of his world. He wrote to all the bishops of Italy in a rage against the Lombard King, first husband of Theodelinda, "the utterly unspeakable Authari who at this Easter lately past forbade that sons of the Lombards should receive Catholic baptism—for which sin the Divine Majesty has cut him off from seeing the Feast of the Resurrection in another year." He rebuked the Catholic Queen Theodelinda for following Istrian bishops in the schism caused by the "Three Chapters" and for withdrawing from communion with Constantius, Bishop of Milan, a zealous adherent of the Fifth General Council which had condemned these bishops. He refused without hesitation the request of the Empress Constantina, wife of Maurice, that he send to her from Rome the head of St. Paul for the honouring of a church she was building in Constantinople. It was not, indeed, to be expected that Gregory, with his intense veneration for relics, would send away to the East so precious a possession, and John the Deacon states clearly that the Patriarch of Constantinople

[89] *Epp.* IX, 66f.; Paul. Diac. *H.L.* IV, 20; 28f.

had encouraged the request in hostility to the Pope. Another letter from Gregory to the Empress begs her to use her influence with Maurice to lighten the burden of taxation imposed on the people of Corsica and Sardinia.[90]

With Maurice the Pope's correspondence is marked by dutiful reverence, even by acknowledgment of the Emperor's power in matters spiritual, yet by loyal upholding of what his own conscience bade at all costs. He was horrified when Maurice ordained that no one holding public office in the government might become a monk, no one, moreover, who had been enlisted as a soldier. "Let my Lord ask himself, I beg, who among former Emperors put forward such a law? Let him consider carefully whether it ought to be declared. Let him think well before he forbid men thus to leave the world when the end itself of the world has come near. Lo! there will be no delay! Amid heavens ablaze and earth ablaze, and elements flashing and crackling with fire: with Angels and Archangels, with Thrones and Dominations, with Principalities and with Powers the tremendous Judge will appear! If when He is forgiving the sins of men, He accuses you of opposing His will herein, what excuse, I beg, will you find? . . . As subject to your order I have caused this law to be sent abroad throughout different quarters of the earth. But I also declare by this letter to my most Serene Lord that this his law is by no means pleasing to Almighty God. Therefore in both directions I have done my duty. I have shown obedience to the Emperor, and I have not kept silent on what I deemed right toward God." [91]

Not only from his Papal throne did Gregory wrestle respectfully with the ruler of the Roman Empire in the East, but he also waged a long and bitter struggle with the Patriarch of

[90] *Epp.* I, 17: IV, 4; 33; 30: V, 38; Joh. Diac. *Vita*, III, 56.
[91] *Epp.* III, 61.

Constantinople. For "John the Faster" had dared to declare himself "Universal Bishop," a title which Gregory interpreted as claiming that this one Bishop had alone been truly appointed in the universal Church. Letters upon letters were poured out from the Pope's hand in a passion of remonstrance against this usurpation, as he held it: to John himself, to the Emperor, to the Empress, and to bishops of the East. That John himself did not see in this light the title he assumed made no difference. Gregory would allow none but Rome to claim the honour of Chief Bishop in the world; that Constantinople or any other See should use a title which seemed to him to arrogate to itself not only this supremacy, but the only lawful bishopric on God's earth, was horror and grief untold. And so, when Eulogius, Bishop of Alexandria, turned the tables by respectfully addressing Gregory himself as "Universal Bishop," Gregory turned his indignation on his friend and forbade him ever to use the title for any man. Not Saint Peter himself, he wrote to the Emperor, was thus named. With the recalcitrant Patriarch he pleaded that the last hour was now at hand, shown by evident signs: "What then, dearest brother, will you say in that terrible examination of approaching judgment, you who are eager to be called in the world not only Father, but *General* Father?" Pride, hypocrisy, disobedience are the qualities the Pope ascribes to him who would be guilty of such scandalous behaviour, worthy of Antichrist himself. His anguish broke out afresh when Cyriacus, Patriarch after the death of John, continued to append the same title to his official signature. It remained unabated at the day of Gregory's death; the Patriarch was still "Universal Bishop" in the Churches of the East.[92]

The tragic end of Maurice has been told for us by Byzantine historians. We read of the Emperor's aristocratic reserve,

[92] V, 37; 39; 41; 44f.: VII, 30: VIII, 29.

unwelcome to the Byzantine mob; of his fatal urging of discipline and thrift; of the rebellion of his soldiers and the rising of his people, armed by himself against his own power; of the flight of the Imperial family across the water under cover of night; of the massacre of father and four sons at the harbour of Eutropius. We read of Maurice, convicted by outer and inner vision of his sins, crying out in submission to Divine justice and revealing with his last words the pious fraud of the servant who tried to substitute her own little boy for the baby prince she nursed. We read, too, of the crowning of the tyrant Phocas, "a man of drunken savagery, monster on earth, of face as a Gorgon, chief worker of our troubles." So a Greek writer described him, and Constantinople loathed his name when eight years later he came himself to an untimely end and Heraclius reigned in his stead.[93]

Maurice fell and Phocas seized his power two years before Gregory died. One might wish the tragedy of the East had been two years later. Then it would not have been necessary to record that the Pope wrote to Phocas, as Augustus and Emperor, the year after his usurpation: "Glory to God in the highest, Who, as it is written, 'changes times and transfers kingdoms.' . . . Sometimes, when the merciful God wills to refresh with His comfort the hearts of many, He advances one man to the height of rule, and by human bowels of mercy pours the grace of Divine gladness into the minds of all. We believe, then, that quickly we shall be strengthened by the abundance of this gladness; we who are happy that your benevolent Piety has attained the Imperial throne. Let the heavens rejoice and let the earth be glad, and by your benign act may the people of our grievously harassed State now be

[93] Evagrius, *Eccles. Hist.*, V, 19; VI, 1ff.: Theophylact, *Histories,* VIII, 5ff.: Theophanes, *Chron.* ed. de Boor, pp. 283ff.; p. 296; Joh. Diac. *Vita,* IV, 17ff.; George of Pisidia, *Heraclias, PG* XCII, 1317: *Chron. Pasch. ibid.* 981; Bury, *Lat. Rom. Emp.* (ed. of 1889), II, pp. 197ff.

lifted up in merriment." Now, he writes a little later, we shall
at last find some one bold enough to fill the office of Papal
legate in the Eastern Court, an office vacant the last two years;
now shall the Imperial consort, the Empress Leontia, recall
the Catholic zeal of Pulcheria and of Helena, mother of Con-
stantine. Let angels in heaven sing praise to God and men on
earth give thanks.

As in the case of Queen Brunhild, the other side of the
picture must be shown. Maurice had wounded the Pope in
his deepest longings for Italy's political and spiritual welfare.
News, here again, travelled very slowly, coloured by personal
messengers, and perhaps Gregory had not understood in all
its horror the sacrilegious slaying of Maurice and his children
when he wrote thus to the new Emperor and Empress. He
certainly did not know what the reign of Phocas was to bring
forth, and, as ever, he hoped by courtesy and tact to gain
goodly fruit for the Church. Under Phocas, indeed, the Pope
did gain his ends: truce with the Lombards, support against
the schismatic partisans of the "Three Chapters" in northern
Italy, against the abhorred title of "Universal Bishop"
addressed to the Patriarch. Yet we should gladly wish deleted
the record of this writing to Phocas.[94]

A few words should be added on some of the more personal
letters. Some of these are to women. At Constantinople
Gregory formed friendly relations with Rusticiana, a lady of
very high rank, and remembered her with grave rebuke from
his Papal seat in Rome. Apparently she was no Paula or
Etheria. First of all, she threw over her resolution to go on
pilgrimage in the Holy Land, and when at last she did go
as far as Mount Sinai, she returned in most unseemly haste.
"I am afraid," the Pope writes, "that your Excellency paid

[94] *Epp.* XIII, 34; 41f. Hartmann, ed. Greg. *Epp.* II, note on XIII, 34;
Lib. Pont. ed. Duchesne, I, p. 316, and note 1.

very little attention with your mind to the holy places you saw in the flesh." Nor would she obey Gregory's repeated admonitions that she should visit the shrine of holy Peter: "Why you delight so much in Constantinople and forget Rome, I do not know, and so far I have not been honoured with any explanation." . . . "Please do not keep on writing 'your handmaiden' in your letters to me," a third letter admonishes; "once would be quite enough. As Bishop I am now servant of all; I, who was once your servant before I was thus ordained."

Theoctista, sister of the Emperor Maurice, receives two long letters from Rome. One thanks her for alms, and bids her continue zealously her work of educating the little princes, her nephews; the other gives her much spiritual instruction and comfort in a difficult time when unkind things were being said about her by the lighthearted Byzantine populace. Her theological opinions, it would seem, had been called in question; she was a lady much addicted to study. Gregoria, Lady of the Bedchamber to the Empress Constantina, sends a pathetic appeal. She is terribly worried about her multitude of sins; would not the Pope please write back that he has had a special revelation from the Lord that they are forgiven? We do not know how far she was consoled by the grave answer that the Pope did not hold himself worthy of particular visions. As for her sins, the mercy of the Lord is truly very great. But penitents have no business to do aught but sorrow after a godly manner for their sins all the days of their life; so may they come at last to eternal bliss. Clementina, who lives in Italy, is likewise a trifle feminine. She is afraid Gregory is offended with her? He assures his glorious daughter that all is well. He regards her with true fatherly affection; why does she not write more frequently?[95]

[95] *Epp.* II, 27: IV, 44: VIII, 22: VII, 23: XI, 27; VII, 22; IX, 85.

There is a charm, indeed, in Gregory's letters not always found among monastic counsels. His care for his men friends was incessant. Libertinus, ex-Praetor of Sicily, who has fallen upon hard times, receives twenty suits of clothing for his servants: "Please do not be offended at this little gift from St. Peter's Treasury; it will bring you great blessing." Theodore, physician to the Emperor Maurice, is gently rebuked for neglecting to read his Bible. Gregory sends him a present of a duck and two little ducklings: "To thank you for your love; so that as often as your eye lights on them you may remember me, even in the distractions of your strenuous life." The letter calls up a pleasant picture of this busy doctor, obediently snatching a few moments for "the singularest and most excellent Book that hath been extant since the Creation," while Mother Duck and her offspring waddle at his feet.⁹⁹

Important for the study of Gregory's conduct as Pope are the letters written to Venantius, a noble of Syracuse, who had fled back to the world from the cloister to which he had vowed his life. Gregory warned him urgently of his danger, but did not reject his friendship. He even admonished the Bishop of Syracuse to say Mass in the house of Venantius if requested to do so, though he sent his permission in a message addressed "To Venantius Ex-Monk and Patrician." When Venantius was dying, the Pope wrote again to this same diocesan, urging him to beg Venantius even at the last hour to return with penitence to his forsaken state. With the same breath Gregory took thought for the two little daughters of this ex-monk, Barbara and Antonina. We have two letters which he wrote to them. The second ends: "I am glad to receive your present of two cassocks with the message that they are your own work. All the same, I do not believe the

⁹⁹ *Epp.* X, 12; V, 46, and Ewald's note 3, p. 346.

message. You are trying to win praise for the work of other people, and I do not think you have ever yet put hand to spinning. Never mind! I hope you may love to read your Bibles, and that when Almighty God gives you husbands you may know how you ought to live and keep house." Gregory was not too happy in writing to little girls.[97]

Throughout the years of his Pontificate we gain from time to time glimpses into the Pope's inner self, revelations, above all, of suffering in body and in mind. One of the most vivid descriptions of his physical pain is given in a letter to a bishop in Arabia: "I was so sorry that I could not enjoy the visit of Abbot Candidus as I would; for he found me sick and left me still feeble. For a long time now I have not been able to get up from bed. Sometimes I am tormented by gout; sometimes some strange and painful fire swells out through all my body; very often the burning and the pain struggle together within me, and both body and spirit fail. But there are many other weaknesses and ailments, too; I could not possibly describe them all. In a word, so steeped am I in noxious poison that it is sheer penance to me to live, and I long eagerly for death, the only possible remedy for my troubles. Most holy brother, beseech the mercy of the Divine Love, that He may graciously lighten His scourging toward me and give me patience to endure. . . ."

Even greater sympathy, if possible, is due to the soul that from beginning to end of these fourteen years longed ceaselessly for its monastic peace. There is space here for only one lament, written to John, Abbot of Mount Sinai: "What does it mean for us, this governing of the Church? It means that we are tossed by the waves of this world, frequently overwhelmed, but lifted up again from the deep by the protecting hand of heavenly grace. So do you, who live your tranquil

[97] I, 33: VI, 40f.; XI, 23; 25; 59.

life in so great serenity and peace, you who stand safe as it were on the shore, stretch out your hand of intercession to us, sailing, or rather, foundering; help us all you can by your prayers, as we struggle toward the land of life." [98]

While he still grappled thus with practical problems of every nature, there came from Gregory's pen that most popular book of spiritual fairy tales, as true and as well-beloved to the children of the Church in the Middle Ages as any legends of worldly beauty and beasts. It was written during 593 at the request of some of Gregory's friends in Rome; [99] partly for the encouragement of souls tempted to despair, partly for the Pope's own comfort. God was surely in His Heaven, even if all was not right with the world; and what surer sign of this than the deeds of great men wrought by His grace still abounding on earth?

The *Dialogues*, then, were composed in such intervals of leisure as the Pope's life in Rome allowed, cast in the form of narratives told by Gregory to "my most dear son, Peter, the deacon, my intimate friend from his earliest youth and my companion in the interpreting of sacred Scripture." In the introduction at the beginning of the first book he is said to have found the Pope one day utterly cast down at the thought of his own miserable life, as compared with those of the heroes of sequestered contemplation; whereupon he begged his Father to tell him of their doings.

The sources of these tales of wonder do not appeal to modern secular criticism. Gregory's care for accuracy is usually satisfied by naming his informant: whether some bishop or priest or abbot or "certain religious men," or, once, even "a certain poor old man," with whom the Pope fell into conversation. But part of the story is often true, and always all of the moral; so we shall do well to read with pleasure and

[98] XI, 20; 2.   [99] III, 50.

profit undisturbed these sermons which have been the meat of wayfaring men all down the centuries. Some of them we have already met in connection with St. Benedict, in that priceless second book. The attentive and delighted Peter often asks for explanation at the end of a tale and is duly instructed in sound teaching of the Church; in this the work recalls the interviews of Cassian and his friend Germanus with the Abbots of the Desert, or the telling of the *Life* of St. Martin to his friends by Sulpicius Severus.

The four books of the work hold much of interest in their reflection of ways and manners in this sixth century, especially among religious people. The Pastors of the Church, it appears, were sometimes formidable Christians. Gregory tells of the Abbot of Fondi near Terracina, who flew into a fearful rage against one of his monks, and, when he could not find a stick, caught up a footstool and beat the poor man's face black and blue. Next day the brother was obliged to go out from his monastery on some errand and was asked by sympathetic friends of high station whatever was the matter with him? He replied: "Yesterday evening for my sins I came into contact with a footstool, and this is the result." Thus he honoured both his Lord Abbot and our Lady Truth, and his humility brought his Superior to repentance. Another monk, dwelling on Mount Soracte, was equally sensible of his Abbot's high station. When one unlucky day he had broken into pieces a glass sanctuary lamp which he was washing, he fell before the altar with loud groans of anguish, and prayed most fervently for help. The Lord, at any rate, was merciful, and when he lifted up his head, the lamp lay before him whole.

But all this pales before the righteous indignation of Boniface, Bishop of Ferenti. His Lordship had been invited by a certain nobleman of that town to dinner after Mass on the Feast of St. Proculus Martyr. Now Boniface was a very holy man and addressed himself first to chanting a pontifical grace. Just as he was beginning, a man with a monkey suddenly appeared before the door and began to make brazen music. "Alas! alas!" cried the man of God in his wrath, "the wretch is dead, the wretch is dead! Here have I come to dinner. Not a word have I yet uttered for the praise of the Lord, and that fellow comes with a monkey and beats his brass. Go of your charity and give him to eat and drink; but know that he is a dead man." He was, soon after; for a great boulder fell on his head as he was leaving the house. One dares to think his punishment rather severe! So, surely, was that of the miserable woman who brazenly approached the cave where a certain hermit named Martin lived on Mount Marsicus. Martin, Gregory tells, had vowed never to look on women again, not because he despised them, but through fear of temptation. So the woman went to see for herself, and ended her life that same day, as one highly displeasing to Almighty God.[100]

Similar prudence was exercised by a priest in charge of a cure in Nursia. He not only held his wife as a sister but looked on her as his enemy, and, though they lived in the same house, forbade her ever to come near him or to minister to his needs. When they were both feeble through age and he had been forty years ordained, he fell dangerously sick of a fever. At last the poor old lady saw him lying so still that she thought he must be dead and crept near to find out whether he still breathed. But with his last gasp he burst out: "Away from me, woman! There is still a little spark of fire in me. Take away from it your fleshly straw!" Shortly afterward he departed this life under escort of Saints Peter and Paul themselves.

Well-known names frequently occur. There is a pleasant story, though its details cannot be trusted, of Paulinus, Bishop

[100] *Dial.* I, 2; 7; 9: III, 16.

of Nola in Campania. He had given away all his goods to the
poor and his purse was empty, when one day a widow came
begging him to help her ransom her son who had been carried
off to Africa by the Vandals. Paulinus answered that of gold
and silver he had none. However, she might take him himself
as slave and captive of the Vandals in her son's place. The
woman for long refused to believe the Bishop was in earnest;
but her scruples were no match for his desire of martyrdom.
So they journeyed together to Africa, where Paulinus obtained
the young man's release and served King Gaiseric's son-in-law
as a gardener. Eventually King Gaiseric had a bad dream
and Paulinus was revealed as prophet and bishop; so effectu-
ally, indeed, that he returned home in the company of many
Romans, freed together with himself.

Two Gothic Kings also appear, each under condemnation.
As an example of the lasting fire that awaits the bodies as
well as the souls of the wicked after death, Gregory declares
to Peter the fate of Theodoric the Ostrogoth, King of Italy,
as told him by a Papal overseer named Julian. A connection
by marriage of this man had landed on one of the Lipari
islands on his way from Sicily to Italy, and found there a
holy recluse who declared to him that Theodoric was dead.
"God forbid!" was the reply, "we left him alive, and no such
tale has reached us." But the hermit persisted in his story:
"Yesterday at the ninth hour, stripped of belt and shoes, with
his hands bound, he was led along by Pope John and the
Patrician Symmachus and was hurled into the crater of this
volcano here." Gregory goes on to tell that the hour of Theodoric's death was found to have been exactly this very time,
and concludes that the King had well deserved this punishment from the men he himself had killed.[101]

Several stories tell of Totila the Goth: how he dined with

[101] *Dial.* IV, 11: III, 1: IV, 30.

a bishop who was blind through advanced years but gifted with inner vision, and handed him a cup of wine with his own hand, to see whether the holy man really could discern whence it came; how he misjudged another saintly bishop, thinking him the prey of strong drink because his face was ruddy; how yet another he threw to a most savage bear in rage at the escape of Roman soldiers, and how the bear licked the bishop's feet in presence of Totila himself and many who had come to see that sight; how he put the bishop of Perugia to a terrible death when he had taken his city in the seventh year of siege; how he thirsted with insatiate fury for the blood of Fulgentius, Bishop of Otricoli, whom the Lord snatched from his hand by a miraculous storm of rain. Gregory could not forget the ruin that had been wrought by the Goths when he was a child.[102]

To the *Dialogues,* also, we owe the story that made Hermenegild of Spain a Martyr of the Church, though secular historians offer a very different narrative. Gregory here represents the Visigothic Prince, not as rebelling against his father King Leovigild, but as captive at his hands for the sake of the Catholic faith, commanded by him to receive communion in the dawn of Easter Day from a heretic, a bishop of the Arian creed of Spain. According to this narrative Hermenegild stoutly refused, and the King's rage brought his captive to execution.

The devil, of course, looms large and fierce in this work of spiritual combat. Once he seized a pious nun; she had imprudently breakfasted off a lettuce leaf in her convent's garden without making over it the sign of the Cross. His complaint was very bitter when Abbot Aequitus drove him away: "What fault was it of mine? I was merely sitting on the lettuce and she came along and ate me!" Another time he entered into

[102] III, 5f.; 11; 12f.

a wedded wife who slept comfortably at home instead of keeping vigil the night before Saint Sebastian's Chapel was to be dedicated to the Lord.[103]

Yet the devil was no match for holy Saints. Bishop Datius of Milan was warned against sleeping at Corinth in the beautiful big house he had selected. You can't stay there, men said; the devil haunts it. So much the more reason for taking it, replied Datius, and promptly went to bed under its roof. In the dead of night the ancient enemy awoke its echoes with terrific noises; he roared like lions and bleated like sheep, brayed like asses, hissed like serpents, grunted like pigs and squeaked like rats. The Bishop was much annoyed at being disturbed, and showed it; he taunted the devil with trying to be like God when he could only succeed in imitating the beasts. At this Satan, if I may put it so, says Gregory, actually blushed for shame and departed in high dudgeon.[104]

There are many stories of animals of various kinds. Martin of Campania lived three years with a serpent unharmed, though the devil was its tenant. Deacon Peter shivered when he heard this. Another time Satan appeared as a hog, running up and down among the people gathered to celebrate the converting to Catholicism of an Arian Church in the Subura at Rome. Gregory himself was officiating on this occasion and dedicated the Church to St. Agatha, for whom he had great devotion. He declares here that the priest and many of the congregation saw this sight, though he does not say he witnessed it himself. Elsewhere we read of a good snake, guardian of the garden of the Abbey of Fondi, and of a swarm of caterpillars leaving the garden of Bishop Boniface to peace at his command. This man of holiness began his miracles early. When still a "little boy of God" living with his mother, he used to keep hens in the front yard of their cottage. One day

[103] III, 31: I, 4. St. Hermenegild's Day is April 13.   [104] III, 4.

he saw a fox carry off one of his prizes, and rushed into the church: "O Lord," he cried, "is it Your Will that I shouldn't eat of my mother's food? The fox is eating her hens!" The prayer savoured a little, perhaps, of the future prelate, though Gregory stresses his humility. But the hen was saved, and the fox fell dead.[105]

A bear kept watch over his sheep for Florentius of Nursia, who had such power with God that he killed by a thunder-storm myriads of snakes infesting a certain deacon's cell. One of the most delightful stories tells of a horse which belonged to a nobleman of Corinth. It was so gentle that his wife used to ride upon it and made it her special favourite. It happened that Pope John the first came travelling to the city, and when he needed a horse, the nobleman courteously lent him this one for its mild character. After a while, to the lady's joy her horse was returned, and she immediately decided to go a-rid-ing. But, Gregory relates, "in no wise could she do so. For after having so great a Pontiff on its back, it utterly refused to carry a woman; it neighed and snorted and shook and kicked till the nobleman was obliged to send it back with a petition that His Holiness would accept it as a gift." [106]

Visions occur in plenty: of things of Heaven and things of Hell, vouchsafed especially to the dying, who often speak with the tongues of prophecy. The fourth book is devoted to death and life after death, and holds the famous narrative which was the forerunner of countless mediaeval visions of the land beyond, rising to their highest level in the *Divine Comedy*. It is the tale of Peter and of Stephen, who returned to earth after a passing hence caused through sickness, and related, like Er in Plato's *Republic*, what had befallen them in their journey to and from this death in the midst of life. Here Gregory ends with this warning: Let us who are still on the

[105] III, 16, 30: I, 3; 9.   [106] III, 15; 2.

march through this world strive to live unto God and to help
our fellow-travellers in the same way, remembering that not
miracles, but obedience is its paving. Let us offer with love
and prayers our oblation at the altar for those gone before.
"And so, my son Peter, I am bold to say that after death we
shall not need the Sacrifice of our redemption, if before death
we ourselves shall have been made a sacrifice unto God." [107]

The *Dialogues* reaped a rich harvest in later days. Bede
loved them and drew upon their words. His visions of Fursey
and of Drythelm followed in the train of those of Peter and
of Stephen; his prose *Life of St. Cuthbert* shows markedly
their influence. In the same eighth century Pope Zaccharias
the first, the correspondent of St. Boniface of Germany, translated these same books into Greek for the benefit of his coun-
trymen. In the ninth, Werferth, Bishop of Worcester, rendered them in Anglo-Saxon for King Alfred, that the English
might likewise learn counsel and encouragement. Throughout the Middle Ages their readers were legion. [108]

The commentary on the Book of Job, originally a series of
informal instructions which Gregory gave at Constantinople
to the brethren who shared his house, was revised and continued at St. Andrew's and finally completed after he became
Pope. [109] Here, then, under title of the *Morals,* we have thirty-
five books full to brimming point of that same symbolical interpretation which we ·found in the *Pastoral Rule:* the same
extravagant building of theories of numbers, the same paral-
lelism of outer circumstance and inner meaning, brought to
bear on the minutest detail. The method of teaching is a
triple one. The facts of the narrative are well and truly laid

[107] IV, 36; 60. Plummer, ed. Bede, *H.E.* vol. II, p. 294; B. Colgrave in
Bede, his Life, Times and Writings, ed. A. Hamilton Thompson, p. 215.
[108] W. Levison, *ibid.* p. 127; Bede, *H.E.* III, 19; V, 12. See also
Browne, *King Alfred's Books.*
[109] trans. *Library of the Fathers,* vols. I–III.

as foundation; the fabric of symbolism is then built up; finally, the whole receives its light and colour in the moral and spiritual meaning which the mind of Gregory painted thereon.

This labour of many years of love was dedicated to Leander, Bishop of Seville, as one who had shared its beginnings. A letter written to him forms its introduction. Gregory prays that faults of style may be forgiven on account of the years of bodily suffering which have severely tried his mind and endurance. Moreover, it is not incumbent on him to teach with the art of a rhetorician, and the writer has had no care for such. He has not sought to avoid cacophonies or barbarisms; his prepositions have been left to take care of themselves: "Because I am quite sure it is unseemly to fetter the words of the Divine Oracle by the rules of Donatus." [110] The text used is that of Jerome's newer edition of the Bible, though from time to time the older version is called on for additional witness. As Gregory explains it: "The Apostolic See, over which God wills me to preside, uses both; so may the labour of my study find also in both its support."

Very few scholars in these days, one supposes, would have the desire or the courage to plough their way through this manual of the Church's teaching in the sixth century. It tells of theology dogmatic, moral, pastoral and ascetic; of God in heaven and God incarnate on earth; of angels and of demons; [111] of sin and of sacraments; of active works of mercy and of contemplative prayer; of grace and of free will; of the mystery of evil; of virtues and their gaining; of priests and their people; of rulers and their subjects; of heresy and schism; of temptations and of trials. Doubtless the listeners heard with reverence, patience and pleasure. In the last chapter the writer reproaches himself that something of human

[110] *Epp.* I, 41: V, 53 (595 A.D.); 53a (ed. Ewald).
[111] The Whitby *Life* especially declares the Church indebted to Gregory for his teaching on the Angels: c. XXV.

enjoyment has crept for him into this pure offering for the glory of God. Every line does savour of Gregory's delight as he revealed to his sons the thoughts he had struck so frequently in ploughing the knotted soil of truth. At the same time, he had no desire to see them forced upon those who could not appreciate their teaching. A letter to a Papal agent in Ravenna complains in 602: "I am vexed to hear that my brother and fellow-bishop Marinian is having my commentaries on blessed Job read in public at Vigils. It is not a popular work, and hinders rather than helps uneducated hearers. Tell him to have instead commentaries on the Psalms read at Vigils; for these are excellent for training laypeople in good ways. Besides, I do not wish while I am alive that any writings of mine should come easily to the notice of men." [112]

Gregory sent, however, the first and second parts by his own hand to Leander; his only copies of the third and fourth parts, he told the Bishop, he had given to certain monasteries. In the seventh century the Bishops of Spain sent Taio, Bishop of Saragossa, to Rome to recover these missing portions, and he wrote back to Eugenius, Bishop of Toledo, of his labour and joy in copying them. Later days coloured this visit with legend. It was said that requests of Taio for the manuscript of the *Moralia* met with continual delay on the ground of difficulty in unearthing it among the multitude of the treasures of the Papal Library. At last he could bear it no longer and begged the vergers of St. Peter's that he might spend the night there in petitioning the Apostle for this end. In the middle of the night a sudden flood of radiance streamed out from the depths of darkness, and Taio was amazed to see a procession of Saints enter, lanterns in hand, accompanied by chanting of psalms. Two of them, gray-haired and clad in white robes, approached him as he lay prostrate, nearly dead

[112] *Epp.* XII, 6.

with terror. But they asked him kindly why he was there, and when they had heard his tale, as though they knew it not already, they bade him be comforted and showed him the place where the manuscript lay hidden. They were, of course, Saint Peter and Saint Paul. Gregory also was of the company, and our Bishop had the supreme happiness of a word or two with his dear Saint. He even plucked up courage to ask whether Augustine was not there too? "That most glorious man?" replied Gregory. "He is in a higher place than I." Thereupon the whole vision quickly disappeared. At the tale's end there comes a pleasant sequel. The clergy of Rome, it runs, were much impressed when at the Pope's request Taio told of this experience; ever after they respected him highly, though they had always thought him slow and stupid before.[113]

Other parts of the Bible were subjects of other commentaries by Gregory. In the same letter to Ravenna mentioned above he remarks: "My beloved son Claudius has written down from memory some observations which he heard me make on *Proverbs,* the *Song of Songs, the Prophets,* the *Books of Kings,* and the *Heptateuch.* I have been too ill to put them into writing, and he did not want them to be forgotten. But when he read them to me, I found that his version was very poor, quite different from my own words." The Pope then asks the sub-deacon John, to whom he is writing, to collect all the copies made by this Claudius, Abbot of the Monastery at Classis, and to send them to him.[114]

Of any books under these names which might be of Gregory's work, we possess now only Commentaries on the *First Book of Kings* and the *Song of Songs.* The question is still undecided regarding each of these writings, whether it be by

[113] *PL* LXXX, 723ff.; Isidorus Pacensis, *Chron. PL* 96, 1257ff.; Ewald, ed. *Epp.* I, pp. 352f.; Dudden, I, 412, note 2.
[114] *Epp.* XII, 6.

Gregory himself, or the version of Gregory's oral teachings badly written up by Claudius, or merely a forgery. But it is generally held that the *Commentary on the Book of Kings* is not by the Pope. It would be a happy addition, if only for the sake of its words: "Instruction in secular literature helps us toward knowledge of spiritual writings"; though these very words rouse suspicion against Gregory's authorship. The *Song of Songs* may possibly represent something of Gregory *via* Claudius; it is also possible that Columban is referring to this work in his petition to Gregory to send him a book of this name. The same holds good of Ildefonsus of Toledo, who also mentions such a writing from Gregory's pen. The gravest doubt surrounds yet other works printed by the Benedictine editors together with the attested Gregorian corpus.[115]

For the form of his narrative Gregory craved neither poverty nor riches. His sole desire was to present its teaching in a medium practical, clear, easily understood, yet not unfitting, so far as might be, for its great matter. The Pope who would not ride on a donkey or an inferior horse because he was a Pope would not clothe his words on Divine truths in ignoble dress; he remarks at the beginning of his *Dialogues* that he has not reproduced the exact words of his authorities, since the rustic idiom of country speech would not be suitable in a written work. He never forgets that he was born of a noble family and educated in the best schools of Rome; his language, though it is marked by the lapses from Cicero's Latin current in his time, is always cultured, if plain, dignified, if workmanlike. We may be thankful that he does not spin for

[115] See Bardenhewer, V, pp. 298f.; Schanz, pp. 613f.; Lau, *Gregor I der Grosse*, pp. 319ff.; Dudden, I, pp. ixf.; Columban, *Epp.* p. 159; Ildefonsus, *De vir. ill.* c. I. For text, with the Benedictine arguments for genuine authorship against Goussainville's attack, see *PL* 79. Cf. also D. B. Capelle, *Rev. Bénéd.* XLI (1929) pp. 204ff. The *Liber Paterii* (*PL* 79, 683ff.) consists of a collection of extracts from Gregorian writings begun by Paterius, a friend and secretary of the Pope (see Joh. Diac. *Vita* II, 11), and continued in the twelfth century.

us the ornate complexities of Ennodius. But neither does he descend to the simplicities of Gregory of Tours.[116]

He died on March 12, 604, the day on which the Church keeps his Feast. Legends afterward clustered about his name, often repeated by word or by painter's art. Two may be recalled here. A dove often rests on his shoulder or whispers in his ear as he looks out at us from mediaeval pictures. During the famine that followed his death accusations were thrown against him as one who had brought the people to want by extravagance in spending the public funds, and certain men longed to burn up the books he had written. They had even succeeded in destroying some, when Peter the Deacon, the "dear son" of the *Dialogues,* declared on solemn oath that this was sacrilege. Had he not often seen with his own eyes the Holy Spirit in form of a dove whiter than snow, holding its beak against his lips? [117]

The other story is the Legend of the Mass of Saint Gregory. It tells that the Pope one day was in the act of administering holy communion to a noble lady of Rome when she recognized the likeness of bread which she herself had made and offered to the Church. So she smiled in unbelief when he extended toward her the Host, with the words *Corpus Domini nostri Jesu Christi,* judging it foolish to speak so with regard to bread of her own making. Gregory promptly withdrew from her the Host and placed It on the altar. Afterward in the sight of all the congregation he prayed, and lo! for a moment the Host stood revealed to human eyes as of the true Body of the Lord. The woman believed and humbly made her communion, when the vision faded again into the likeness of bread.[118]

With Gregory, as we have said, the Middle Ages ended

---

[116] See Sr. Mary B. Dunn, *The Style of the Letters of St. Gregory the Great, Cath. Univ. Amer. Patristic Studies* XXXII, 1931.
[117] Paul. Diac. *Vita,* 28; Joh. Diac. IV, 69.
[118] Paul. Diac. *Vita,* 23; Joh. Diac. *Vita,* II, 41; Whitby *Life,* XX.

their long travail in the womb of Europe and came to birth. His faith in prayer and its heroes and miracles was theirs. His mighty conception of the spiritual fatherhood of the Bishop of Rome over all the Churches, of temporal administration extending over many lands and peoples, harked back to the early centuries of Rome's government and laid its mark forever on the Papacy of days to come. "Consul of God," his epitaph named him. It was a fitting title. Yet to the Roman prerogative of supreme power exercised in justice he added the Christian grace of mercy to Romans and to Gentiles alike. His legacy to the centuries that followed was not, indeed, unmixed with evil. But he ruled his world faithfully with a pure vision of holy charity, and all the trumpets sounded for him on the other side. To the English he stands between Ninian and Aidan: one who led them from pagan darkness into a light which the shadows of the Dark Ages already lengthening around his path could never subdue.

SELECT BIBLIOGRAPHY

PROCOPIUS : *History of the Wars,* Loeb ed. vols. III–V, 1919–1928.

—— *Anecdota (Secret History),* Loeb ed. 1935.

J. B. BURY : *History of the Later Roman Empire,* vols. I and II, 1923.

—— *The Invasion of Europe by the Barbarians,* 1928.

EDWARD GIBBON : *Decline and Fall of the Roman Empire,* ed. Bury, vols. IV–V, 1909–1911.

T. HODGKIN : *Italy and her Invaders²,* vols. III–VI, 1896–1916.

—— *The Letters of Cassiodorus,* a condensed translation, 1886.

F. GREGOROVIUS : *History of the City of Rome in the Middle Ages⁴,* trans. Hamilton, I, 1900.

LOT-PFISTER-GANSHOF : *Histoire du Moyen Age,* I, 1928.

H. GRISAR : *History of Rome and the Popes in the Middle Ages,* Eng. trans. ed. Cappadelta, vols. II–III, 1912.

F. LOT : *The End of the Ancient World,* trans. Leon, 1931.

W. P. KER : *The Dark Ages,* 1911.

H. ST. L. B. MOSS : *The Birth of the Middle Ages,* 1935.

SIR CHARLES OMAN : *The Dark Ages⁶,* 1923.

——*England before the Norman Conquest⁶,* 1924.

W. G. HOLMES : *The Age of Justinian and Theodora,* vols. I and II, 1905–1907.

E. K. RAND : *Founders of the Middle Ages²,* 1929.

C. FOLIGNO : *Latin Thought during the Middle Ages,* 1929.

C. C. MIEROW: *The Gothic History of Jordanes,* 1915.

BOETHIUS: *Consolation of Philosophy,* ed. E. K. Rand, with trans. of "I. T." revised by H. F. Stewart, 1926.

—— *The Theological Tractates,* ed. E. K. Rand, trans. Stewart and Rand, 1926.

H. F. STEWART: Boethius: an Essay, 1891.

H. R. PATCH: *The Tradition of Boethius,* 1935.

C. H. HASKINS: *Studies in the History of Mediaeval Science,* 1927.

E. GILSON: *The Spirit of Mediaeval Philosophy,* trans. Downes, 1936.

M. de WULF: *History of Mediaeval Philosophy,* I⁶, Eng. ed.³, 1935.

H. RASHDALL: *The Universities of Europe in the Middle Ages,* ed. Powicke and Emden, vols. I–III, 1936.

O. M. DALTON: Gregory of Tours: *The History of the Franks,* trans. and commentary, vols. I and II, 1927.

SIR SAMUEL DILL: *Roman Society in Gaul in the Merovingian Age,* 1926.

T. SCOTT HOLMES: *The Origin and Development of the Christian Church in Gaul,* 1911.

D. TARDI: *Fortunat,* 1927.

E. BRIAND: *Histoire de Sainte Radegonde,* 1898.

L. ECKENSTEIN: *Women under Monasticism,* 1896.

F. J. E. RABY: *A History of Christian-Latin Poetry,* 1927.

—— *A History of Secular Latin Poetry in the Middle Ages,* vols. I and II, 1934.

ALBAN BUTLER: *Lives of the Saints,* revised Thurston and Attwater, 1926–1934.

W. J. REES: *Lives of the Cambro-British Saints,* 1853.

H. WILLIAMS: ed. and trans. *Works* of Gildas, 1899.

—— *Christianity in Early Britain,* 1912.

SELECT BIBLIOGRAPHY

J. E. LLOYD: *A History of Wales,* I, 1911.

EUGIPPIUS: *Life of Saint Severinus,* trans. G. W. Robinson, 1914.

C. F. ARNOLD: *Caesarius von Arelate,* 1894.

A. MALNORY: *Saint Césaire,* 1894.

BARING-GOULD and FISHER: *Lives of the British Saints,* vols. I–IV, 1907.

COUNT DE MONTALEMBERT: *The Monks of the West,* vols. I–III, 1896.

ADAMNAN: *Life of St. Columba,* ed. W. Reeves', 1874.

JONAS: *Life of St. Columban,* Univ. Pennsylvania, *Translations and Reprints,* II, 1902, No. 7.

J. A. DUKE: *The Columban Church,* 1932.

—— *History of the Church in Scotland,* 1937.

LOUIS GOUGAUD: *Christianity in Celtic Lands,* trans. Joynt, 1932.

J. F. KENNEY: *Sources for the Early History of Ireland,* I, 1929.

W. A. PHILLIPS: ed. *History of the Church of Ireland,* I, 1933.

JOHN RYAN: *Irish Monasticism,* 1931.

W. K. LOWTHER CLARKE: *The Rule of St. Benedict,* 1931.

PAUL DELATTE: *Commentary on the Rule of St. Benedict,* 1921.

F. CABROL: *Saint Benedict,* trans. Antony, 1934.

CUTHBERT BUTLER: *Benedictine Monachism',* 1924.

E. G. GARDNER: ed. *The Dialogues of Saint Gregory,* translation of ann. 1608.

GREGORY THE GREAT: *The Pastoral Rule,* trans. Bramley, 1874. *Pastoral Rule;* Selected *Letters,* trans. Barmby, *Nicene and Post-Nicene Fathers,* XII, *Morals on the*

Book of Job, trans. *Library of the Fathers,* vols. I–III, 1844-1847.

G. F. BROWNE : *King Alfred's Books,* 1920.

F. HOMES DUDDEN : *Gregory the Great,* vols. I and II, 1905.

P. BATIFFOL : *Saint Gregory the Great,* trans. Stoddard, 1929.

INDEX

ANN ARBOR PAPERBACKS

reissues of works of enduring merit

The University of Michigan Press   *Ann Arbor*